£5

CU00913930

# FOCUS ON RUGBY

# FOCUS ON RUGBY
## An International Coaching Book
# Carwyn James

Based on the television series
*Focus on Rugby*

*Produced by Opix Films in association
with S4C, BBC Wales, and RTE*

**Stanley Paul**
London Melbourne Sydney Auckland Johannesburg

Stanley Paul & Co. Ltd

An imprint of the Hutchinson Publishing Group

17–21 Conway Street, London W1P 6JD

Hutchinson Group (Australia) Pty Ltd
30–32 Cremorne Street, Richmond South, Victoria 3121
PO Box 151, Broadway, New South Wales 2007

Hutchinson Group (NZ) Ltd
32–34 View Road, PO Box 40–086, Glenfield, Auckland 10

Hutchinson Group (SA) Pty Ltd
PO Box 337, Bergvlei 2012, South Africa

First published 1983
Text and illustrations © Opix Films 1983

Set in Linotron Univers Light by
Input Typesetting Ltd., London SW19 8DR

Printed in Great Britain by The Anchor Press Ltd
and bound by Wm Brendon & Son Ltd,
both of Tiptree, Essex

British Library Cataloguing in Publication Data
James, Carwyn
    Focus on rugby.
    1. Rugby football
    I. Title
    796.33'32        GV945

ISBN 0 09 150271 3

# Contents

# Acknowledgements

Carwyn's untimely death meant that he could not see his last book through to publication. However, we feel sure that if he had been there to write these acknowledgements, he would have wished to thank: all the players and coaches who contributed to the book, for their willingness to discuss with him the finer points of the game he loved; his colleagues at BBC Wales, especially Gareth Price and Brenda Thomas, who gave him so much support; producer Ray Marshall and director Terry Ryan of Opix Films with whom Carwyn worked closely on the television series from which this book originated; Bob Shepherd, who researched the photographs and who spent many hours checking through Carwyn's original manuscripts; Roddy Bloomfield at Stanley Paul, who nurtured the book to fruition; and, perhaps, most of all, his friend and fellow *Guardian* writer, David Frost, who made an important contribution to the book's final preparation. Though Carwyn had submitted the entire manuscript and selected the pictures before his sudden and tragic death, it was David Frost who, at short notice, undertook all the technical editing, proof-reading and captioning which are so necessary to the final product.

There are probably many others, who Carwyn would have wished to thank. We can only apologize for any omissions.

# Photographic acknowledgements

For permission to reproduce copyright photographs in this book the publishers would like to thank Associated Sports Photography, Colorsport, *Glasgow Herald,* John Harris, George Herringshaw & Associates, Kemsley Picture Service, Opix Films Limited, Alan T. Richards, *Scotsman* Publications Ltd, Sport and General Press Agency Ltd, Bob Thomas, *Western Mail and Echo* Ltd and Elwyn White.

# He believed...
# and we believed in him

*Gerald Davies*

The room remained silent for a while. To an unbelieving crowd, unaccustomed in his ways and grown old with being second best, Carwyn James had brought his prologue to the tour to a close. The four nations, each distinctive from the other, shall be one. The challenge ahead will be met.

'Let me say this,' he said at the Park Lane Hotel, 'let me simply say this,' with his right hand waving, school masterishly, in the air, with the inevitable untipped cigarette held between first and second finger, 'I believe that we will win the Test series in New Zealand.'

To some, the new Lions, it was no more than a much-needed bolster to wavering confidence. Others, much longer in the tooth, saw it as a carefully manufactured boost to morale, a coach trying to cut something of a dash. There was no outrageous effrontery in his bold claim, though there may have been just a tinge of ingenious impudence. At any rate, the seed had been sown. As the tour progressed, and long before the issue had been settled, his measured tones, his unerring choice of words, his utter though quiet conviction had found receptive ears and responsive minds. We believed him as he had always believed in himself. We flew, almost unnoticed out of London. We returned to a changed rugby world and it was not going to be the same again. It changed dramatically for him. From the quiet groves of academic life first in Queen Elizabeth Grammar School, Carmarthen, then Llandovery College and, finally, at Trinity College, Carmarthen, he emerged as a national figure in Wales.

He was not of the common mould of rugby men. He was the philosopher king of the rugby world. As a coach he tried at times to persuade and convince in the most astute and democratic fashion. On other occasions he guided, as all the best teachers do, in such a way that the player, like the fortunate pupil, would be surprised to find a wonderful discovery for himself. Since the discovery is your own, or appears to be so, the reward is that much sweeter and infinitely satisfying. The glory was his as it was ours. The twain, player and coach, meet in glorious harmony.

For all the time he devoted to rugby, he never lost his sense of wonder in it. And he never wanted to lose it. Rugby should not be reduced to the commonplace. It should continue to delight and surprise.

His was a scholar's mind. He could speak Russian fluently and had an abiding interest in the drama of that country. He could just as easily debate the subtle ironies of Chekhov as unravel the darker mysteries of front-row play. And, more difficult still, see the humour in both. Whilst all about him people became animated, full of nervous chatter, he would remain calm and, if called upon, could produce a succinct analysis of any match. A marvellous player in his own right, he had a devastating jink and could always be counted upon to drop a goal in almost every game. Or so it seems now to me. It was to see him play that I went so often to his beloved Stradey. If he only played twice for Wales then he more than made up for it, in his own mind, by coaching Llanelli to that famous victory against the All Blacks in 1972 and winning the Welsh Cup in four consecutive seasons. And many thousands of miles away made Rovigo the champions of Italy.

He had a passion for Welsh poetry as well as the literature of other nations and in his writing brought a poet's sensitive mind to bear on a rugged and boisterous game. Occasionally, just occasionally, he saw rugby aspire to that condition and its players transformed into artists. He drew extensively on those other interests of his as a way better to understand a game which, in Wales, has its roots firmly established in its culture and tradition. It was unthinkable of him to isolate rugby from any other aspect of Welsh life.

A miner's son in socialist west Wales, he subscribed fully to the idea of excellence and he believed passionately, where talent was concerned, in the existence of an elite. He was a product of a community which, given a glimpse of what was possible, yearned for ideas and unprejudiced thinking.

A week ago at the Tabernacle, Cefneithin, where he was a deacon, a remembrance service was held as a tribute. There could have been no better illustration of the range and depth of feeling and friendship which he inspired. Politicians and poets, deacons and doctors of medicine and philosophy were there. Lawyers and lecturers, miners and fellows in faded duffle coats. Rugby men who understood not a word of the all-Welsh service. And an Eisteddfod Arch Druid who wittily told of the day he shook hands with Colin Meads. All loyal friends who came to pay a final homage to Carwyn James, a man who effortlessly bestrode their differing worlds. All in all we shall not see his like again.

January, 1983

# Introduction

At the end of the seventies and the beginning of the eighties rugby football lost its way a little. The only country in the world which played with confidence and with a belief in itself was New Zealand, but even the All Blacks, during an unreal, politically tarnished tour of their country undertaken by South Africa in 1982, found that the tough and talented Springboks were still a world power.

New Zealand has tended to go its own way. If there are lessons to be learned, and there were some on offer in 1971, they learnt them and they usually came back on top. The other countries of the world keep a close watch on developments in Great Britain and tend to copy what is best. That particularly applies to Australia and South Africa. France still has too strong a hold on Europe.

I am strongly of the opinion that a second coaching explosion, similar to the one we experienced in Britain in the mid sixties, is overdue. Similar, but with a different emphasis. The new coaching emphasis, I feel, must rest less on the team and the unit skills and much more on the individual player.

Already, I am pleased to say, the coaching staff of at least two of the four home unions have contributed positively to the new thinking. The RFU has published several pamphlets on positional play and the WRU has conducted practical sessions and seminars on individual skills. An acceptance of this kind of thinking will mean a different attitude towards coaching from now on.

Back play – that is, half-back and threequarter play – has declined dreadfully in the relatively short period of less than a decade. The aim of this book, therefore, is to re-assess the contribution of the individual within the unit. To maintain a balance, forward play is discussed by Graham Price, Billy Beaumont, Murray Mexted and Jean-Pierre Rives, all of them experienced and highly competent performers.

Andy Irvine discusses the role of the full back in the modern game, Mike Slemen the role of the wing, and David Richards that of the centre. Ollie Campbell, the outstanding player of 1982, analyses fly-half play while Dave Loveridge is the chosen scrum half.

The views of all these players were gained by interview and are presentations at length of material which formed part of the television series 'Focus on Rugby'. Where necessary their comments and mine are illustrated either graphically or by the use of photographs.

Coaching is discussed with Bob Templeton of Queensland who, within the last eight years, has brought two Wallaby teams to Britain on major tours. Tom Kiernan, a former full back and captain of Ireland and the British Lions, analyses his role as the present coach of the Irish Triple Crown winning team and gives his views on the importance of individual skills.

The basics, the habits or the fundamentals are always all-important no matter how the game evolves. Equally important and equally fundamental is fitness or physical conditioning. The specific fitness of individual players within the game is presented by Tom Hudson, the Director of the Physical Education Department at Bath University and Dr Bruce Davies, Director of the Human Performance Laboratory, University of Salford. Tom was a colleague of mine for a number of seasons at Llanelli Rugby Football Club, whose coaching staff he still advises and assists.

I hope that many aspiring young players and coaches of the game at all levels derive as much pleasure from watching the television series and from reading this book as I did from preparing them.

# 1 What is Wrong with the Game?

I am just old enough to remember the time when professional cricketers entered club and county pavilions by a different door from amateurs. While the separation might raise a good few eyebrows today, the concept of the amateur and the gentleman is one that we should re-examine where rugby football is concerned.

A gentleman (as I dimly perceived in the mining village where I was born) was not entirely disapproved of even if occasionally indolent, nor was a certain insolence frowned upon, especially if it resulted in the exhibition of a certain style. These two qualities may seem strange bedfellows in a new book about the skills of a game, but I often feel we could do with a good deal more indolence on the part of governing bodies, who seem to have a genius for doing the wrong things, and a parallel insolence on the part of players who, increasingly dragooned, are in danger of becoming little more than treasurers' chessmen.

A gentleman player, an amateur, should have the right to choose whether or not he wishes to play. If at the conclusion of his career he is seized by the muse and he wishes to put pen to paper, then that too is his non-professional, uncompromising right. If from the age of nine or ten he has been pressurized to play in huge national stadia with mini coaches exhorting him to win maxi cups, then at least he should have the opportunity later to bite the hand that has allegedly fed him.

More than anything, we are in need of plain speaking and a sharp reappraisal of a structured game that sometimes seems to me to lend itself more to the creation of balanced account books than to cater for the simple satisfaction of players. The game, let it be said again and again, is for the enjoyment of the players. Money, whether we like it or not, permeates administrative thinking, and that is most ungentlemanly. Rugby football is our aristocratic inheritance and not something we have entered as a trade: we should value it as such.

As for indolence, I should like to see that word painted in gilt and embossed on a plaque in that august room at the East India Club in St James's Square where our law makers, members of the International Rugby Board, periodically meet. Rip van Winkle should have had a second nap there.

Twenty years of sleep would have left us free of interference with the line-out laws which have become more and more irregular and complex; it would have saved us from a complete devaluation of the skill and the courage of tackling which led to a permissible knock-on and the pile-up; and, more recently, it would have prevented the law makers' frantic zeal and tactical naivety which will soon result in a change in the scrummage law whereby hookers may now scrape or forage for the ball before it leaves the hands of the scrum half.

Twenty or so years ago the respective unions began a tentative embrace with coaching but, in my view, despite a lengthy courtship, the marriage has not been fully consummated; rather, it is widely divorced from the true aim of the game, while at the same time we have all become professionals without noticing.

It is not the chink of coin which disfigures but the regimentation imposed to make the turnstiles click. When the gentlemen and players went their separate ways there was an unwelcome distancing but few doubts about status or direction.

More importantly, that most elusive of qualities, the natural flair of the intuitive player, is currently so rare that we wonder what we have done. It is not so much that the baby has gone down the plughole instead of the bath water as that we have taken the fun out of the whole of the participant's childhood. Immediately after the cradle comes the grave, the grave of fierce competitive football without the joy of lazy Saturday mornings and a bit of a yarn and a joke in between.

What, then, is wrong with rugby football now? Let's start with a brief comparison. My first view of a rugby ball was from my father's shoulders, peering over the hedge at the end of the garden to see the village team playing. Although there were times when you wouldn't think so, the lads, as I later understood, played friendlies for the fun of it.

It was natural to want to play like them, two friends against two on the road with a hedge as one touchline, the school wall as the other. We were not allowed to play on the playground so we made do with the road. In these internationals I learned to sidestep and to swerve because being tackled meant being hurt. It was something to be avoided, getting hurt.

Come May, the touchlines became boundaries, three stones uphill marked the batsman's end, one only for the bowler, and when the same sponge ball was recklessly dispatched into the hayfield or over the school wall, it was six and out. In a puritanical age when there was no Sunday cricket I once batted for ten painful days; no one spoke to me but they appealed often! Leg before was not allowed so I was extravagant with my legs and with the wide, heavy bat; and in the manner of an old photograph I had seen of a bearded wonder, I ostentatiously cocked my left elbow high into the sky.

At the council or primary school there were no organized games as such, although our headmaster was a Welsh cap, having hooked for Wales in the year that the undefeated All Blacks and George Nepia came. But he, W. J. Jones, never talked about it. In the village, however, we ate and breathed rugby, although thankfully it was never organized by our elders as it is today for the under-elevens. We did our own shambollic organizing. From the village school we moved, undersized and eager, to the grammar school. The war was on, no formal games were possible and the allotments had changed the rugby pitches to potato patches as we dug for victory.

Victory achieved, I played my first match for the school at the age of sixteen as captain, probably because my pavement skills had been noted and my experience with the village senior team was known. A year later I played fly half for the Welsh Secondary Schools team and my debts to the pavement and a golden era without organization had begun.

At a tender age I had realized that rugby football was a game in which I could survive provided I was elusive. There was a place for my frail nine stones amongst others much more robust if, like

the Welsh outside halves I was beginning to hear about, I could survive. Folklore was already heady.

In the village I had seen a sidestepping genius who was as quick as a fish. When he was drowned on HMS *Hood* I deeply mourned the loss of a natural rugby player. There is still, even now, much of him left in the village and maybe in other parts of the world. Influences pass on.

Before the war I remember walking three miles to see Haydn Tanner and Willie Davies play for Swansea University. I was about seven then and no doubt images were present in my mind and a conception of half-back play was taking shape. At seventeen, when I first played for Llanelli whilst still a schoolboy, the only inspiring coaching I'd had was the chat of former players and caring schoolmasters. Nothing, not even a tiresome tackling session before playing against the French Schoolboys, had dampened my enthusiasm and I came into senior rugby with a freshness that would today be unthinkable.

The masters in charge of team games knew no spirit but the amateur one. They put in the hours because they loved the sport. Came, alas, the destruction of one of the best educational systems in the world. Came the levelling down process. A disbelief in Plato's gold, silver and brass. All children are equal and none is more equal than another. Comprehensives. The new in word. Big and beautiful. Hours of business: strictly nine to four. Special responsibility allowances a must. Preferably no Saturday morning games.

The history master confines his activities to history. The track-suited professional, weighed down by coaching certificates and manuals, takes over a clientele more interested in physical recreation than education. Choice is the operative word in the comprehensive. A flirtation with half a dozen team games is preferable to the discipline of one. The disciplines of gymnastics are as repugnant as the disciplines of spelling and counting.

The sadness of the age is a lack of understanding of the needs of children. They love discipline. Without it there is chaos and that is the state of too many of our schools at the present time. No wonder the private education sector is thriving. The primary aim of education, surely, is to make children, whatever the cost, literate and numerate. The aim of games coaching, too, is to make children literate and numerate in the skills of a game. The schools, by and large, are failing in their duty.

This was the general feeling expressed by qualified WRU coaches, many of them schoolmasters, at a conference held at the Sports Centre in Cardiff on 4 July 1982. Present were all the members of the investigative committee, under the chairmanship of Ieuan Evans, set up to explore what is wrong with rugby at the present time. It is, I have no doubt, as much a European as it is a Welsh problem. Now for a moment of contemplation.

## The second coming

Rugby union in the northern hemisphere awaits a new stage of development. After the coaching explosion of the mid sixties we are already late entering the second coaching phase.

When Wales lit the fuse on the first British coaching explosion, the fuse itself had been meticulously manufactured by the English. In other words, the caring English did the work and the cunning of the Welsh did the rest.

Mallaby since has pontificated on the state of the game, Burgess on the state of play, and both reports are tidy, despite the dust.

There is a sceptical school of thought, English rather than Welsh, which does not see the need for investigation. Be that as it may, now that the committee has been called, I hope that its findings, following thorough research, will be presented right from the shoulder. That is the least I expect from the Evans report.

It troubles me that the youngsters of today discover and lose the joy of playing before they are of secondary-school age. The mini-rugby game was created with the best intentions, but screaming mums, doting dads and the competitive urge have given it the image of a monster.

Recently there was a mini-rugby festival for the under-ten-year-olds at the Arms Park, played by sixteen teams from an original entry of nearly 200. One concerned father told me that his worried son, who was 'competing', had not slept well for

Mini rugby: its level of competitiveness makes it a monster. It destroys the wonder and enjoyment which youngsters should experience in rugby

a week in the fear that he would make a mistake at the National Stadium.

As a matter of principle and discipline – let alone the preservation of the seating at the Arms Park – I would not allow junior schools internationals to be played there any more. It was cruel, to say the least, to see the under-eleven match on a full-sized pitch as a curtain raiser to the under-sixteen international between Wales and England.

To play at Wales's National Stadium should be an honour reserved for the senior schools and the youth. Let us preserve in the youngsters a sense of wonder and achievement as long as possible.

I sincerely hope that the committee, in their discourse on cultivating the right attitude, will come down strongly against competitive rugby before the age of at least fifteen. At this stage the most that can be achieved is the learning of good habits in the most enjoyable manner possible.

When youngsters are playing for trophies, the emphasis is on winning. Many of the holders of coaching certificates, and others, teach them exactly as they would a senior team; that is, by teaching the unit skills of the forwards and the backs separately and then the team as a unit.

Drill, teaching by numbers, moves – the kind of pressure rugby which the seniors play – is of greater consequence, it seems, than teaching the individual. This is bad, unthought-out coaching.

Too often we see players reacting like unthinking robots. Hiding behind moves – moves which are called before the ball emerges from the set piece and when its quality is, as yet, unknown – is the escape route for the robot. That coaches have hidden behind moves as in American football is, I am afraid, a fact of life. The obvious example of this is the crash-ball tactic, already a boring cliché, which has, unfortunately, ruined classical centre play so that this is unseen by the present generation.

The Bleddyns and the Butterfields must suffer agonies during current international matches. How one longs to see more and more tries like the one David Johnston scored for Scotland against Wales in the spring of 1982, an outside break in overdrive from a set scrummage.

Since youngsters are taught at so early an age there should not be any bad habits. Why is it, then, that almost all scrum halves in first-class rugby are technically so imperfect? Why is it that even midfield players use the spin instead of the wrist pass?

The question 'why?' goes on and on until we have to make the point that a coach, like a proficient doctor, must be able to diagnose the ills and the faults and has to set up a clinic.

Coaches are so concerned with the team effort that the individual is neglected during training. Coaching a full team is less exacting and less demanding intellectually than perfecting individual skills. Practice, someone once said, makes permanent, and not necessarily perfect. The measure of perfection depends on the teacher. I'm deliberately using the term teacher and not coach.

Since 80 per cent or so of team coaching is concerned with the forwards and the production of the quick ball, although we may not think so, the backs tend to be neglected. Too many accept the naive assumption that teaching the backs means teaching moves.

The main concern of the coach should be the quick transference of the ball from scrum half to wing with each member of the chain being able to take and give the ball in one stride. If this is achieved at least 100 times perfectly in one session, the coach has earned his money. There are many first-class teams who do not accomplish it once during a season. Without dwelling on the point, may I state simply that current players at all levels fail to discriminate between the use of the first-phase ball and possession won at subsequent phases.

Quick transference, I would say, is the golden rule at the first phase, but quality possession at the second and the third means that a player must often draw his opponent. The failure of international players to cope when they have three against two, or two against one, is a failure of coaching.

## A general concern

I received many concerned letters in response to a piece I wrote on this theme in the *Guardian* on Saturday, 17 April 1982. All agreed that far too much pressure was put on young children before they were of secondary school age. There were, it was claimed, certain areas in the UK where mini rugby was considered too childish and where the youngsters were forced to play competitive fifteen-a-side rugby.

Equally, where the mini game is encouraged, the coaches were more concerned with winning cups and trophies than with teaching the skills for fun and enjoyment. A coach of the mini game for five years with London Welsh, Mr Neil Kinnock, the Labour spokesman on Education, puts his case and mine forcibly:

17 April 1982

Dear Carwyn James,

I always enjoy your pieces but your *Guardian* column today had me cheering. I'm taking copies to pass around mini coaches. Many of them are very sympathetic to your view but if we are able to change attitudes and practices (not to say the morality) the message needs to come from people like you. Critics of the mini game have mainly contented themselves with talk of abolition. That's neither practicable nor desirable. Your theme that tournaments (a properly medieval title) should be abolished gets to the root of the problem. The kids like lifting the cup. But they would rather play rugby, so three-cornered, half-hour-long friendlies which give them two decent games and plenty of time for training, no worries, no long travel and no despair at being knocked-out-because-of-a-fumble-on- the- line-in-the-semifinal would fit the pedagogic and the rugby interest much better than the torture of tournaments.

I think that the issue is important now because mini rugby, instead of refreshing the game with a generation of confident, competent, adventurous youngsters, is simply reinforcing the drudgery of the adult game. Coaches who should (and do) know better are afraid to let the kids down by training them in the real virtues and taking the risk of losing against the regimented sides. And other coaches seem to be using the boys to make up for their own sporting inadequacies and personality deficiencies so they foster the zombie game.

There are still – and always will be – lots of lads with rugby talent and even more with lovely dogged interest. Mini-rugby at its best helps and encourages both and could provide a marvellous foundation for the continuous improvement of the game. But that will only happen if the kids *enjoy* themselves and that won't come about if they are doing little more than being crew members on coaches' and parents' ego trips.

I'm just finishing my fifth season as a mini coach. It will be my last. My lads have done well – they haven't lost twenty games in the two hundred or so that they've played. But the main pleasure for me has been the sight of boys developing sporting skills and attitudes, and the main delight has come from the boys who started with the lowest natural ability and now play the game well because they understand and enjoy it. Some of the stimulation has come from competitive rugby and they couldn't and wouldn't have learned without pressure. I've got this strong feeling, however, that they would have learned more if they hadn't been subjected to tournaments and everything that goes with them.

Things will get much worse as the mini game gets older so we ought to change it radically now.

No need for reply. I'm just glad to get it off my chest – again.

Regards,
Neil Kinnock

It was encouraging at the coaching conference to find that the chairman of each seminar, in presenting his report, put the schools problem first and the same points were made over and over again:

1. That competition at a tender age was bad.
2. That in breeding negative attitudes there was no enjoyment left.
3. That the skills of the game were either not taught or taught badly.
4. That there had been an appreciable lowering of skill level attainment in schools and that fresh ideas were needed.
5. That games lessons were not used to teach skills but to coach teams. In pursuit of victory, the attitude was too often negative.
6. That young teachers were conditioned not to work unsocial hours and that extracurricular activities were being neglected.
7. That there was a need to encourage more teachers to help.

Much of what was said, sadly, was but a plea to turn the clock back. The need for the Evans Committee was implicit in the comments made. The game was taking a different shape in the name of progress but it was an unacceptable shape. It was time to take stock, call a halt and either turn the clock back or restructure entirely for the wellbeing of the game in the eighties.

I must say I like the suggestion that an award or a certificate be given to youngsters as a reward for attaining a certain level of skill proficiency.

## Club-centred

There is much concern in many areas that rugby football is becoming more and more club- and less school-centred, with the inevitable result that there is an intensity of pressure placed on promising young players. Clubs are so organizing boys' and colts' rugby that the poor schoolboys, as one headmaster put it, 'are being pushed, cajoled, even bullied into playing an astounding and alarming number of hard matches.'

Some headmasters miss the point that school rugby under the old system, before the advent of comprehensives, was flourishing far more than it is now. In fairness to the WRU, a special committee was set up to investigate the situation but apart from restructuring or streamlining the different schools' unions, little was done to have an effect on the grass roots.

Local clubs, seeing the new apathy, decided to take the law into their own hands. If they could organize mini-rugby they could organize the lads at other levels as well, and many headmasters were too weak to forbid their pupils to play for a club, a right which they have.

Not so Mr Afan Daniel, the headmaster of Gowerton School. Its forerunner, the grammar school, produced Tanner and Davies, Lewis Jones, John and Onllwyn Brace, Peter and Alan Stone, Norman Gale and a host of other superb players: 'After forty or so years as player, coach, referee, assessor and headmaster, I think we are facing the most serious crisis in rugby that I have known.'

His views are shared by many colleagues in Wales. He goes on:

There is added pressure of all kinds from clubs and, alas, from parents, many of whom are active in club circles and the majority of whom can be beguiled by club blandishments. Boys of eleven and twelve, playing well and honourably at school, are often whisked off to play a second match on the same day; certainly Sunday morning rugby is not uncommon and weekday evenings are also used in early and late season. There are representative sides at many levels and matches can be hard and bitter. I see fresh and keen boys of great talent at eleven succumbing to the pressures, declining in verve, spontaneous talent and interest, and leaving the game in increasing numbers at thirteen, fourteen and fifteen, or surviving as half the players they gave early promise of becoming.

The message is loud and clear. The WRU must stop clubs organizing rugby between the age of eleven and sixteen. That is easily done, but we are still left with the problem of the bad schools who don't offer the opportunity of playing at these age groups. If the status quo is maintained, no amount of recommendation by the Evans Committee will change matters for the better.

It seems to me that the WRU will have to be more positive and attack the problem another way. The union should appoint a couple of fully qualified teacher/coaches to go round the schools to encourage young masters to join teaching courses on the skills of the game. In a materialistic age, the schools will have to make it worthwhile for those masters to spend their time on extracurricular activities.

I must also make the point that it isn't enough to teach the skills of the game to a would-be coach. A qualified coach must also be guided in the art of teaching, the art of communication. So far this hasn't been done and this is where the system is breaking down. We must train literate coaches.

## Youths or colts rugby

The formation of the Youth Rugby Union was an important development in Welsh rugby. Players like Derek Quinnell and Phil Bennett who left school at the age of fifteen plus were now being coached and encouraged to play in matches of a pretty high standard.

Again it has to be said that there are schoolboys playing for their school who are also persuaded to play for a youth team. There is a definite need for liaison and a much better feeling between clubs and schools. WRU local members probably don't like to intervene when the clubs are in the wrong (and they usually are) because it may lose them votes and their seat on the union, but I have no doubt that positive intervention is necessary.

In its annual report the Youth Union has never shirked its responsibility, and time and again Mr E. B. Davies, the secretary of the Union, has referred to the violent trend in the modern youth. Many players have been severely disciplined. There is no doubt, however, that these young men need better teachers who will demand a disciplined, controlled performance and they certainly need much better and more sympathetic refereeing. Too many raw and green referees are allowed to serve their apprenticeships in youth rugby.

## The clubs

On the question of rough, dirty and violent play, I have no doubt that the responsibility lies with club coaches and committees whose job it is to stop the rogue elephants or the psychopaths from playing. There *are* psychopaths playing; we know who they are but the clubs pretend that they are nothing of the kind.

Referees, too, have their responsibility and they need the support, which by and large they are having, of the disciplinary committee of their union when they send a player off the field. My angry comment to the international panellist referee who prided himself on not having ever sent a player off the field was that it was about time he started to referee. He was not on the same refereeing plane as Kevin Kelleher, Larry Lamb, Gwynne Walters or Ivor David. These superb arbiters never shirked their responsibilities and they won the respect of the players.

There is a need for competitive rugby. I applaud Scotland for their leagues, Ireland, England and Wales for their cup competitions. Since Welsh rugby is highly competitive without a league structure for the top clubs, I would do without one for the moment and certainly until there is a marked improvement in our playing standards. The only added incentive we need now is the joy of playing quality rugby which spectators can enjoy.

All players are asked to play far too many games in Wales and that may apply to England as well. The life span of a rugby player in Ireland and Scotland is at least five years longer. The root of the evil, as always, is money. Club treasurers rule. A suitable Christmas card from the national coaching director should be sent to each treasurer with the simple message: 'Don't kill the goose that lays the golden eggs.' They are killed. By the time they are thirty, the stars of the game have had enough. An average of fifty and more matches per season have taken their toll.

I favour the squad system. This provides a group of twenty-four to twenty-six players who, with careful thinking from the coach, who considers age, ability, experience and the strength of the opposition, share the games so that it isn't necessary for any top-class player to make more than thirty club appearances per season.

The greatest problem is the insistence of clubs on having selection committees. These are the self-important men who suffer from the ex-player's as-it-was-in-my-day syndrome; who have heard the word 'squad' but never understood its meaning. In pursuit of a win they select the best available team for every game. Some clubs in Wales, and I could name them, still think that the selection committee is more important than the coach. And some coaches, I'm sorry to say, are so subservient that they haven't even a vote on the selection committee! No wonder our game is suffering.

## The laws of the game

Rugby's rule-making body is the International Board, which consists of two representatives of the eight leading rugby countries in the world, the four home unions plus South Africa, New Zealand, Australia and France.

The representatives on the board are nominated to serve by their own unions and there is ample evidence to suggest that they are nominated for the wrong reasons. Some of them, no doubt, are efficient administrators, sound business men, but few of them are expert in the laws and the tactical evolution of rugby football.

One of their most incompetent performances ever came in the meeting held in March 1982. They seemed completely out of touch with the modern game: they disregarded the areas which required immediate attention – the penalty which is killing the game, the tackle and pile-up (that is, laws 18 and 19), the shambles known as the line-out, and the deliberate slewing of the scrum which disrupts clean possession – and, pursuing strange tangents, they messed around with the offside line at the line-out and, perhaps without realizing it, they legalized scraping in the scrums.

They should all have been shown the yellow if not the red card. The chairman of this laws committee, Hermas Evans, the president of the WRU and a serving member on the IB for fourteen years, was so incensed by their incompetence that he has resigned. In conversation and in an interview given to Clem Thomas of the *Observer*, Mr Evans said, 'I am annoyed and disappointed over the board's dealings with the laws of the game and I want people to know that members of the board are not doing their homework.'

## The recent background of an evolving game

Before embarking on any new changes of law, the members of the board should have reminded themselves of how the game has been evolving in recent years and should have analysed carefully why, at the moment, it is in danger yet again of losing the way. Why, they should have asked, is the standard of play so low and why is it that referees have become overimportant and can decide the results of matches? This is the recent background as I see it.

Top-class rugby union, as in the mid sixties, is yet again in a state of deep depression. The substandard quality of the Five Nations Championship during the last few seasons, particularly in the standard of back play, is so worrying that changes of law alone will not save the game, but they are necessary.

The 1964 committee responded courageously by setting a pattern for the future and that, although now outdated, remains the pattern of today's game. The hindmost foot became the new offside line at the scrummage and 10 metres – 10 yards then – from the line of touch was the obligatory position for those not taking part in the lineout except for the scrum halves and the wings on the throwing-in side of the field.

Unfortunately, the positive thinking of the lawmakers, designed to liberate the backs, eventually had the converse effect. Before the law change the back row and the opposing halves were virtually in a hand-shaking position. The poor halves had to develop the survival instincts of a hunted forest animal, but that kind of quick reaction made the chase fascinating.

The change in the offside law developed not the instincts but the thought processes of the halves. From being conditioned to the Pavlovian reflexes, they became more dependent on the intellectual appraisal of a situation.

All fly halves, however, were not overendowed with the grey matter, which led to the next step and the curse of the modern game; that is, the calling of a move before the ball has emerged from the set piece. As the scrummage forms, the fly half will call 'miss one', 'dummy scissors', 'scissors and loop', and so on, and, regardless of the quality of the emerging ball, the players become like puppets on a string or a stocking in the hands of Santa Claus as they go through with the move.

The greatest contributory evil towards the break-up of modern back play, however, has been the introduction of the crash-ball. Our backs are still at it: hunks of manhood with madness in their eyes bulldozing their way down the centre of the field, content to be picked off short of the gain line by larger hunks from the opposing back row selected for the purpose.

When Ian MacRae of New Zealand first started this ploy in the sixties he was used as a battering ram who expected to be tackled. He knew that his purpose in life was to set up the artificial platform for the second-phase attack once his colleagues had accomplished the nirvana of life, the winning of the tackled ball by means of the ruck, New Zealand's creative contribution to world rugby.

Wales's back play for some time has been a pathetic apology not only to MacRae but to the cloud of witnesses who have graced the international field for a century, but every one of the five nations has lost sight of the beauty of back play. Crowds now clap at the sight of the kick-ahead and pay £12 for the privilege.

The fulfilment of the ultimate agony which we are now experiencing was delayed in 1970 by the introduction of the dispensation law, which restricted the kicking of the ball into touch on the full from outside the player's 22.

Enter the attacking full back and the demise of the 'safer than houses' type of custodian who was at best a pain in the neck. Further means of breaching the defence were now not only possible but almost obligatory, with the inclusion of a running full back, which we had already seen in the play of Ken Scotland, Terry Davies and others and, of course, innumerable rugby league practitioners.

In the early seventies, however, the line-out laws were changed by the introduction of spacecraft, for want of a better phrase, and overnight the referee came into his own. For a decade he has become more and more important. Offences by the score were revealed to his grateful eyes as he whistled the melodies which led to more and more penalty goals.

He has, in effect, become the winner and the loser of a game, assisted even more by the definition of the tackle law, which for years devalued the tackle and which conceived the pile-up – a more illegitimate child than the line-out, fathered, I regret to say, by the unthinking International Board.

We have suffered the new tackle law for some time now, but brilliant attacking possibilities have been thwarted by the phraseology which states that 'a tackled player must release the ball immediately'. Why not 'a tackled player must not hold the ball'?

In my mind's eye I can see superb forward support play, ripe for further continuity, ended by the referee's interpretation of a badly written but worthy law. Devaluing the penalty to two points for minor offences and keeping it at three or even making it four for the major ones of foul play might help. But I sincerely hope that the committee of senior citizens will not have mellowed to the extent that they leave the line-out and other major infringements to the mercy of referees and willing psychopaths. A reintroduction of the line-out laws of the early fifties or early sixties might benefit the two-handed jumper and the game considerably. I would also do away with the mark, award only two points for the drop goal and only allow the third player to drop a goal from a free kick.

The true spirit of the game, surely, is not in belting the leather, in crash-balling, raking, scraping or late tackling. At the moment the minor offence, incredibly, is still equal to the major. The laws need simplifying. Referees must become less and less important.

## Blunders and more blundering

It was in the context of this kind of background that the IB abrogated its responsibilities:

1. The member countries of the southern hemisphere, despite the fact that Australia had suffered adversely on their tour of the UK, would not change the wording of the tackle law.

For season 1982–83 an innocuous change was made which may prove equally ambiguous. Meanwhile, reports of varied interpretations of 'the tackled player releasing the ball immediately' are coming through from down under.

In his last match before retiring, one match too many, Gert Bezuidenhout in 1982 allowed Ray Mordt, a tackled player, to play the ball off the ground and Transvaal went on to win against the Five Nations Invitation XV in extended injury time. The large video screen at Ellis Park, Johannesburg, showed the action replay while the crowd laughed and jeered at the referee's incompetence. In 1976 the same referee probably cost New Zealand the series against South Africa, but his bias on that occasion, and I was there to witness it, hastened the decision to have neutral referees.

Incidentally, I regret that Scotland refused the offer of neutral referees on their short tour of Australia in the summer of 1982. I wish they would understand that it has taken a tremendous amount of lobbying to get an important principle accepted. The principle will die a death unless there is a constant interchange between neighbouring countries and the countries of the two hemispheres. To have a Kiwi refereeing in the Five Nations Championship in season 1982–83 complements partly the invitations already accepted by Clive Norling, John West, Ken Rowlands and others to referee in the southern hemisphere.

As a postscript I hasten to add that I don't like the idea of action replays at rugby grounds because unless the word of the referee is final and unquestionable we are heading for disaster.

2. It has become abundantly clear in recent seasons that the penalty goal is of much greater significance in international rugby than the try.

Wisely the IB decided at their 1981 meeting that member countries should record accurately the penalty kick awards at matches of different levels during the 1981–82 season. Wales was the only country to comply. Armed with revealing statistics, Wales wanted law changes but England and New Zealand said immediately that they were not prepared to alter anything.

The average number of penalty kicks per match is 21·6. When the free-kick infringements for technical offences are added the figure is considerably higher than the 21·9 for 1976.

The figures for international matches are even more worrying:

(a) The average number of penalties per match is 24.
(b) Eleven matches out of fourteen were won by penalties.
(c) 219 points were scored from penalties, 179 from tries.
(d) The ratio of penalty kicks awarded for foul play per match is higher for internationals than other matches.

A breakdown of the penalty awards for different offences is most revealing and warrants a detailed, meticulous study from the law makers which, so far, has not been forthcoming.

Instead they concern themselves with meddling in areas which would have been better left alone. I refer in particular to the scrummage and the line-out.

(a) To law 20 a new section, section 10, is added: 'Play in the scrummage begins when the ball leaves the hands of the player putting it in.'

The official 'reason' given is to emphasize when play actually begins and to bring similarity to the line-out.

How naive can you get! Who cares whether there is similarity between the scrummage and the line-out. It is absolutely irrelevant except to the woolly thinking of fuddy-duddies trying to convince themselves that they are doing the right thing. This is a classical instance of the need for indolence! In fact the game would be better off had the meeting not taken place.

If the scrummage starts only when the ball leaves the hands of the player putting it in, it will be perfectly legal now for hookers, something which has been happening in Australia and New Zealand for a long time, to practise their striking – so, whether the IB knew what they were doing or not, and I'm sure many of them didn't, they have legalized the unworthy practice of scraping, which may lead to a lot of trouble. It will be so foreign to our referees in the northern hemisphere.

(b) The philosophy of the board on line-out play, law 23B, led to the greatest blunder of all because with one destructive stroke they were completely contemptuous of all tactical thinking relating to this set piece. This was their wording:

It has been decided to eliminate the 'furthest player' concept at the line-out, as imposing unnecessary restrictions within the fifteen metre limitation. It is considered that the furthest player concept is now frequently used in an attempt to contrive a penalty and that a fixed position would be more satisfactory in setting the maximum length of a line-out. This will allow any number of players in the line-out formation, subject to other conditions imposed by Sections 1, 2 and 3.

The coaching organizers in the UK, no doubt aided and abetted by other acute thinkers, got together and put forward a strong case in defiance of this fundamental change. As they had done a few months before over the binding of the tight-head prop, the IB, to their credit, admitted ignorance and lack of foresight and they decided to rescind the minute relating to 'the furthest player concept'. So, back to square one for season 1982–83.

By now many members of the board, knowing that they are not up to it, are feeling more than a little sheepish. The next move is clear, I would

have thought, and I'm not the only one, by any means, who feels strongly that an evolving game needs the finest expertise available in the world of rugby.

I fully understand Mr Hermas Evans's frustration. He says:

I have come to the conclusion that the board is not capable of making changes of law. It does not have the machinery, the time or the necessary expertise to do so. After all, the IB members are put there for a variety of reasons, usually as senior administrators, but they are certainly not experts on law. The board should therefore give the brief to people who (a) have the time; (b) are expert at law; and (c) know the game. This means co-opting referees, coaches and players.

Well said, and not before time. The amateurish approach of our law makers is destroying a fine spectator sport. Fresh minds are needed to spring-clean the game from top to bottom.

On the question of amateurism it has taken a journalist to question the IB ruling in a court of law. Dissatisfied with the judgement in favour of the player in question – J. P. R. Williams – the *Telegraph* and John Reason lodged an appeal. Since the case was sub judice during the board's last meeting, the law concerning amateurism and professionalism remained under consideration for the next year but, unquestionably, there is a definite tendency towards a broadening of attitudes.

A number of former players have written their autobiographies. I would ask the board to come clean and announce which players were professionalized and why others have remained amateurs. The list is a fascinating one: Colin Meads, Fergie McCormick, Grant Batty, Sid Going, Chris Laidlaw, Fred Allen of New Zealand; Steve Finnane of Australia; Willie John McBride of Ireland; Ian McLauchlan and Gordon Brown of Scotland; Fran Cotton, Roger Uttley, David Duckham and Billy Beaumont of England; Barry John, Mervyn Davies, Gerald Davies, Gareth Edwards, J. P. R. Williams and Phil Bennett of Wales.

It is a formidable, if incomplete, list of rugby knowledge and expertise which the board could call on, when deprofessionalized, to help them in their predicament. The game can hardly afford to lose men of this calibre. Unfortunately, as in many walks of life, professional committeemen are jealous of expertise and specialized knowledge. Let the board realize that the doors and the windows of the East India Club are now wide open and that the long sleep of the sympathetic rajahs on the walls will be more and more disturbed if they persist with their incompetence.

## Grass roots

What the International Board does matters in Keri Keri, Cardiff, Cape Town and Catania. Whether the game the world over is school- or club-centred matters. It also matters whether mini-rugby is for the instruction of the young learner or for the ego trip of Dad and the big-time coach. It matters to me that coaching, everywhere, has lost its way. That is why the remainder of this book is concerned with the teaching of the individual.

# 2 The Coach and the Coaching Method

## 'The proper study of mankind is man'

In the immediate postwar years the Soviet Union and her satellites promoted intensive mass-coaching programmes in different sports. I well remember seeing, in Bucharest in the early fifties, scores of youngsters moving their tennis rackets in unison with a couple of instructors who called and demonstrated the basic shot. The drill, without the ball, was most impressive. So was the music.

How well those youngsters coped with a moving ball I shall never know. Without any ball sense, many, I'm sure, fell by the wayside. The Nastases came through the system. For every Nastase there must have been thousands of nonentities. Models in front of mirrors, and no more.

We live in an age of mass coaching, sport for all, jogging for the also-rans, marathons for the millions, and I know that too much of our coaching of team games is directed towards the group rather than the individual. Rugby coaches, too, have lost the way. They have conveniently forgotten the importance and the value of individual skills within the team effort.

There is little difference these days, it seems to me, between a rugby coaching session in Invercargill or Inverness, in Durban or Dubai. Each has a rigid, frigid air of finality about it. Each reflects the manual more than the man. Unheeded are the words of Pope regarding the proper study of mankind. Unheeded is the individual who, in the coaching session, is but a letter or a number and never a name.

Inevitably the session starts with a warm-up, with or without a ball. It is followed by a practice, of the unit skills, with the forwards and the backs splitting up to rehearse in different parts of the field. Difficulties arise because the coach cannot be in two places at the same time. Difficulties arise, too, because the forwards need a more prolonged session. The proceedings are usually brought to an end with an unopposed or a semi-unopposed game.

It is a convenient and safe formula for any coach to follow. Provided that the players are sufficiently skilful, within the units the formula can prove successful. It is also a safeguard behind which the unimaginative coach can hide, the coach who is well versed in the modern jargon. 'Gain and tackle line', 'effective area' and such phrases roll easily off the tongue and the memory, demanding few or no thought processes. The purpose of coaching, like teaching, is to exercise the intellect.

In the mind's ear I have often heard John Burgess's persistent Lancastrian voice ringing out the -ink and the -ing like the pealing of bells as he exhorts his men to do some thinking.

Another superb motivator was New Zealand's Fred Allen, perhaps the most demanding of all coaches I ever met. 'If you feel so bored, you don't have to play, Piney,' was a typical curt comment to Colin Meads, who had failed to suppress a yawn during one of Fred's provocative perorations. Unlike many of his compatriots, Fred Allen encouraged his players to think.

Fred Allen, Danie Craven and the writer at Stellenbosch at a barbecue following the Springboks' winning series against the All Blacks in 1976

Dr Danie Craven, or Mr Rugby as he is called, now in his mid seventies and already the president of the South African Rugby Board for over a quarter of a century, has never stopped thinking about the game. His doctorates are the result of much thought and discussion and practical application at the University of Stellenbosch. The game the world over owes a deep debt of gratitude to this giant among rugby men.

Another original thinker on the game is John J. Stewart, the principal of an agricultural college in Wanganui. J.J. was highly successful with the All Blacks in Great Britain in the mid seventies when they comfortably defeated Ireland on the Saturday and Wales in midweek. In 1975 his tourists should have been the first ever to win a series against the Springboks in South Africa.

I first met him in 1971 when the Lions played the Wanganui–King Country combined team, captained by Colin Meads and coached by J.J., a man feared by the rugby establishment for his outspokenness. He possessed a genius for diverting the press away from previews and injuries and such dull matters. On this occasion each of his players was handed a copy of a prayer written in J.J.'s inimitable style provoking them to ponder on the basic do's and don'ts of the game.

Amen I say unto you that whosoever shall pass the ball under conditions more advantageous to the opposition than his own team will be cast aside.
Verily let it always be that our defence will be desperate and those who set up second-phase play behind the forwards shall feel the wrath of the Almighty.
May we always remember to concentrate not on winning but on not losing.
It will come to pass that the ball shall be kept ahead of the forwards, and in so doing may we always remember it can be done by passing or kicking, and kicking is simple, and as we consider these and other faults let us be mindful that he who adopts the involved dog position in the rucks shall be smote with a bucketful of water.
From these sins and the national selectors may the Lord protect us.
Dominus Tackle, Dominus Tackle, Dominus Tackle.
Amen

The prayer, alas, went unheard by the Dominus who, on this occasion at least, listened to a simpler prayer in Welsh, the language of heaven. But the players of both sides read it and some understood it better than others. Like myself, J. J. Stewart is of the opinion that rugby football is a thinking game.

## A thinking game

Rugby football is a thinking game. The word 'think' and the imperative of the verb should be heard often in a lively coaching session. The players should be challenged to think about the game, to think and to memorize and to recall in the correct order the exercises they may have done in a skill sequence.

During a line-out session, as a brief interlude, the thickest forward may be asked to reveal the line-out signals of the opposition. A laugh or a chuckle may shorten the agony, and a slight digression on signals is permissible.

Any kind of ambiguity should be avoided. A word sign beginning with the letter 'p' was the call for the forwards to go right. When Gareth Edwards, typically, called 'psychology', half the forwards went left. The Welsh team, incidentally, use the Welsh language although most of them are ignorant of it as a daily means of communication.

I was quite amused, probably because in Wales we never use the pronoun 'thee', to observe that Ray French in his characteristically down-to-earth dissertation, *Running Rugby*, uses the 'me to thee', 'thee to me' call for the scrum half and the number 8. Acceptable and less ambiguous for the lads of Cowley and the North of England than other parts, I'm sure. The least ambiguous and the most surreptitious sign I ever encountered was by Arthur Summons, the Wallaby fly half, who pointed the toe of his right foot in the direction that mattered.

Calling signals or decoding them should keep players alert. Another wakey-wakey contribution is the use of the whistle: two blasts and all the players must fall flat on their faces, three means six press-ups and four is to stand again. I'm a great believer in constantly reminding players orally and by practice how important it is to get off the ground immediately.

It isn't easy for a twelve-stone scrum half to get up quickly following a dive pass. Imagine the effort for an eighteen-stone forward! It is a skill and it should be taught as a skill. For a perceptive thinker I would offer the subject: 'The undiscovered skills and the forgotten arts of all football games' for a post-graduate degree, probably a doctorate.

Incidentally, in case you are asking yourself the question, I reserve the one blast on the whistle during the action for a deficiency in technique. Play carries on but the point has been made. More about this later when I discuss my Italian experience to make coaching points. This was an invaluable experience, really, because it made me rethink my philosophy and approach, following a longish connection with top-class material at Llanelli and with the British Lions.

It was almost like teaching youngsters in the junior school again with the accent on the basics, the fundamentals, the skills and the habits, and forgetting, more or less, that there were forwards and there were backs. They all had to learn the individual skills. An awareness of this simple fact could be the salvation of the game in the eighties. Players need to be shown the way, but above all they must be encouraged into action.

## Too much talk

I have a feeling that coaches generally tend to talk too much. Talk provokes talk and too much of it can lead to indiscipline.

In my first week as a schoolmaster I learned that silence is golden. Chattering children hate a silent teacher. Silence suggests strength. Silence, I have found, provokes silence and obedience.

I shall never forget my first training session at Rovigo in northern Italy. I knew no Italian. Most of the players knew no English. Fortunately, the hooker, Paolo Ferracin, spoke English quite well and I gave my instructions through him. I first asked him if the boys always talked so much in a training session. He laughed and said that they

Paulo Ferracin of Rovigo: a fluent hooker and fluent in English

were Italian! If you want to be heard in Italy you have to speak louder than the next guy.

My first instruction, naturally, was that no one should speak. Imagine their disbelief. Like naughty children, two of them tried me out and for their curiosity they spent the next twenty minutes in almost solitary confinement, fifty yards apart, running around the adjoining pitch while in the blissful silence I gave quiet voice to the falling eventide and the encircling gloom, which bewildered my Italian friends even more.

What a joy, once they had learned the value of silence, to see them working hard in training and to observe their discipline in matches against garrulous opponents who inevitably quarrelled amongst themselves when things began to go wrong. Their silence and their disciplined approval easily won for them the championship of the first division and a private audience with the Holy Father, John Paul II, at the Vatican. The following day Sanson Rovigo played inspired rugby against Frascati, the home of my favourite *vino bianco secco*.

With or without wine, the tongues of too many coaches are too loose. They will insist on delivering lecturettes during a coaching session. My advice to any aspiring coach is to cut the chat to a minimum.

One of the worst examples I ever witnessed of a coach who loved to hear his own voice was in Villa Dose, a small village in northern Italy. I had been asked to assess him. It was a bitterly cold night, the kind of night when I cursed my luck and yearned to be beside a coal fire. The coach, an Argentinian who prided himself on his Italian, dominated the session with words and more words while the players were hanging around getting more and more miserable in the freezing conditions.

I soon relegated him to the touchline and took over to conduct a short, sharp session full of running and passing and amusement. Even the elephants in attendance chirped and twittered as if they had swallowed nightingales, while the Argentinian cuckoo moved on to another nest.

He was replaced by Alex Penciu, a Rumanian exile, who had played brilliantly for Locomotiva against Clem Thomas's All Whites in 1954 and again as a full back against R. H. Williams's Scarlets in Moscow in 1957. I spent hours discussing those matches with Alex and also the coaching methods of Vogel, now exiled in Buenos Aires.

The Holy Father

## The fitness addict

Another type I can't abide is the immaculately tracksuit-clad coach who, although past it, turns the clock back and leads the field to set the pace for the running-around-the-paddock bit. I would hope that my players could set and maintain a faster pace than I could.

This type of coach, too, will insist on demonstrating particular skills badly. A coach should never demonstrate unless he has perfected the art. Choose the best performer in the squad and let him demonstrate. Use the expertise that you have around you, comment briefly on the points to look for in the skill and let the lads practise.

The better coaches will accept the fact that certain players may have a more specialist acquaintance with a particular aspect of play than the coach has, that other players may be able to demonstrate better, and that they should all be fitter than he is. It is bad psychology to reveal the shortcomings of a player in front of others. Equally bad at the end of a hard session, when most of us are gasping for a fag, is to see our 'fitter-than-thou' coach, after he has dismissed the players, setting off on another round-the-field jogging trip in full view of the dressing room.

## Diagnosis and the cure

A coach should be able to diagnose what is wrong with his team. If he is unsure, then he must look for expert opinion in much the same way that a family doctor calls for the help of a consultant. Once the ill or the ills are diagnosed, the coach must set up a clinic to provide the correct treatment.

Because the players didn't have the natural ability of the Welsh lads that I had coached for years, I found my two-year Italian connection more challenging and eventually most rewarding.

I had a great deal of sorting out to do in the first couple of months and I soon discovered that I was alone in all matters that related to the team. The *dirigenti*, the Rovigo committee, were really only concerned that we should collect two championship points every week.

Having always believed that rugby football is a benign dictatorship and that the best committee is a subcommittee of one man, it was an ideal situation in which to be. The enlightened Rovigo committee never dreamed of interfering; they didn't even ask who was in the team, preferring to find out from Luciano Ravagnani in *Il Gazettino* or from Sandro Andriolli in *Il Resto del Carlino*.

In other words, I was allowed to stand or fall by my own judgements, a situation with which I wasn't too unfamiliar, having worked with an enlightened captain in John Dawes and a considerate manager in Doug Smith in 1971. I also had the advantage of knowing how to keep a squad of twenty-four or twenty-six players happy from my coaching experience with Llanelli, where a coach's word was law and where a selection committee was an anachronism.

I still can't abide the principle of five selectors. To find five who think alike would be to doubt the parentage of some. I hate the inevitable compromise. A coach has the vision and he must select his own men to project the vision. For holding such views I have been called arrogant, Clough and other names, but I'm afraid that even age hasn't mellowed my strong feelings on the subject.

A committee of selectors does, of course, protect the coach. Without such a cushion it can be a lonely job. Mine was lonely at Rovigo, but I preferred it that way, knowing that I had to produce the right results and that I had to fall in love with the magic of two points. The Monday morning championship table said it all.

So did the World Cup in Spain say it all for Enzo Bearzot who, for many seasons now, has had to suffer and endure the slings and arrows of lesser men. An enlightened coach of the national side, he kept faith with his vision of a game that is only pleasing to the eye when the skills of the individual are beautifully presented. His team were not as skilful as Brazil but they were conditioned by the Italian first division to concede little and to counter-attack from deep positions. He also kept

faith with Paolo Rossi who took over the match-winning mantle of Roberto Bettega.

For me the season in Italy started quite well. We won in the rain at Parma. My opposite number was David Williams, for many years a close friend. Like soccer managers and coaches, we sat in our separate *panchinas* near the halfway line. Dai, an exile in Italy for some dozen years, spoke the language fluently and he maintained a remarkably biased commentary for the whole game, punctuated by the occasional bit of Welsh invective directed at the referee.

From that first match I held strong views about coaches offering a constant stream of advice to unthinking players. It is bad for the players, for the game and the refereeing. I'm pleased to record that for the following season the Italian Federation accepted this point of view and the coaches were banned from the touchline. Dai's ultimate comment was, 'Don't worry, I'll make myself heard from the stand!; and he did.

Three coaching and training sessions, two evenings and one lunchtime, fully attended, were an adequate preparation for the one match. One session for two matches is the norm in Wales. When necessary, the players made themselves available for an individual-skills session. Despite a fair start to the season, I didn't feel that we were playing anywhere near as well as we should.

Another challenge I had to face was the Italians' dislike of playing away from home. Like their wine, they travel badly. Sure enough, the shattering blow came at Rome, all too soon, against a strong side called Algida which included All Blacks Andy Haden and Frank Oliver as well as a number of other internationals. We lost by a margin of more than twenty points. On the following Tuesday evening came the post mortem. They wanted to know why they had played so badly.

Not a punch was pulled. The following points were made:

1. Discipline. Silence. Accept the decisions of a referee, however bad.

2. No quarrelling amongst yourselves. Accept responsibility for dropping a poor pass, don't blame the passer.

3. Do precisely what Dirk Naude, a six-foot-eight tough South African lock, tells you. Against Algida the play of the forwards was much too loose. Both props played like butterflies. The

Italians, like the French of the early fifties, love running wildly with the ball and much of their passing is loose and ill-directed. They ran away from their support.

4. Every player must tackle. Against the Romans there was far too much shadow tackling. First-time tackling from the back row is a key factor in a successful team.

5. The half backs suffered because the ball was retailed too slowly. If the forwards hold the ball at a set piece, then they must drive before releasing it.

6. We must work harder on the quick ball from the line-out and the scrummages.

7. The rolling maul was done well enough. Movement must be maintained with the forwards taking the initiative and preferably scoring the tries. If the maul is rendered static don't take the easy way out and release the ball to the scrum half. By then defences are reorganized and it is, in all probability, a poor ball.

8. A lack of experience at fly half meant that far too many bad options were taken.

It was this last point that they were all waiting for. They thought, and I knew there was quite a strong opinion in the team and in the town, that I was selecting the wrong fly half. There was, it could be said, a Zuin faction and a Bettarello faction. Both fathers were famous ex-players, both coached a squad of youngsters at the club, and both were good friends of mine if not of one another. Loredano Zuin was an experienced player and a fine tactical kicker. He had played for Italy, he could set his threes going and he usually took the correct option. He was rather long-legged, slowish off the mark and not my idea of a fly half. I preferred him at inside centre or full back.

Stefano Bettarello was a youngster, barely eighteen years old, small, Iberian looking, quick, restless, a beautiful punter and place kicker – but he made mistakes. I had to choose. My assistant, Franco Vecchi, wanted to play safe and select Zuin. I felt it was my duty to develop the obvious talents of a lad who resembled Phil Bennett and had many of his better qualities.

I may have lost the championship in my first season because of this decision. We easily won it in my second when Stefano was the leading points scorer in Italy. Since then he has won many a game for his country.

I told the team that I felt it was my duty to give Bettarello the experience of playing in tough championship matches. I also admitted that as yet he didn't have the vision of Zuin or Bernard Thomas of Llanelli, who had played for Rovigo for the previous two seasons. But, with patience, he would be a most competent player sooner than later.

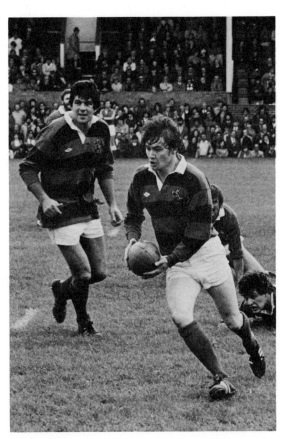

Bernard Thomas who was Bettarello's predecessor at Rovigo

I felt I had to devise a system whereby I could transmit automatically to the players what was a good ball or an indifferent one. The method I used was quite simple. Being a firm believer in the quick transfer of ball from scrum half to wing, I would practise this for hours every training night with a Llanelli division comprised of players like Selwyn Williams, Phil Bennett, Bernard Thomas, Ray Gravell, Roy Bergiers, J. J. Williams, Roger

Davies, Andy Hill and others. I didn't bother with moves, but I insisted that they should all be able to take and give a pass in one stride.

Once that pattern had been set, the possibilities were enormous. It was a pattern that my coaching mentor, T. P. Williams, and I had coached at Llandovery College and it was the very same pattern that the Lions of 1971 enjoyed playing. To instil the pattern into less gifted players called for infinite patience, lots of encouragement and occasionally a hard word when their concentration lapsed.

This was the drill. Unless the taking and the giving of a pass was immediate and perfect in execution, I would blow on my whistle. They were not to stop; they carried on with the movement

T. P. Williams of Llandovery College, a perceptive coach

which was still an exercise in trying to make good from poor. Being constantly blasted for imperfect technique helped the players no end. In fact their progress was remarkably quick, proving, if it needs proving, that coaching is not about waving a magic wand but hard work and constant vigilance.

Once the drill had become second nature, I allowed them the luxury of threequarter moves, the kind of moves which took them away and not into the cover. Unwittingly, New Zealand did the game an injustice by creating a crash-ball tackle situation and thereby setting up an artificial platform for second-phase play. In the wake of Ian MacRae's crash-ball tactics in mid-field, 'to MacRae' has become an acceptable and meaningful

infinitive. Then came Joggie Jansen in South Africa, Ray Gravell in Wales, and a host of minor imitators. Inevitably, the majority of other countries slavishly followed suit without being able to ruck cleanly from the platform in the manner of the Kiwi forwards.

From my observation the world over, I'm sorry to say that only a few coaches are well versed in the drill of producing a rhythmic threequarter line. Even at international level the standard of play generally in the late seventies and the early eighties has been unacceptably low. I don't think rugby suffers too much from overcoaching but rather from poor coaching.

Coaches who don't think enough. Content with their certificate and their badge, they go through the motions of what they were told to do at the coaching course. There is a basic sameness and a boredom in their sessions.

Units and teams are essentially boring. Individuals are interesting. Coaching, like teaching, is about helping the individual. If his skills are good and ever improving, the sum total will be so much better.

Teach the simple things well would be my advice to any aspiring coach. Break the skill down, teach the parts, then teach the whole skill in relation to other players and a game situation. A skill for its own sake is irrelevant. Perfecting skills in positional play, by the way, is the province of another part of the coaching session or, maybe, the concern of a brief weekly clinic with a particular player.

For the moment let's forget the warm-up and proceed with the session. Not the Invercargill one but an individual-skill session which should form the coaching base at any level.

## The skill is the father of the move

The poor coaches only teach moves.

Early in any coaching session it is worthwhile to take a back or a forward move as a basic to be performed, analysed and performed again. At this juncture the performance of the skill is more important than technique.

1. When the backs are passing the ball along the threequarter line it is good for three or four forwards to line up with the coach and run in front of the backs as they practise and for the

same number to run behind them. Their presence implies pressure play – both cover defence and support. In fact it is always interesting to note, when play breaks down, who is there first to kill the loose ball. A more practical method is to employ the front five ahead of the backs and the back row behind them.

2. An interesting forward ploy is the peel. The peel, incidentally, was introduced to the game by the French in the early sixties. I first came across it at Mosney, to the north of Dublin, when Jean Prat came over to help run the first coaching course organized by Des Scaife and Judge Charlie Conroy on behalf of the Leinster Branch of the Irish Rugby Union. No one as yet had heard of the peel, the newest creation of the inventive French.

The peel became such a successful and worthwhile ploy the world over that the law makers were soon using the word in the law book. It was a classic case of an acceptable tactic becoming a potent part of an evolving game.

For players, even for the French, it was a most demanding ploy. There are a number of precise skills involved; progression through the different skills is all important:

(a) The ball must be thrown in from touch accurately. Incidentally, it was at one of these Irish coaching weeks that I first became involved in the discussion concerning who should throw the ball in from touch. Almost immediately there was an agreement that one player was preferable to two. I will not analyse the merits or demerits of each forward position now. Suffice to say that your thrower is your best line-out jumper and that, since almost anyone can be coached to throw, the hooker is as good as any. Keep a careful eye, however, on the role of the hooker during and immediately after the line-out because many are using this responsibility as an excuse for roving and playing a butterfly type of game.

(b) The ball must be thrown accurately to number 5 or 6 in the line-out. If to 6, then 5 and 7 must form a protective wedge for an accurate deflection by 6.

(c) With all the forwards facing front and turning towards the opposition, 3 can start his run to take the ball once it has left the thrower's hands.

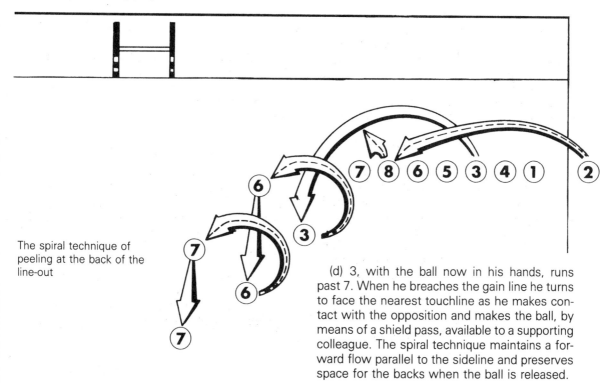

The spiral technique of peeling at the back of the line-out

(d) 3, with the ball now in his hands, runs past 7. When he breaches the gain line he turns to face the nearest touchline as he makes contact with the opposition and makes the ball, by means of a shield pass, available to a supporting colleague. The spiral technique maintains a forward flow parallel to the sideline and preserves space for the backs when the ball is released.

The peel at the front of the line-out is equally potent and has the advantage of creating even more space for the back division. I found it an invaluable ploy on the narrow grounds of Canada.

The perfection of the peel is an excellent example of the need to master a number of skills before the move can be executed. Early on in the history of the peel it was laughable to observe even international players performing badly because they hadn't appreciated the necessity of using the swivel or the shield pass, with the result that they sent their colleagues on a cross-field, worthless mission.

In the front of the line peel 2 throws to 4, 4 deflects to 6, 6 passes to 7 and 7 passes to 8, etc.

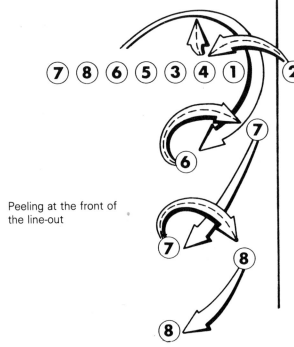

Peeling at the front of the line-out

## Handling exercises related to support play

The following, used extensively by the Lions in 1971, combines a number of skills and is a superb way of teaching support play. It is also demanding physically and proves the point that players can attain a pretty high level of fitness while working on the basics.

The whole field is used and the squad may be divided into groups of five or six players.

### *First exercise* (support in depth)

Number the players 1 to 6 and line them up in a threequarter formation. Pass the ball accurately and swiftly from 1 to 6. 6 then throws the ball along the ground for 1 to pick up at speed, 1 throws the ball for 2, 2 to 3, etc., with the arc getting wider and wider so that the whole field is used. The second line of players may start when the first are halfway through their exercise and then a third and a fourth, etc., may follow.

In this exercise the support is deep.

### *Second exercise* (midi support)

Threequarter passing, 6 runs wide and as he falls to the ground he propels the ball up for 1 to take,

who follows suit and makes the ball available to 2. This means much closer support. The means of transference may be altered to the fashionable current tackle law and the expected release of the ball.

### *Third exercise* (close support)

Threequarter passing, 6 runs wide and carries the ball on the outside or trailing hip, 1 rips the ball away from him and repeats the process running wide and making the ball available to 2. In this exercise the swivel or shield pass action may be used or it can be used in addition as a fourth exercise. In both, the support play is close.

So we have progressed from deep to midi to close support.

May I suggest that players should be encouraged to think of other skills which may be used within the same framework?

Skill and support play ▷

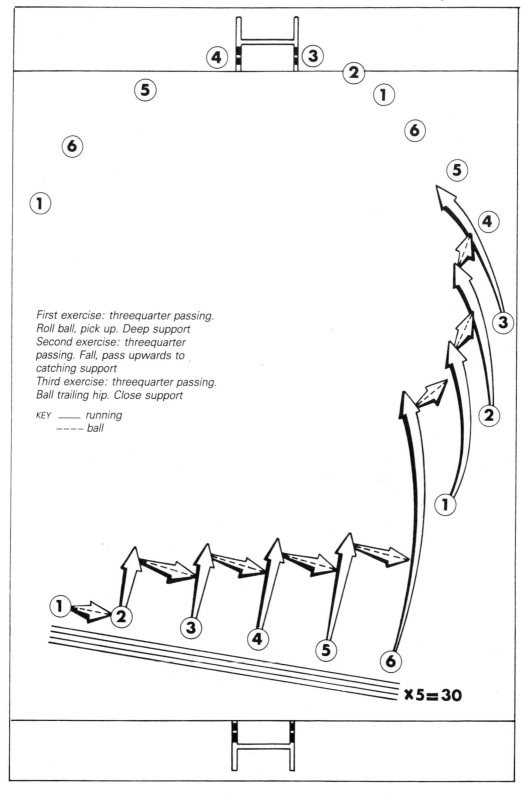

First exercise: threequarter passing.
Roll ball, pick up. Deep support
Second exercise: threequarter
passing. Fall, pass upwards to
catching support
Third exercise: threequarter passing.
Ball trailing hip. Close support

KEY ——— running
- - - - ball

×5=30

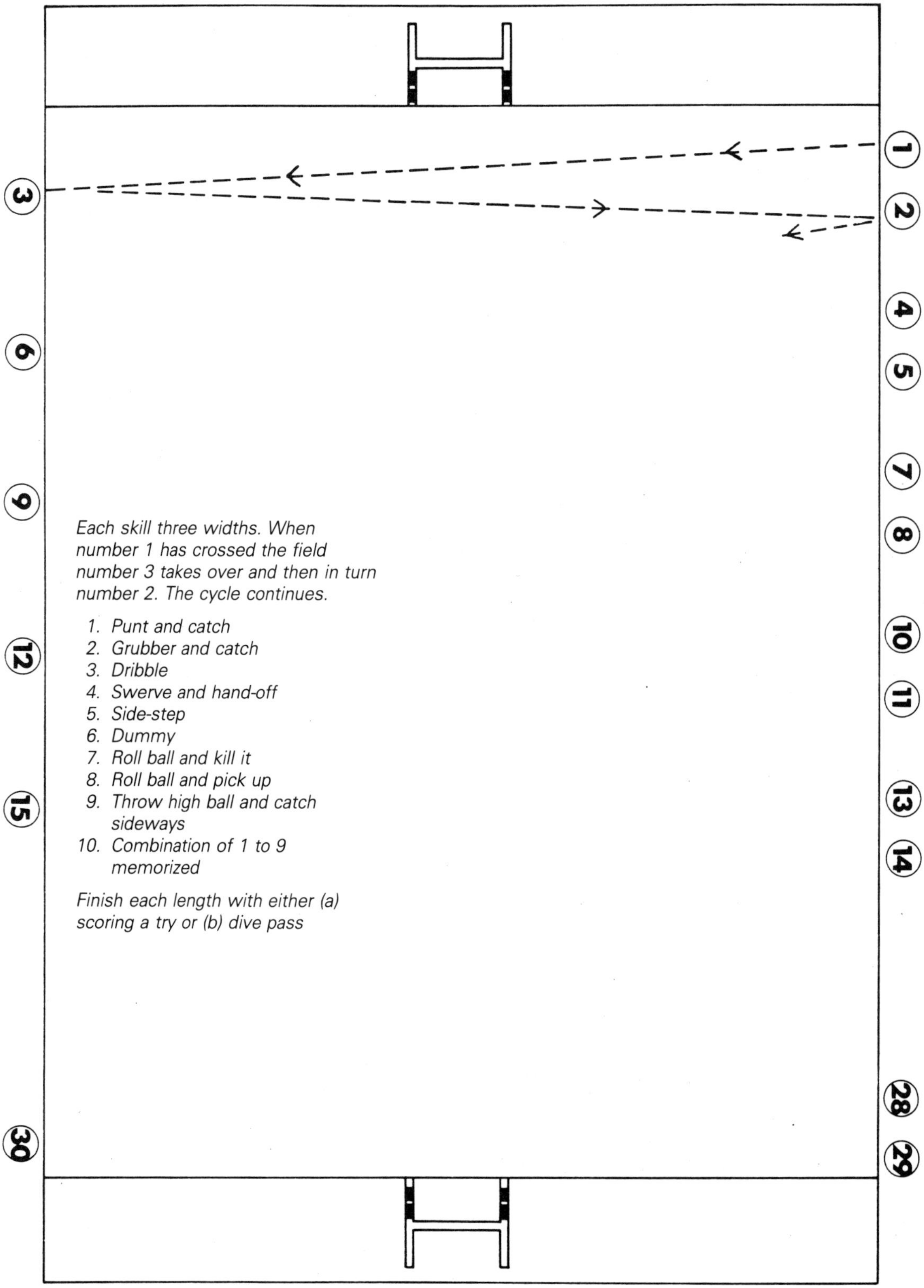

Each skill three widths. When
number 1 has crossed the field
number 3 takes over and then in turn
number 2. The cycle continues.

1. Punt and catch
2. Grubber and catch
3. Dribble
4. Swerve and hand-off
5. Side-step
6. Dummy
7. Roll ball and kill it
8. Roll ball and pick up
9. Throw high ball and catch
   sideways
10. Combination of 1 to 9
    memorized

Finish each length with either (a)
scoring a try or (b) dive pass

# Skills for all

Now for the other more general individual skills that every player should have. With a squad of thirty, ten balls, two players at one end and one immediately opposite, work across field, slowly at first and then more quickly, as the skills are learned and mastered. There is a sufficient time recovery to allow for a long session.

Passing and handling skills may be introduced, all the kicking skills including the punt, the drop and the grubber, and they should be done with both feet. It is important for all forwards to practise skills which they may not use often in a game: there will come a moment during the course of a match when they will be grateful that they have been taught what is, for them, an unlikely skill. In this round of ten skills, allow the players the chance of thinking of one themselves, and as a final flourish ask them to perform the round in the correct order.

For variation the same skills may be practised in a straight line with a runner adding a little pressure and competition. Can the runner, for instance, beat the quickness of the pass up and down the chain? Then change the runner.

A games element may be introduced as well. For example, passing deftly in a circle with an occasional throw at a player's legs in the middle of a circle. Ask for similar games to teach quickness of movement. They are a lot of fun and there is time for that.

I should stress that all these skills should be done at speed. Once the players have been shown how to perform, they must seek to better themselves. An occasional word of encouragement from the coach helps enormously. Incidentally, may I again note that perfecting the technique of positional play is another matter.

While in the games mood, I would stress the value of other team games to maintain interest in the skills part of a coaching session:

(a) *Soccer* – it was significant, perhaps, that Barry John carried a round ball around both islands of New Zealand for three and a half months in 1971. Soccer is a superb game for teaching balanced running with the ball, for encouraging accurately struck and sensitively weighted passes, and for illustrating the value of intelli-

gent running off the ball while the player holding the ball cleverly times his passing into the open spaces. In a game in which no player has the ball in his hands for a minute or more during the full eighty minutes, running off the ball of necessity is an invaluable exercise.

(b) *Rugby League* – the thirteen-a-side game is an exercise in maintaining possession no matter how severe the pressure. While standing or when thrown to the ground the tackled player must not lose the ball even though he may have wanted to fire a short, sharp pass on the burst to a colleague in support. League promotes the smother tackle, the mauling, all-in-wrestling type tackle more than the classical, traditional-type tackling again now rewarded in Union despite a recent devaluation period.

# Tackling

By 1983 I have no doubt that the IB will have seen sense and offered a simply defined and easily interpreted tackle law: 'A tackled player may not hold the ball. . . .'

May I stress yet again that the individual skill session is not the time to perfect the tackle technique. The clinic for the individual is better. Rather, it is the time and the place to seek the joy and the abandon of tackling.

Progression, again, is important. In this instance, developing a technique by building confidence. With the tackler and the tackled of a similar physique, start by tackling static, then at a walking pace, a little faster and eventually flat out. Confidence comes from not being hurt.

For that reason it is the position of the tackler's head that is all important. The tackler must get used to an opponent who has a high knee-raising action and he must also learn how to cope with a hand-off, which particularly applies to the side-on tackle. It is important to practise this tackle from the left and from the right.

I would encourage youngsters to learn the side-on tackle first. Then the head-on and the smother tackle.

The most difficult tackle, probably, is the one from behind. For comfort, the tackled player's heels must be avoided by getting that much closer to his body, hitting him just above the knees with the shoulder and gripping him tightly round the legs.

◁ General skill practice for a rugby squad

Cliff Morgan side-on and low under Ted Woodward's hand-off

It is important to emphasize over and over again the positive nature of tackling. A strong tackle can turn defence into attack. Such tackles are just as important as the corner-flagging, try-saving tackles performed, as we well recall, by some of the great back-row players. A tackling front five is a tremendous bonus for any team.

## Cover defence

Most coaches, in my experience, work on set pieces (like scrummages, rucks and mauls) going forward. It is quite amazing to see the transformation in players when their minds have been conditioned to perform these unit skills by running backwards first.

Work with the whole fifteen. Throw the ball behind the forwards. They run back and when they have overtaken the ball they will perform the various skills of the ruck – e.g. the half turn before entry parallel to the touchline. They will grab a colleague and, as they enter the ruck, the upper half of the body will get into a scrummaging posture. They will drive in controlled fashion over the ball, giving plenty of protection for the scrum half.

When the coach blows his whistle, the scrum half passes to the fly half. This means that the whole threequarter line and the full back have also run back and got into a position for attack or defence. Reassembling your forces in this way, and the constant practice of it, is a positive psychological way of teaching cover defence without even mentioning the fact.

I must confess that I only became aware of it by chance. During the first few weeks with the Lions in New Zealand I did a great deal of my work with the forwards going back before going forward. Their level of fitness rose appreciably and when the All Blacks continually attacked early on in the first Test, I found that our cover defence was superb. The lads were so used to going backwards before performing that it had become like a conditioned reflex to them.

## The forgotten skills

I shall concentrate on three which, although hardly used in the modern game, are as relevant today as they ever were.

### Dribbling

(a) Dribble, with the inside-of-the-foot method, legs splayed wide and moving the ball from one foot to the other. Keep the ball close to the feet at a controlled pace, not too fast, keeping the body forward, head down and still all the time with the eyes directly over the ball.

Dribbling: inside-of-the-foot method

(b) In the outside-of-the-foot method the legs are closer together. Back spin is imparted which keeps the ball close. With an experienced performer this method allows for speedier dribbling.

Dribbling: outside-of-the-foot method

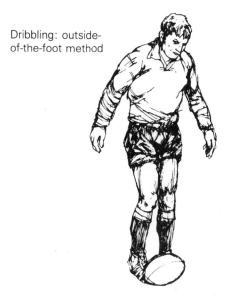

In an era of disruptive wheeling at the scrums, forwards should be taught to dribble. It is a most positive way of countering the disruption and setting up a powerful counter-attack with the ball at the feet. It would be a thrill to hear a Murrayfield crowd once again calling, 'Feet, feet, feet, Scotland. . . .'

Group dribbling

Training Run.                                      3. 5. 71.

                                                        Carwyn James.

30 players        10 balls.        2 hrs (approx.).

1. <u>Warm Up</u> : round paddock in groups of 3, passing ball (lateral, one-
       handed, overhead etc.). Keep moving the ball.
          Stop now + again for body exercises.
       Ball games : 3 v 3 (dispossess by touching opponent or ball touching ground).
               6 v 6 League (5mins) ; Touch (5 mins).
          Accent : Running, Exercising all muscles, ball-handling, VARIATION.
                                                        Total : 20 mins.
                                                              to 25 mins.
2. <u>Individual Skills</u> : Halves passing, Centres – variations on midfield break,
       Wings throwing in, then outside break, Full Backs high punts,
       catching, line-kicking plus cutting the side-line.
       Props – mechanics of scrummaging, Locks – two handed catching
       and deflection, Back-row – defence + attack from Scrum.
       Coach moves around, keeps eye on all groups. Total : 15 - 20 mins.

3. Unit skills : J.D. in charge of Backs. Accent on ball-handling.

{  H   x x x            Quick chain passing – then : 1. Picking up ball in arc.
        x x x                                        2. Falling + passing.
        x  x                                         3. Shield passing. etc.
   Backs      Competitive Relays : Running + standing positions.
              Ball games. Must have plenty of variation.   Time : 40 mins.
              (Teach one ploy in each session. Today : Counter attack from high kick.

       Forwards :  CJ + 2 pack leaders.   Intro. Strength exercises for scrummaging.
          1. Scrum : Tight grip, lowering knees, straightening leg, concerted shove.
+ Half Backs.    Move up + downfield, 8 going down together, Tight head 8 man shove.
          Accent : Control, Discipline, togetherness.          Time : 20 mins.
          2. Line-out : Signals. ① Two lines working separately – 3, 5, 7, peel.
+ Wings.                 ② Together, contesting. Concentrate 3 + drive.
          Accent : Compressing, tightness.          Time : 20 mins.
       4. Two 15s – CJ + JD.  Unopposed. All ploys – concentrate today on Counter-Attack. 20mins
       5. Forwards – RJMcLoughlin, Strength Training.  Backs Sprinting CJ.  10mins.

## The cross kick

A classical manoeuvre, once upon a time; hardly seen any more. A wing threequarter on the outside swerve, realizing in good time that he can't beat the cover, places a high cross kick into the middle of the field which his forwards have anticipated. Practised to perfection, this simple ploy can lead to many a stirring try.

## The outside swerve

A well-executed outside swerve used to be one of the real aesthetic pleasures of the game. We see it seldom now because of the new offside line at the scrummage and particularly at the line-out.

At the first phase, therefore, it is rubbish to call on a mid-field player to draw his man, as crowds still do, when that opponent may be 10 metres or more away. At the second or third phase, however, it is so important that players draw their men in order to try to release an outside player.

For this reason coaches should practise the four to three, three to two, two to one situations. Set these groups in opposition, draw your man and time your pass.

Then encourage the ball carrier to veer slightly away from his opposite number and half-draw the next opponent. This is the way to teach the outside swerve. A lengthening of stride by the ball carrier in the area between the two opponents gives him the thrill of making the break and taking a colleague on the outside with him who accepts the scoring pass.

He who quotes himself must be mad. I take the liberty, however, of including the notes on a coaching session I gave the Lions almost a dozen years ago and published in Gabe David and David Frost's joint analysis of the tour. I placed great value on individual skills then and if the sessions worked with thirty of the best players in these islands, then I feel more concerned than ever that they should still be taught. It may well be the emphasis that the game needs at the present moment the world over.

# 3 The Full Back

## Assessment of the position *Carwyn James*

If Andy Irvine had played in the thirties or in the immediate post-war years I doubt very much whether he would have wanted to play full back. In those days full backs like Howard Davies and Gerwyn Williams of Wales and George Norton of Ireland, as I remember them, were bona fide custodians, the last line of defence. Their assets were fielding, kicking and tackling and little else was expected of them.

It would be unthinkable to play a full back who couldn't tackle or preferred not to tackle. I remember the occasional artist who had the knack of arriving just too late to bring off the crunching tackle near to the corner flag!

### Tackling

The skills of tackling are a must for any aspiring full back even in the modern game which demands the support of a covering wing three-quarter. The shrewd tackler will shepherd his opponent in the direction which is the more advan-

J. P. R. Williams: here the arch-tackler himself resists a double tackle

tageous for a sure side tackle but he must always be prepared for the frontal confrontation with an eighteen stone mobile forward. In recent times J. P. R. Williams is the prime example of the tackler par excellence.

The paragon of all full backs for me, maybe because I played with him for the best part of a decade, was Terry Davies, a former captain of Wales and a British Lion. He had mastered all the traditional skills and he was also a fine attacker.

It is an interesting fact that Terry Davies, a full back, played at fly half for the Royal Navy in 1953 and the following spring I was selected to play at full back for the Navy although I had played most of my rugby at fly half. I have no doubt at all that it is a tremendous advantage to have had experience of two positions which are interchangeable.

## Positioning

Following my experience at full back with Devonport Services and the Navy I was a much better tactical kicker at fly half on my return to Llanelli. Terry Davies was prompted to write the following in 1961 about the positional play of a full back:

'When positioning yourself the man to watch is the opposing fly half. He is the hub of the opposition's tactical play. He dictates their play, it is he who decides whether the ball is moved to the left or the right. Watch for his signal to the scrum half at a set scrummage. If you can spot the signal you can get into position quickly, prepared for the break-through or the diagonal kick. If, for instance, the ball is worked quickly to the wing and you see that he is well looked after by the cover defence, move back to the middle of the field to counter the cross kick.

'For a line-out, position yourself 15 to 20 yards from the touchline giving yourself ample time and room to cover both sides of the field. In the case of a loose scrum (i.e. ruck or maul) position yourself directly behind it keeping an eagle eye again on the opposing fly half.'

It has always been the source of much pleasure

Terry Davies: master of the traditional skills and a fine attacker

to me to watch the canny positional play of the great full backs. There they are, always unhurried under the high ball or reaching confidently for the diagonal along the ground. It was for me, equally, a pleasure to see a Barry John, with pin-point accuracy, premeditated, destroy as giant a full back as Fergie McCormick.

New Zealand have never had the grace to admit that this happened in the first Test at Dunedin in 1971 and the dropping of McCormick was partly responsible for the All Blacks losing the series. Other fly halves like Phil Bennett and Ollie Campbell are capable of such destruction but they have lacked the mental hardness or the killer punch of a Barry John.

## The high ball and falling on the ball

Without courage, oceans of it, neither is possible. The high ball or the garryowen is still a major tactic in the modern game. Less so falling on the ball

because of the forgotten art of dribbling and the making available of the ball following a tackle. Down and up like lightning is the current mode of play.

## Fielding and kicking

Kill two birds with one stone by practising with another player. Practise taking the high and the low ball at different positions. In fielding, the ball should be taken into the body with the arms forming such a cradle that the ball is tucked away. Never allow the ball to move away from you in the process of fielding; on the contrary, move into the line of flight and get under the ball at every opportunity. Don't trust a bouncing ball. As you field, turn your body sideways so that if you misfield the ball will travel backwards and the knock-on will be avoided.

When it is your turn to kick make the flight of the ball different for your colleague by experi-

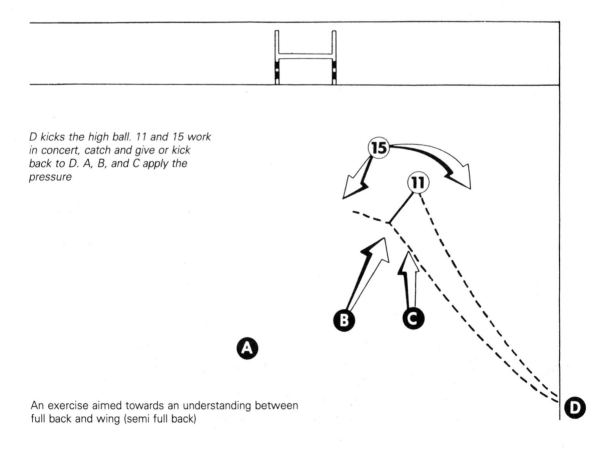

*D kicks the high ball. 11 and 15 work in concert, catch and give or kick back to D. A, B, and C apply the pressure*

An exercise aimed towards an understanding between full back and wing (semi full back)

menting with the way you place the ball on your foot. The angle of placement – and let there be no light betwixt ball and foot – is all-important. Immensely so for the screw kick and its safe delivery over the touchline. For the fly half and the full back, saving the energy of the forwards is all-important.

In my first week in the Royal Navy I discovered the essential difference between English and Welsh rugby. When I found touch for the English the pack leader praised loudly, 'Thank you, James!' I never received such courtesy at Llanelli. Twenty brilliant, screw-kicking touchfinders went unheeded. One wayward and my parenthood was disputed.

For successful spin or screw kicking hold the ball at the precise angle at which you intend to cut the touchline, letting the lace (or where the lace should be) hang over and away from its destination. That lace weight in the good old days was all important in giving the ball added weight on that side to help the spin. Then by stretching a taut foot, kick with the instep across the ball at the end of your follow through. To help your follow through, and this is a Terry Davies secret, try and touch the tips of your fingers after kicking the ball, which, incidentally, also helps to balance the body.

In punting or place kicking I have always stressed the importance of making sure that the upper part of the body is leaning slightly forward, that the follow through is absolutely essential and that you don't look up until you hear the applause.

## As an attacker

It is a most interesting fact that in his treatise on full-back play written twenty years ago Terry Davies doesn't say a word about the attacking role of his position. And yet Davies could be and often was as fine an attacker as any today.

A number of us in West Wales were fortunate to have played with Lewis Jones, one of the finest attackers of all time. The Welsh selectors didn't really know what to make of him or where to put him. His natural impulse was to run with the ball and his honest philosophy was to let 'them', the opposition, score two tries and he would collect three. That he could kick goals gave him an extra confidence which many would call arrogance.

A classical place kick, here taken by Bob Hiller of England and the Lions

Jones played cat and mouse with any defence. I have never seen any other player with his facility to move from a lazy second gear to a graceful over-drive in a few paces, leaving behind him a trail of clutching arms and prostrate bodies. If there ever was a genius on the rugby field it was Lewis Jones.

Without question he was an attacking full back; that is, when he was invited to play in that pos-

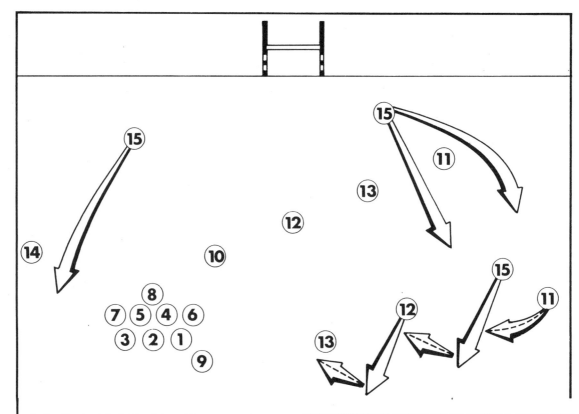

Left: *On the blind side, links with scrum half or with the wing. Top right: On the open side he may join the line between 13 and 11, or outside 11.Bottom right: He may take an inside pass from the wing (11) and link with the inside centre (12) to change the direction of the attack*

Full back attacking options

ition. Unfortunately, he became a league player much too soon but he was a natural for a game which has always nurtured the counter-attack.

Following Jones came Ken J. F. Scotland, another fine attacker who paved the way for the likes of Andy Irvine to play in the modern idiom. Such has been the concentration on attack that all full backs by now need the pace and the skills of a wing threequarter. No one has combined the two positions better than Irvine.

Ken Scotland, an attacking full back who paved the way for such as Andy Irvine

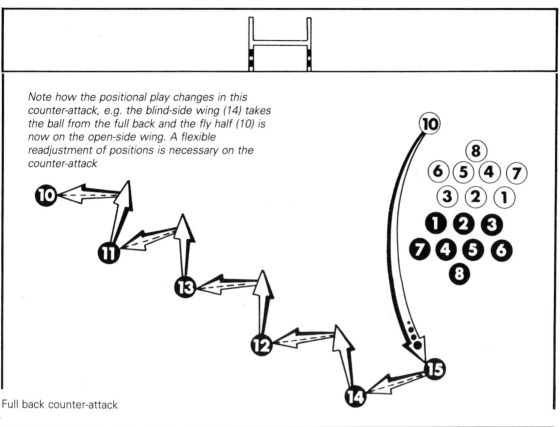

*Note how the positional play changes in this counter-attack, e.g. the blind-side wing (14) takes the ball from the full back and the fly half (10) is now on the open-side wing. A flexible readjustment of positions is necessary on the counter-attack*

Full back counter-attack

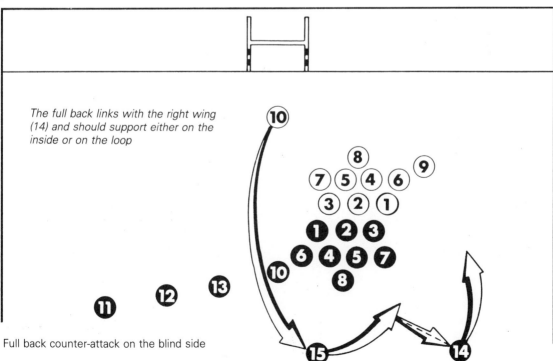

*The full back links with the right wing (14) and should support either on the inside or on the loop*

Full back counter-attack on the blind side

# Introducing the player *Carwyn James*

Andy Irvine is a natural! A schoolmaster's dream of the pupil for all positions in the backs. He has pace, quick reflex actions, and his timing is impeccable, the timing of the artist in any moving ball game.

In the fifties he would have probably been an international fly half. In the seventies it was almost inevitable that he should belong to the peripheral three, as I like to call the wing threequarters and the full back.

On the 1974 Lions tour of South Africa Irvine played on the wing with J. P. R. Williams at full back. Scotland on forty-seven occasions have chosen him at full back, on four occasions only on the wing. It was on the summer tour of Australia in 1982 that he broke Sandy Carmichael's record of fifty as the most capped Scots player.

His right boot, of whatever design or colour, has figured more than any other on the television screen. He will be remembered more for his prodigious kicking from his own half than for the accuracy of his place kicks from close range. He has served Scotland and the Lions well.

Terry Davies and Ken Scotland were attackers from full back. Davies was like a rock under the high ball, so was J.P.R., and they were both enthusiastic tacklers. Irvine's forte was never the defensive game but in his boundless energy and his facility in turning defence into attack. He, perhaps more than anyone, has successfully explored the angles of attack from full back. The counter-attacker par excellence.

Irvine will not be remembered as the traditional custodian but as the man of his age who contributed towards making the wings into semi-full backs and the full back a potent attacking force.

# The player *Andy Irvine*

I don't think there was any particular influence on me as a full back. In my early days I used to do a fair bit of catching and kicking with Lyn Tatham who was the Heriot's coach at that time, but obviously, through the years, you pick up points from other players. I think J. P. R. Williams was probably the best player to learn the art from because he was very solid. In coaching terms we've rarely had a club coach.

I was unlucky in that I never had the chance to see Ken Scotland play because he finished just before I started. Having said that, Ken is a member of our committee and in fact a couple of years ago was chairman of our selectors, and in this capacity he used to come out and train with the lads. Even now, as regards catching and kicking the ball, he is hard to equal.

They say that Ken Scotland was the first of the so-called attacking full backs, and obviously I can't comment on that because I didn't see him; but certainly playing in practice matches and in games of touch rugby and so forth at our local rugby club, Ken still has a fair turn of pace and an eye for the gap.

My main philosophy on full-back play, I suppose, is to think of the lads in front of you, to make sure that when the ball is kicked to you, you catch it,

and that if you're finding touch, to find touch, and if you make a tackle, to make it count. Having said that, I still feel that it's very much the position from which to attack, but at international level,

The full back is nowadays very much the position from which to attack

especially, you've got to make sure that your basics are right because even a half chance in international rugby is snapped up. You can't afford to make any mistakes at all, the pressure is so intense.

With regard to kicking, I'm very much one-footed; I prefer my right foot. Having said that, there are instances in games where even though you're on your left foot you can always get onto your right foot. Phil Bennett was the best that I can think of and, to a certain extent, Tony Ward's very good at it; the half jink onto the good foot and bang! But even they, I'm sure, have had to use the left foot on some occasions. Though you would certainly never get as much distance as you would with your good foot, as long as you keep your concentration there and put the ball in touch safely, even if it's 10 or 15 yards short – it still does the job. There are very few players I can think of who are equally good with both feet; in fact, I can't think of any just now.

Sometimes it is necessary to use the less good foot; you may not get the distance but with concentration you can still do the job

I also can't think of any fly half I've played against who would put in a diagonal to force you to use your left foot or your bad foot. I think it's a very difficult thing for a fly half to do because if the ball bounces that bit short and you've got 10 yards to take on a winger, you might be down the touchline and in for a try. I believe that Barry John gave Fergie McCormick a real roasting in the first Test on the Lions tour in 1971, but that's about the only time I can think of a fly half really tormenting a full back.

In the modern game the full back tends to liaise more with his wingers and to a certain extent wingers nowadays aren't the out-and-out attacking players that they used to be. They've got to have many more strings to their bow than just to be able to run and sidestep, and certainly at international level we communicate to a very great extent. We work on it and practise, we have particular calls about who can veto what and so forth, and I think it's absolutely vital, when you play with new wingers, to have all the codes and the communication down to a fine art. There are certain wingers I prefer playing with because I know their style of play and we know where to find each other. I think that develops through communication and practice and playing with each other.

I couldn't screw kick until I was about nineteen or twenty – in fact I only played full back full time when I was about eighteen and a half or nineteen. It was during my second season at club level playing full back that I really worked on kicking, and after about four or five months' really hard practice the screw kick started to come naturally; even now I don't think I'm a great kicker, but usually I can put it away when I want to. I quite often place-kick to touch, but that's mainly in windy conditions when we want to slow play down and give the forwards a bit of a breather. I think also, in certain conditions, place-kicking tends to be much more accurate and you can get longer distances as well.

When I place the kick, I always kick round the corner. I think that stems from my days of playing soccer; also the boots nowadays tend to be very soft, like slippers. I can't think of any rugby boots with hard square toes. I think if you kicked straight these days with the boots they make, you would probably break your toes. It amazes me to see the Australians, for instance, coming over here and trying to kick toe-on with soft rugby boots.

When the Australians were here, Paul McLean probably suffered because of the type of ball we used – the Gilbert ball. It's slightly more pointed than the ball they would normally use in Australia, but I think also that people overlook the fact that

The back three can be a formidable force by developing their liaison through practice and rehearsed communication

Conditions dictate that Irvine choose to place-kick and also require Roy Laidlaw to take on the not-so-pleasant task of holding the ball. Note the round-the-corner approach

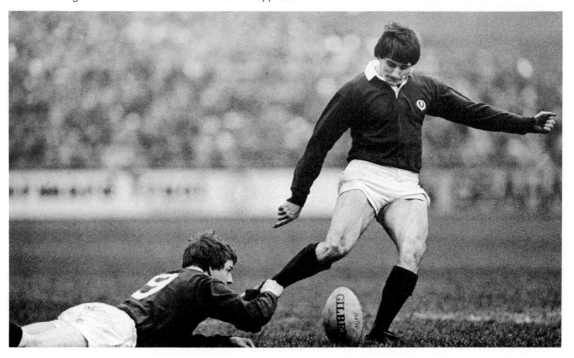

in Australia the kicking conditions are so much better – the ground is usually pretty hard, you can tee the ball up nicely and it's usually dry as well. In these conditions it's so much easier to kick well. I think McLean suffered over here because of the ground conditions and also because of his style of kicking.

The boots today are like soccer boots, apart from the ones the forwards play in; but certainly all the backs play in soccer boots. They're all very soft, very comfortable to wear and very light so that they assist your running. I can't think of any boots now that give you protection by being high in the ankle and protecting your toes. If there were boots like that, I don't think I would wear them because I'm sure I would feel psychologically slowed down by them. I would like to play in running spikes if it were legal.

It doesn't have to be the full back who takes the goal kicks; as long as they go in it can be anyone in the team. I've always been a goal kicker, I think, from my soccer days. I started playing

Timing, left-foot position and follow through. Let them flow naturally for a first-class kick

rugby when I was thirteen, which is relatively late I suppose. I was always a reasonable soccer player, and kicking a rugby ball I've always found relatively easy. I think goal kicking is a bit like golf – the more you practise at it and the more you get a set rhythm, the better you are going to become at it, but I must confess I haven't practised as much as I should have over the years. I think that's partly because of time, and also I feel that when you're practising goal kicking you've really got to try to get into the right atmosphere. You've got to have a very good ball for a start – there's no point in practising with an old ball. I think you've also got to have somebody who will retrieve the ball and kick it back to you. You will never be able to get an atmosphere and a crowd round you in practice, and I've no doubts at all that when you get a few thousand in a stadium, that brings an extra 5 or 10 yards out of you; but I think the big thing about goal kicking is, in practice, you've really got to use a match ball. A new Gilbert, I think, is worth 5 yards on one that's been used in two or three games because there is a bit more bounce and spring in it.

Theoretically, when you're analysing kicking, again it's a bit like golf. I think one word that describes the whole thing is timing. Then there is the position of the left foot and the follow through. But my own personal feelings are that the more I think about it, the worse I kick. I'm better when I just let it happen, let it flow naturally. For instance, I don't have a particularly big follow through. The best photograph I can think of is of a kick that Phil Bennett converted against the All Blacks in 1973 in one of their tours to Wales when he and Joe Karam had a kicking contest – there is a tremendous photograph of Phil with his right foot way above his head. I personally never reach those heights. It's basically because I'm fairly stiff in the hip, and for someone that doesn't follow through I can still get a fair degree of length. There are classic styles of kicking and I'm sure that if you really analysed it and worked hard at it you could make the perfect goal kicker, but I haven't come across him yet.

The positioning of the head is very important in goal kicking as well. You must, as in golf, keep your eye on the ball until you've connected, and even then I suppose you should keep your eyes on the ground until you hear the applause from the crowd. If you lift your head, then you've got no idea where the ball is going to go. Again, my own views are that although you're thinking about all these things as you run up to take the kick, in that split second when you're about to connect with the ball there are so many things running through your mind, you've really got to let Mother Nature take over.

With regard to positional play from a full back's point of view, there are very many factors to consider. I always treat my positioning as a personal duel against the opposing fly half, and it very much depends on whether he's right-footed or left-footed, whether he's a big kicker or a short kicker,

The head position, with the eye on the ball until you hear the applause

whether or not he's got a long service from his scrum half or a quick service. In ideal conditions, with no wind, from a line-out you're almost directly in line with the fly half, and from scrum situations you're between the scrum and the fly half.

These are very much general terms and a lot depends also on the players around you: if you've got a particularly quick winger on your side you could perhaps ask him to cover an extra 5 yards of territory that you might normally cover yourself. Wind makes a very big difference. If there is a strong cross-wind you could find yourself standing 10 yards to the side, the way the wind's blowing, and also, if the wind is up and down the field, against the wind you tend to lie that bit deeper because the kicks are going to be that bit longer to you. Positional play is very important: there are full backs who you might think are out of position, but in fact they're thinking about it all the time, and when the ball is kicked you find that they are in the right place at the right time.

I'm sure it would also help a full back to have had experience of playing in other positions. I've played on the wing many times, and in defensive situations it is very important that the wing and the full back know what they're doing – who is taking the last man, and so forth. But with regard to positioning yourself against kicks, I'm sure it would be very helpful if a full back had the opportunity of playing fly half. I've never played fly half, and I think it's something that would have helped me in my positional play. I think also that if you've had a chance to play in the centre, it might also be quite interesting because nowadays the fly halves sometimes slip the ball out and let the centre do the kicking. From a full back's point of view it is much more difficult to cover a kick from the centre because, once you see the fly half passing the ball, you are tending to start your run across the field, just in case the winger's put away. It's very, very difficult, if you're going flat out, to stop your run, change direction, and either take a high ball or the short chip over. In that context, England use Dodge and Woodward to some extent to do the relief kicking, both of them left-footed, both of them big kickers, especially Dodge, and also quite accurate. In the Scottish team we tend to use Jim Renwick to do some auxiliary kicking instead of John Rutherford.

Cross-kicks these days tend to be a forgotten art. I've rarely had problems with cross-kicks, mainly because you're almost on the winger yourself in your covering role as a full back so that when he cross-kicks, it tends to be your blind-side winger who's taking the ball. Cross-kicks can be either very, very difficult if you get man-and-ball situations or, if they're poor kicks, they can be absolute heaven because they give you a beautiful ball with which to counter-attack. But cross-kicks are seldom used these days. I think the French, and possibly the All Blacks, are the only two national sides who still use them quite regularly.

Tackles are also absolutely crucial with regard to full-back play and obviously it helps greatly if you're a big lad. If you've got 14½ or 15 stones, then you're usually going to come off best in any tackle. The frontal tackle straight on is in many ways the most difficult. You really can't afford to mistime it because if you do, you're going to be brushed aside. I think a lot depends on the amount of space your opposite number has. If he's got 10 or 15 yards to run at you, then the odds are that he's going to beat you because he's calling the tune, especially if he's quick. If he's a winger, he's got the opportunity to go inside or outside you. You've also got to try to judge whether or not your cover defence is with you. If it is, you can tend to cover the outside so that if he does come in, the cover defence is going to nail him. I think the golden rule from a full back's point of view is 'never be beaten on the outside' because usually the winger or whoever's beaten you on the outside has got a clear run into the corner. With regard to big heavy forwards coming at you, I've always found that a very difficult thing to deal with. The chances of stopping them dead in their tracks are pretty slim, and really you've got to try to either slow them down or, hopefully, if they try to beat you, to take them round the ankles. But if they run straight at you, it's very difficult, certainly for someone my size.

With regard to cover tackles, they are much easier, and you can rely on speed because in the cover tackle you've got time to pick your man off, and I think this is where having pace is very, very helpful from a full back's point of view. If the full back has played a bit on the wing and so forth, and he is quick, then he can compete with most wingers. Also bear in mind that the man carrying the ball tends to be that wee bit slower because he does not have both arms free to help him run.

As for marking your opposite number coming into line, we mark man-for-man only when the

Pace enables a full back to make a successful cover tackle

opposition are close to our goal line. If they're out of the 25, our winger tends to come in and leave the last man or the free man to the full back. Away from our goal line the full back can't really afford to take his own man because it would involve him being in line with the centre and winger, therefore leaving a big gap over his head for the kick. So I personally lie deep and take the last man or the man that's been put on the overlap, roughly from our 25 outwards. If the opposing full back happens to be particularly fast, then we might make a point that the winger doesn't let him run. If you're playing against a very dangerous winger, we might ask our own winger to stay with his own man and hope that the cover defence gets to the full back before I have to get involved.

When I'm confronted with a two-to-one situation, I try to stall the attackers by back-pedalling as much as I can, hoping that our cover defence has time to come over. In a recent game against England, Marcus Rose ran straight at me and left Woodward free on the outside. Now, I think that

had I gone in and tried to make the tackle early on, he would probably have put Woodward away for a try. But I tended to back-pedal, hoping for our cover defence to get across in time. I think this is very important: that you try to read the situation as best you can. Also, if you can stay inside both of the attackers and drift slightly, even without any cover defence, it's still possible for one man to take out two. But if the opposition are any good, they should always draw you because two men should always beat one. It's vital for the man carrying the ball to accelerate as fast as he can into the tackle and hence release the free overlap. If you watch the film of that incident, Rose has got about 30 yards to run at me, and I back-pedal the whole time, thinking that Jim Renwick's got him. At the end of the day Jim didn't have him. Rose was silly, because he should have come to me and then put Woodward away.

I personally practise a lot at dealing with high balls because in the modern game that tends to be the main type of kicks opponents use. We also

Catching the high ball

tend to work on the grubber kicks, the kicks coming along the ground to you, and also the chip-over kicks. Done accurately, the small chip kicks and the grubber kicks are very, very difficult to deal with. I suppose the odds are fifty–fifty; nobody can anticipate the bounce of a ball accurately every time, and there are times when you've just got to take a heads-or-tails choice and go for it. If you do happen to get the ball on the run, then you're sometimes put in a very strong position because, with the opposition running fast at you, if you get a nice bounce you can sometimes be past them and set up a counter-attack. But if the bounce beats you then you're quite often in deep trouble. Against Australia recently I had a fairly difficult ball to deal with from a small kick-over. I got the bounce but I didn't have time to put the kick away, and when I tried to beat the tackle off I was about to be clobbered. I tried to find my winger but threw a dreadful pass over his head. These situations are very difficult to deal with, but from the attacking point of view, especially if you've got a lot of chasers, such kicks put you in

If you happen to get the ball on the run you're in a strong position to set up a counter-attack

a very strong position. Ireland are quite good at this – Ollie Campbell and Tony Ward, when they put the small kicks over, seem to exert tremendous pressure. If the bounce goes against the full back, these kicks are very difficult to deal with.

I felt inhibited in the centre, but at full back I have so many options. It is one of the most creative positions on the field. I prefer to attack along the touchline because I can use my winger to generate pace, and because I do not have sufficient power to barge through the middle. At set pieces I am marked out of most games, yet this can sometimes create an opening for a stand-off or a centre. At the top level I tend to be used primarily as a decoy.

From set play a lot depends on the opposition. In internationals we rarely attack from our own half unless the opposition is standing very deep and we can give our winger a quick service. Around the halfway line, overlap rugby is the most effective form of attack but near the 25 the crash-ball tactic is used because it keeps the momentum going.

Normally, if we come up on the blind side of a scrum, I am noticed and I will be marked. You will often see New Zealand number 8s, like Gary Seear, stand back from a scrum on the blind side. This can create chances for the forwards because the number 8, obviously a big defender, is out of position.

From a scrum near the opposition line, you should score five times out of ten. Because it is a man-to-man situation, and there are so many permutations, you should score more often than not. The attackers have all the options, and should take advantage.

# 4 The Winger

## Assessment of the position *Carwyn James*

The forgotten pacemen, as they have often been called, come in all shapes and sizes, as A. J. F. (Tony) O'reilly, himself a proficient practioner, so aptly put it: 'They vary in size from lion to leprechaun, in speed from greyhound to tortoise, in grace and elusiveness from ballet dancer to pampas bull.'

Ken Jones, in the style of an Olympic sprinter, was the classical runner-in of tries, as were John Young, Jim Roberts and J. J. Williams. There have been many big men with hand-offs like sledge-hammers, men like Doug Smith, Ted Woodward, Martin Turner, Peter Thompson – quickish, strong, determined and scorers of many tries. And then there have been the Nijinskies, the individualists, the elusive weavers of intricate patterns which have baffled colleagues, the opposition, the referee, touch judges, spectators and passing seagulls. Take your pick – Gerald Davies, Peter Jackson, Bryan (B. G.) Williams, Grant Batty and A. N. Other; side-steppers, swervers and jinkers.

Unclassified are men like Vollenhoven of South

Tony O'Reilly being jostled by Keith Fairbrother at Twickenham in 1970

Grant Batty of New Zealand, a small provocative bundle of energy

◁Gerald Davies, a study in concentration, in balanced running and with the ball held in both hands to take his opponent's eyes away from the feet and the inevitable side-step

Africa and latterly, because wings are semi full backs, immensely talented players like Blanco of France.

Today's wings, like Mike Slemen, need to be rounded players well versed in the skills of two positions. As we salute their versatility and pursue Slemen's experience may we also share O'Reilly's prayer: 'Long may the joy of wing threequarter play flourish, for there is hardly a more stirring sight than the lonely foray of a solitary figure striding to death or glory into the gathering gloom of a winter's evening.'

# Introducing the player *Carwyn James*

The rugby fraternity at Merchant Taylor's, Crosby, strong in the Jones–Morgan coaching tradition, are fortunate to have the services of Michael Slemen, an experienced and astute footballer. So are the Liverpool club and the Lancashire and England selectors.

Unlike many of his colleagues, Slemen is steeped in both union and league. Frequent visits as a young lad to Knowsley Road gave him a rich league background, personified in the play of Alex 'Alexander the Great' Murphy and in the powerful running of Springboks wing Tom van Vollenhoven, persuaded to leave South Africa by Pilkingtons of St Helens.

The young Slemen was never to forget the importance of close man-to-man marking, the holding of the ball and the smother tackle, the pinpoint accuracy of tactical kicking and the exhilarating possibilities of the counter-attack from full back.

Experienced as a full back and as a fly half, Mike Slemen has used the skills and the awareness demanded by those positions in his role as an England and Lions left wing. As a student of physical education, he understands better than most the need for conditioning, for specialized fitness and the benefit which can be gained from a study of the skills of other ball games.

Only a few players have an overall understanding of the game while they are still performing. Michael Slemen, a shrewd observer, is such an outstanding exception that I see him in the White, Elders, Burgess, Colston, Davis succession.

# The player *Mike Slemen*

It's possibly true that the winger is one of the positions you could do without more easily than others on the field as far as the team is concerned. But it's probably the position that gives pleasure to more people who watch the game than does any other.

I first started playing rugby when I was at secondary school, when I was eleven. There's no primary rugby apart from at a few independent schools and all the state schools play soccer. My rugby coach at secondary school was a man named John Thomas. I mention John because I find at the moment that a lot of lads stop playing after they leave school and I think that the coaches must take part of the blame for this. It's so intense now at schoolboy level that some of the enjoyment is taken out of the game and boys get fed up with it before they've actually even started playing properly. But John had a tremendous philosophy and love for the game so all the lads got the most out of it and enjoyed it.

I played all through school at scrum half. That was because of my size initially, but then I grew about nine inches in a year and so went into the first-team squad. Suddenly the first team realized that I'd changed so much I was having trouble getting down for the ball, so I moved to fly half. That didn't work out so I was stuck at full back; then I played in the centre because we were short due to injuries. But I played for about three-quarters of my year in the school's first team at full back. However, that was just mainly through physique, not because John particularly thought that anybody should play in more than one position.

When I went to St Luke's they thought I was a winger. I stayed there because the fly half, Neil Bennett, was there at the same time as me; he was a year ahead and was ensconced in the position.

I didn't really want to play on the wing but they more or less said to me, 'Well, you'll get a place in the second team on the wing.' Within a very short time I was in the first team. Things went well and so, although I still fancied playing fly half, I didn't rock the boat. I was more interested in being in the first team at college.

The main attribute of a normal winger is speed. I think speed is the most basic quality and the more speed you've got, the better – but it's not the be-all and end-all. I think that the second attribute you need is a safe pair of hands. It amazes me that there are so many wings who've got all the speed in the world but can't catch the ball. In the modern game you are called upon to field the ball and then do something with it.

I don't think size is that important. Obviously it helps: you know the maxim that a good big one will always beat a good little one. As long as

Speed and a safe pair of hands, the attributes of a winger. Note that the ball is held in both hands

they've got the same other things, I'd say that strength is more important than actual size: if you tackle correctly, people will come down no matter what size.

The kind of speed that you need is not so much from a standing position as the ability to go again from threequarter pace, because often you get the ball at the end of a movement where all the backs are moving, so that by the time you get it you're going at a certain pace. The ability suddenly to change pace is probably more important than pure speed.

I try to train for the match situation. I take an actual position on the field and do a specific kind of sprinting. Suppose we take the length of the field, or a certain part of it. I run at, say, half pace, then build up my pace and try consciously to accelerate at given marks on the field, rather than just going out and maybe doing 10- or 25-yard

sprints. This way you can get nearer to the game situation. I do this sort of training with change of direction as well as change of pace. I'll sprint and, at a given place, try to change direction either by sidestepping or swerving; but it has to be very specific. Players don't really take enough time over this sort of thing when they're doing their own training, which is a pity because it can make it a lot more interesting.

Change of pace comes from two things: you need to change the angle of your run so that the angle of your body comes forward, and I think you need to change your length of stride. Your stride becomes slightly shorter to get that initial acceleration and then lengthens again – so it is very specific.

Knowing how and when to change direction is a question of experience – it depends on how your opponent is running. When he's stationary it tends to be different from when he's coming across the field or at an angle. A man who is stationary needs to be sidestepped a lot earlier than a man who is coming across on a converging course, because when a man is stationary you push him one way or lean one way before the

Slemen prefers to beat a man on the outside

sidestep. After the sidestep you must accelerate away to give more distance because if he's stationary he can start moving much more quickly than he could make a change of direction if coming across the field. Once you've beaten him he's got no chance really of coming back. I wouldn't say that I know how the distance between me and another player is right – it's something, I think, which is inside you.

When the man is coming across the field, the easier option is to side-step him. Often you might beat the first man but, the way people cover today, there's a fair chance that there'll be other players there. So you often face an option where maybe you've got one man to beat and you're close to the line, and then the easiest thing to do is to sidestep inside. But if you can go the opposite way, either by a sidestep that way or by stopping a man and then swerving outside, that's

a much better option for a winger if a man is coming across. You must initially slow him down, and the way to slow him down is to go towards him, because if you start coming in towards him as if really to sidestep inside, he's got to stop. The slower you can get him going the better chance you have when you start to accelerate again of him not being able to catch you. So I always give the impression, as I come in, of trying to get into a line where he's between me and the try line so that at that stage he must stop or he'll overrun me. At this point I look to be sidestepping, just a feint of a sidestep, and then I try to accelerate out the other way.

As you swerve outwards, initially, you've come from maybe a dummy to a sidestep inside, but as you drive out again off your inside foot your body must lean a long way towards the touchline. The farther it leans, the quicker you can accelerate because your legs have to catch up or else you

As he speeds away from the swerve, Slemen has the ball tucked in his outside arm

don't stay on your feet. As you come in towards him with the ball, if you can have it in two hands, you have the option to pass, but I would always tuck it inside my outside arm as I swerve away. You've got to be ready to use your inside hand as a hand-off against the man as he's trying to come in to tackle you.

As you lean, you can go much lower, and usually the man, if you're going away from him after you've swerved, will be trying to go low to get you anyway. So you'll be pushing down rather than upwards. In fact, it is easier to hand-off someone who's on the way down because he's not really driving into you, he's still running. He has less force and you can use him to increase your acceleration as you go away.

The hand-off against the low opponent

I think this has been happening even more since the change in the laws where you've got less time in which to distribute the ball. At times, if you're going for a hand-off and it doesn't work, then obviously you're looking to move the ball away if possible. You've got it in one arm and then you're trying to get it into the other one to move it away. It's now become more difficult. Before the law changed you had all the time in the world, and so the skill was to land on your back but, to be perfectly honest, I don't think I was tackled more than a couple of times in three or four seasons. I'm not sure that I'm in favour of the new laws because they can, in fact, make the game bitty and also make for more stoppages. As people put the ball on the floor, others try to pick it up and maybe

fail, whereas previously a man on his back just for that split second only needed to look where the support was and then feed. It kept the game flowing far more than is the case at the moment.

I don't feel the cross-kick is used as much as it could be, but with the way support comes from the forwards and the way backs are being told to get as close to the ball as possible, it's an option that's got to be used very carefully. If you kick away from all your close support, you can sometimes kick the ball to opposition where the opposition can use it very well. But as a move which is thought out and called, and as something which could be tried when the rest of the team know about it, it could be used a lot more.

I practise kicking, but I don't practise cross-kicking very much. It is possible to kick with your inside foot if you're very right-footed, but it's something you have to practise a lot. I'm much stronger on the right foot than the left. I can kick with my left foot, but if I had the choice I would always kick with my right. I also can't kick very well with my left foot when I'm on the run.

I play on the left wing and I prefer it – there are several reasons for that. It's easier to kick right-footed to the left-hand touchline from defensive situations. I also find that I tend to be stronger sidestepping off my left foot than my right. Often you find that, when kicking, whatever leg you don't kick with often tends to be the stronger leg in terms of actual physical strength. This is because that's the leg you stand on when kicking, and so it tends to build up more.

There are many basic differences between right and left wing. One is the ability of people to pass the ball from right to left. People tend to be better at that direction and also tend to make longer passes so that often, going left, you have many more miss moves than going the other way. From scrums near your own line, back-row moves tend to be very good attacking chances and because of the side of the scrum on which your opponents put the ball in, you on the left wing often have to defend against them. In contrast, on the right wing you tend to score from them. John Carleton has scored a couple in his international career, but I've never scored from a scrum in that position. I don't think you get as much ball on the left wing as on the right because, although it's fairly even from line-outs, from scrums it's easier for the scrum half on your own ball to pass the ball to the right. You get the quicker ball going that way as well

A winger has to get involved in the game as much as he can. Slemen, experienced as a fly half, is often used as a kicker

because when the scrum half wants to pass from right to left, the scrum tend to hold the ball and then push it as far as they can away from him to come round to; in other words, to give him all the protection he can get from the scrum half spoiling him. So attacking-wise I think maybe the right wing gets more opportunities than the left, but defensively I think that the left has to work a fair bit harder at times, usually at scrums rather than line-outs.

I prefer a quick ball from the scrums because it is the exception at the moment, and people don't expect it. When it does come, you get a really good chance to move the ball quickly – the unusual is often the cause of tries. I think the ball tends to be held at the back of scrums too much at the moment. The backs should know what's coming, and it should be the backs who decide what ball they want at a particular stage. A team often seems to get into a good attacking position,

John Carleton beats Welshmen Clive Rees (left) and Gwyn Evans to score a try for England in 1982

Slemen argues that the right wing gets more opportunities than the left, but as a left winger he takes the opportunity here of running past Ireland's John O'Driscoll to score a try for England

and the forwards – or the back row in particular – think, 'What a good idea, we'll try and score here,' not thinking that the backs are also in a good position to use the ball.

I remember when the winger used to stand out and never get the ball – it's not so long ago. When I started to play on the wing, which I suppose is only about eleven years ago, I think the situation was changing; wings were already getting more involved. I think this happened because the full back became an attacking force and he opened up more options for the winger. As he became an attacking force, the blind-side winger had to begin to move and cover the places the full back left. It was the change in full-back play that brought a change in wing play. It's changing all the time now because people think more about the game and are beginning to look at the positions which are underused; they are also maybe trying to think of new things. The wing, of course, is one of the positions which has been underused for a long time.

I'd say that for a winger it's a big help to have been a full back at some stage in your career. It's important for younger players who play on the wing, and I speak as a teacher myself, not to stay on the wing for any length of time. I try to move them in, make them play somewhere else. Nobody at the age of twelve is a winger – or he shouldn't be.

Positioning from line-outs depends obviously on the side of the field you are on. If I'm on the same side as the line-out, I tend to stand a bit more in-field than some wingers do because if the ball is kicked back into the box I'll have plenty of time to get back to field it. If you stand across, this will give your full back much less ground to cover and he can move wider. It cuts down the options for the people kicking against you. Obviously, if you're on the open side I'd say as a rule that no winger should ever stand inside the outside post, and I tend to stand maybe 5 or 10 yards farther than that at times. It depends very much on where the opposition winger stands: if he stands very wide, there'll be a reason for it. So you must mark him, even if it means that you'll leave a big space inside. This is something that we work on when we're talking tactically. However far up the field you are, you should never get in front of your centres because if the opposition

Use of blind-side wing on the open side as an attacker. He takes the pressure away from his fly half by giving him more options

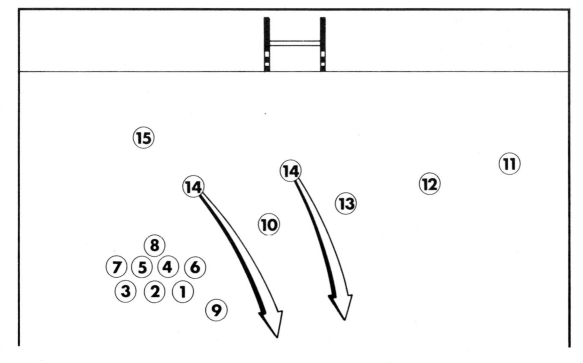

centre breaks in behind, you'll be out of the game. But I stand far enough back to maybe discourage kicks or for me to be far enough back to get them, but also to be in such a position that when my centres are tackling their centres, I should be back up in a position to tackle the winger at the same time.

Positioning at the scrum is more difficult because its position on the field can vary considerably. Obviously, if it's close to your own line, you'll be farther up than if it was in an attacking part of the field. If the opposition have a player who is continually kicking the ball, then you would also vary your position according to what they're doing. But it does depend very much on the way the game is going, what the players are doing, whom you're playing against, and what your position on the field is.

Of course, coming from the North of England, I used to watch a lot of rugby league – St Helens was my first love! But I don't think they play the game to its full potential. Some of the backs never seem to me to be able to make anything from set play. From the scrum it's the only time really when players aren't strung right across the field, and yet you see very few tries scored from that position by using the full back as an extra man. They just seem more interested in close support and passing. I don't think it's got that much to offer to a rugby union coach to pass on, except for the high level of the ball skills that they have – the passing and the taking of the ball at top speed. In terms of spectator appeal and player enjoyment, I think rugby union offers a lot more than rugby league.

My hero when I was at school – although he probably thinks he's not that old – was Gerald Davies. The fact that I actually played against him in two internationals came as a bit of a shock to me. He was the best winger I've seen in my lifetime; he had everything and more. He was one of the few people who could change direction and still keep the pace he'd had before changing direction. His hands were very good, and his tackling for his size was tremendous.

I think it's important that there should be a rapport between a centre and a wing – it's important to know your centre and to know exactly what he's going to do. I played particularly with Tony Bond, a left centre. He was playing with me all the time for Lancashire and, when he first played for England, I found I knew almost instinctively what he was going to do. I knew whether he

wanted me to come short or when he was going to throw a long pass and when he wasn't, in fact, going to pass at all. I think this is something which only comes from experience and from talking about it. The more you play with a colleague, the better.

The centre must be able to give the short, early pass and the delayed pass, so I think the timing between the centre and the winger is all-important. If the winger knows when he's going to get the ball, he can actually get into his run-in before he receives it. Once he gets the ball I think often it's too late for him to start running. If you can actually be accelerating onto the ball, knowing when he's going to give you a pass, it can make all the difference between beating a man and not beating him.

It's very easy to overrun the ball. I used to overrun it more than I do now. But I still have to think all the time about my positioning and the need to vary it according to what's going on in the field and what the opposition are going to do. It's very easy to overrun the outside centre: you think you're in a position where it's all right to run, and suddenly something changes inside you and you're gone.

I think it's very important to know what you're going to do with the ball before you get it, if at all possible. Often this doesn't happen, and what you do is instinctive. Instinctively, you react to situations that you've been in before, and you know what is likely to be successful and what is not. But if you get the chance to, I think you've got to keep your opponent guessing as to exactly what you're going to do. He's not sure from your angle of run where you'll take the ball each time, sometimes taking it wide, maybe coming in before you go out, or sometimes taking the ball starting off close. If you start off close, you tend to find a man who will move fairly close to mark you. He'll stay more or less opposite you, so that as the ball is coming, you move out to take the pass farther out, which means he's got to readjust his line of defence to where you're running.

I don't think that winger is a good position from which to captain a side. Against it is your position on the field and thus your ability to communicate with other people. However, it is a good position in some ways. For instance, you see quite a lot from the wing that forwards who are more involved don't see. The fact that many forwards have been captains of international teams is, I think, purely psychological. I also think that maybe wingers tend to be loners to a certain extent and they don't have the type of personality that lends itself to captaincy. Obviously that's a broad generalization, but on the whole I'd say it's not the best position for captaincy.

I've never thought of myself as a real loner, but I'd say I'm very self-critical. A lot of players who get to the top are self-critical, and that's one of the reasons why they do get there. It's good to have the ability to know when you've done wrong. You may not like other people telling you, but if you actually know it yourself then you go away and do something about it. If you can't see where you're wrong, you're never going to improve.

Tackling was probably one of the weaker spots of my game when I was at school because I was very small, and it was something I had to work on very hard. I'm still not the biggest man you'll ever meet, but I am reasonably strong for my size so it's something that doesn't worry me now. As a winger, I don't think you do that much tackling. If you do your job correctly, you often don't have to tackle; and if the backs do their job correctly, the ball won't get to the opposition wing where he's in a position of space to do anything. The trouble on the wing is that if you give a man any space at all, he's usually quick enough and often skilled enough to stop you and go outside or inside. You tend to be out in the open very much, so that it's one against one – and usually at an important time of the game. You're always seen, so that people realize if you miss a tackle on the wing. Forwards tend to get away with it.

As far as being tackled is concerned, I think the situation has changed considerably with the new definition of the tackle. I don't think I had been tackled for a few years under the old definition you had the time to make the ball available. That is a skill which I think has been lost to the game. It's now much harder to keep the ball alive and moving. Sometimes the easiest thing to do is to have a set way of putting the ball in a position where forwards coming across will know where it is. I've found under the new definition that unless your team is very well drilled and your backing up is very good, it's extremely easy for the opposition to intervene. The object of getting rid of the pile-up has failed because people are still diving in for a ball that's now on the floor instead of being held there by one man.

Another weaker spot for me is possibly pace –

I'd love to be faster . . . but who wouldn't? However, one part of the speed question is the art of being in the right place at the right time. You can then make proper use of what pace you've got.

Pre-season training for me starts at the end of the previous season. On a fitness level I never really stop training, though I do different types of fitness training at various times of the year. Pre-season is the time when you put in the work that's going to take you through the winter – it's basically stamina work. I do a lot of fairly long-distance running, and I always try to do weights for the whole of the summer. I have to work hard in the summer to put on poundage or strength.

Opposing wingers can give you problems. Luckily when I played against Gerald Davies I don't think he got a pass. Stuart Wilson from New Zealand, though, is an instance of a real handful. I must have played against him about six or seven times, and he's got plenty of pace. He's a lot bigger than people think and he does vary his angle of run. I can remember one time in particular when he came inside me before I realized where he was. Not because he sidestepped but because as he took the pass he was already inside my inside shoulder. He's always unpredictable, and if you give him any room you know he can do something. I think, defensively speaking, that you have to attack the difficult wings. You must put them in a position where it's going to be hard for them to do anything. So if a man can come off one foot, you put yourself in a position where it's a long way for him to come off it. If he's slow, you're going to show him the outside; if he's quick you're going to move outside him and make him come inside.

I think the relationship of the wing to the full back is very important. The concept of three levels in both attack and defence is quite right: you have the forwards as the front line, the half backs and centres as the middle line, and then a back line of three. Obviously you can get in each others' way quite easily so you ought to train with your full back a fair amount and know exactly what sort of ball he's going to go for and what he will expect *you* to go for, because at international level it's very often impossible to hear anything that's shouted.

The way we do it is that anything the full back wants he can have. But you tend to know that things that are dropping in front of you are more or less yours. If the ball is in front of the winger,

The back line can be seen as one of three levels in defence and attack. Here full back Dusty Hare is in support of Mike Slemen as Slemen beats Andy Irvine and dives over for a try

the full back has got to go past him to take it, so you might as well take it yourself and he will back you up. If you're turning to go for it, and the full back is close enough, it should be his. Anybody coming onto the ball will take it because he can see exactly what's in front of him: he knows where the rest of the players are.

There are often times when spectators never see the winger and, even though you haven't seen him, he's just run five miles! Sometimes people can't believe that you're really tired at the end of a game. The thing is, if you're playing well, you're never, ever, standing still. You're always moving to cover the eventualities that might happen. If the opposing winger beats the full back, or if he kicks, he's still got you to contend with before he can score – so you've got to move into those covering positions all the time. I'd say that 99 per cent of the time you never do anything in the covering role. But that 1 per cent is what wins the game . . . or saves a game anyway!

The amount of ball you get depends on a number of things. It often depends on the weather: if it's fine, the ball is easily moved and the winger's got more chance of getting it. It depends also on how you play; I do a fair amount of kicking, especially from set situations like scrums and line-outs, so I probably touch the ball more than a normal winger. At international level, if you get three or four passes in each half of the game, you'll have had a lot of ball. It's not unusual to have fewer than three in a half. Really it's up to you to get involved in the game in any way you can; it's a question of how you develop the game for yourself.

It's nice to get the ball early in the game, but often games start fairly slowly. People tend to size each other up, and it might be a while before they get the confidence to move it wide. But if it's possible to get the ball early to the winger they should. I think it's very important for you to get an early feel of the ball and, from my point of view, the sooner you can get the ball in your hands in a running situation, the better.

The amount of speed you have depends to some extent on how you hold the ball. You obviously hold the ball in two hands as much as you can, maybe less on the wing than other players do because you don't have to pass it as much. Often, though, if you're just running flat out you put it under one arm so that you've still got the other one working to move you. Running with the ball in two hands tends to restrict your movement and slow you down a bit.

There are fewer frustrations now than there used to be for wingers, but you've got to be very careful how you go about your game because you've still got a job to do on the wing and that job is part of the whole team effort. You've got to make sure you can do that job before you start doing other things. Some people try to do the other things before they do their own job properly. You've got to be confident enough to know that if you go across to the other wing and things go wrong, you have the pace, stamina and fitness to get back and do your job. You can't do it in isolation. But I find that it's much more interesting to

get involved in the game in many ways.

Confidence comes into it a lot as you get older. As you play the game at a higher level you begin to think more about the game and think where you can improve your team effort . . . as you get older I think people start listening to you.

I like to think that I can beat a man in several ways: that I have the skills necessary to challenge all the things that might come up against me. Running, I can beat a man on the inside more easily than on the outside, especially men coming across. I think that's just basically easier. But you get a lot of satisfaction if you beat a man on the outside, partly because the satisfaction can come from choosing the right option. I think the good player is the one who does the right thing the most often. But you can beat even him – for example, by kicking the ball over his head or past him in some way. However, as I said, often the player who is successful is the one who makes the right choice the most times.

# 5 The Centre

## Assessment of the position *Carwyn James*

In the British Isles and France and their satellites a centre is either a left or a right centre. Not so in the southern hemisphere, and in New Zealand and Australia in particular. In those countries he is an inside or an outside centre, two different animals.

Since the fly half is known as a first five-eighth in New Zealand, the inside centre is known as the second five, and the outside centre is the true, bona fide 'centre'. The second five is a different breed: he is a cross between a fly half and a centre.

A brash definition would claim that the second five is the contact player and the centre a touch player. The second five is the strong, tough part of the chain between two gifted footballers.

Although they may not have been used in southern hemisphere fashion, I suspect that the hard tackling Claude Davey was the second five and the long striding Wilfred Wooller the classical centre; W. P. C. Davies the rugged man and Jeff Butterfield the touch player; Jack Matthews and Bleddyn Williams; Dennis Evans and Cyril Davies; Ray Gravell and David Richards; similarly Paul Dodge and Clive Woodward. John Dawes and Mike Gibson were interchangeable, both had the capacity to play the two roles.

Two contrasting styles of centre play: Ray Gravell of Llanelli, the 'crash-ball' centre, and David Richards, the 'classical' centre

# The crash-ball hit man

In the sixties, New Zealand, with their passion for the ruck (conceived, bred, and nurtured by the men in black), explored means of setting up artificial platforms for the ruck and the resultant second-phase possession. They had the 'brilliant' idea that they would introduce the hit man into rugby football. The ball was transferred by the first to the second five who, on account of the burst, would challenge his opposite number to tackle him. Knowing the ploy, his forwards would get first to the break-down point, the essence of winning the quick ruck ball.

The strong man first used at international level was Ian MacRae. 'To MacRae', a new infinitive in the English Kiwi dictionary, means 'to crash-ball' in mid-field. South Africa followed with Joggie Jansen and we have had a number of imitators since the fashion caught on about ten years ago. It was such an easy manoeuvre that the incredible hulks were queueing up for immediate employment. The fact that we couldn't ruck was such an irrelevance that before long another illegitimate

Bleddyn Williams of Cardiff, Wales and the Lions, the most gifted of centres

child, known as the pile-up, was conceived, which was neither a ruck nor a maul. The game has paid dearly for the introduction of this crude tactic, not only in serious injuries but in the stifling of the natural, skilful evolution of a fluid pattern.

Less so, probably, in Australia and New Zealand, where they have continued to develop their centre play. Throughout the seventies it was a joy to watch the classical centre play of Bruce Robertson aided and abetted by the strength of Bill Osborne at second five. Tony Shaw's Wallabies in the British Isles produced two class players in Michael Hawker at second five and Michael O'Connor in the centre, but they could never be accused of playing the crash-ball game.

It is the UK that has suffered the most, to the point that our back play has probably never been at such a low ebb. Our centre play is abysmal. Choose any two flankers, play them in the centre, and the result would be the same.

To restore faith to my judgement, I have reread Bleddyn Williams, Michael Gibson and André Boniface on centre play: kindred souls, touch players, men of vision. There is nothing more satisfying for the players, or more rewarding for a coach, or more aesthetically beautiful for the spectator, than seeing a centre carving an outside break and timing his scoring pass to perfection.

Of primary importance to a top-class centre is the ability to give and take a pass at speed. The ball, it was always said, travels more quickly than the man, and a well-executed, well-timed pass can beat a man. Alas and alas, and I have continually mentioned this weakness in the context of scrum-half play, there are too few players who can pass both ways with equal facility and skill. By constant practice, however, a player can become equally proficient on his weak side.

Rugby football is a game of angles. A three-quarter line, let us say, when stationary is at an angle of 45 degrees or so to the touchline, and when the centre runs he is on a similar angle. So when he passes, he needs to move slightly in the other direction onto a line running parallel with the touchline. In other words he should fall away as he passes. I don't mean the pronounced public-school fall-away hip pass which was the rage of all textbooks at one time. That kind of pass was so pronounced that it was ludicrous and only makes sense now in a three-to-two or a two-to-one situation when you must take your opponents out of the game.

Bruce Robertson: against Llanelli his classical centre play led to this match-winning try

The principle of the fall-away pass, however, is valid even when a mid-field player is taking and giving the ball in one stride. The modern concept of a passing style is simply to set it there as quickly as possible in a catchable position in front of the receiver. The French flick pass from awkward catchable positions is acceptable, but I don't like the modern trend of spin passing.

Of equal importance to speed of pass is speed off the mark. Fly halves and centres should continually practice 20–25-metre bursts which will stand them in good stead for the mid-field and the outside break. Speed off the mark for all, superb side-stepping off both feet for Bleddyn, for Butterfield a swerve, a tremendous acceleration resulting in an unstoppable change of pace for Lewis Jones and Cyril Davies. Each to his talent: a developed talent.

In the modern game the calling of moves by the fly half has become such a regular routine that it has become too inflexible. A fly half must always remember that he still has a number of options open to him depending on the quality of possession gained, and he should have the strength of personality to cancel a called move if that is his

reading of the situation. Thinking centres will respond immediately to his decision.

One of the finest tactical centres was John Dawes whose presence meant that the right thing was done almost invariably. Mike Gibson says of him, 'His choice of play was as immaculate as his use of the ball.'

Gifted centres will perform well within a suitable attacking framework. Once the fluid pattern has been achieved, then the variations may be used – the mid-field scissors, the dummy scissors, the miss-move (and the missed player must run into a support position for his colleagues on the outside), the loop, and all the variations of the attacking kick.

The more I think about it the more I favour the concept of the second five and the centre, or the inside and the outside centre. In defence it is useful to have a strong tackling inside centre who sets the lead for his colleagues in the threequarter line. It is also of immense psychological advantage to his full back who has the problem of containing an opposite number who is an attacker. For the inside and the outside centre, the full back too if he takes his man inside the wing, the tackling is

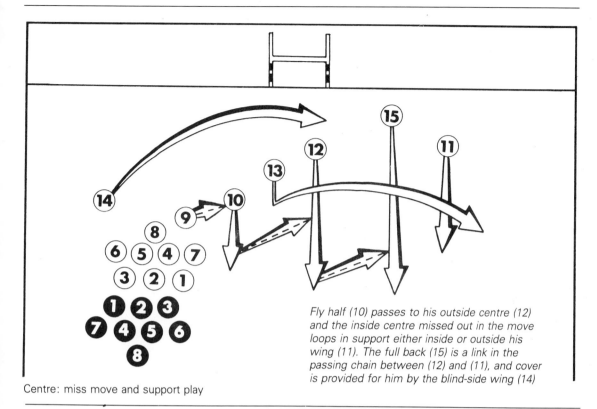

Fly half (10) passes to his outside centre (12) and the inside centre missed out in the move loops in support either inside or outside his wing (11). The full back (15) is a link in the passing chain between (12) and (11), and cover is provided for him by the blind-side wing (14)

Centre: miss move and support play

frontal, probably the most demanding of all tackles.

One of the greatest problems currently facing the coach is to upgrade the standard of centre play. I regret having to say that watching films of the fifties, the sixties, and the early seventies would be far more beneficial than watching any centre play at the moment. I would also say that Dave Richards would have been a greater player during those years.

# Introducing the player *Carwyn James*

Richards, D., of Glynneath, Neath Grammar School, Cardiff College of Education, Swansea, Wales, Barbarians, British Lions was born to be an international fly half. That promise was fulfilled at schoolboy level, but later it was discovered that his imperfect kicking technique, the small matter of bending the knee on impact, would hardly allow him to challenge Bennett, Bevan or Davies for the Welsh number 10 spot.

So Richards, fortified by a sharp pace and a keen awareness of the mid-field running game, became a centre. Not the second five-eighth crash-ball type of player but a bona fide centre by southern hemisphere standards and definition. Not that he was used in this role in a land ruled by left and right – left and right flankers as well as centres.

David Richards, is an exciting player who has never totally fulfilled his promise. This is not entirely of his own making. It is in the centre position, more than any other, that a marked decline in standards is noticeable in the modern game.

Perhaps Richards was born ten, maybe fifteen, years too late to be considered one of the greats in the world of rugby. The sadness is that he had it in him to be one. Injuries marred a number of his performances and denied him international appearances for the Lions.

For me, the immensely talented David Richards represents a half generation of neglected players.

# The player *Dave Richards*

Some people maintain that a centre needs a strong physical presence because of the tackling required. In recent years teams have tended to include a big centre along with a smaller one. But the game now is going towards more fluency behind the scrum, so that perhaps physical presence is becoming less important.

Basically the role of a centre is to feed your wingers and get the back line moving smoothly. There are times during the game when you can be taking passes which are low, high, hard, soft, and you must judge these situations as they come and be able to transfer the ball cleanly to your colleague.

The outside half certainly has a bearing on how a centre performs during a game. He can make you look a good or bad player. He must strive to give you the right ball at the right time. You line yourself on him in attack and defence.

I'm not an advocate of ten-man rugby, although I realize that it has to be played from time to time. As a centre you're not involved in that type of game. I like to have the ball in my hands as often as possible, and if I don't have it every couple of minutes at least during a game, I feel that I'm not contributing as much as I possibly could towards the play.

When you haven't got the ball you've got to be able to put pressure on the opposition. You'll go through a number of games in which you don't get the ball. You've just got to make your opposite number feel that you're about. You've got to tackle him, force him to make the wrong decision in passing or kicking. Often people in the stand don't realize that although you haven't had the ball in your hands, or you haven't made a lightning break, you've often put pressure on the opposition which causes your side to gain possession. A centre is just an extension of an outside half, and he's obviously got to be able to read the game like an outside half.

The long raking kicks to the corner are the most vital kicks an outside centre can make. A fast flanker may be able to get out onto your outside half, and then the outside half is standing still giving you a quick ball. You're then trying to get

In the back line the centre, always in the middle of the chain, practises taking and giving a pass

Side-stepping practice helps you get past a determined defence

the ball in front of your forwards, which means you can either kick it to the blind side or put in a long diagonal kick to the corner.

Perhaps their defence is very good and the opposing full back is already coming into the line to mark your full back. So you see an opportunity to tip the ball over the top, push it through the middle, and then you've given an opportunity for your outside centre to get to the ball first. But it's all about reading situations from the mid-field.

There are times when the gaps are not there, but if you run at a certain angle at your opposing centre from the inside centre position, for instance, you can also draw the outside centre in. By going straight in mid-field, you're checking the opposing back line. Now if you can check the opposing two centres enough, a long pass will sometimes put somebody else into a gap. You're always looking to create space for other people, even if there's not a gap there for yourself.

What we try to introduce into the Swansea back line is lining up very, very deeply; that is, about 2 yards behind one another. This means that, provided we're having decent sorts of ball, we can give a player just a yard extra to decide whether he's going to take his opposite man on, whether

Two mid-field tactical manoeuvres
The loop: moving outside for a quick return pass can take a defender out of the game. Richards, having passed to Wyatt on the inside, loops round behind to receive the return pass on the outside
◁The scissors: the secret is to keep the ball hidden from the defender. David Richards and Mark Wyatt demonstrate

Intense concentration and the correct alignment for the next attack

Tackling practice is crucial

he's going to kick, pass, or whatever. So angles, as far as a line man is concerned, are vital, and I believe this gives you that much more time to decide what to do.

I was originally an outside half until Wales picked me in the centre and obviously, at outside half, you don't have to do much tackling. Lines of defence for outside halves and centres are different, so I just had to line myself differently. I'm not a big chap, but I tend to go at an angle to try to bring down a man. Tackling is what I've had to tighten up quite considerably. Stan Addicott, our Swansea coach, helped me during training by getting tackling bags out or even using people just to run at me so that I could align myself properly. Luckily I've got a bit of pace, so I try to start inside a man to show him perhaps a gap on the outside and then tackle him from the side, which is always easier than a head-on tackle.

Every training session with our local club is with the ball, whether it's passing, catching high balls, or whatever. We go through the basics because you tend to forget sometimes to practise these things. You can become a little rusty like everybody else.

A basic handling exercise

I think a centre will probably need 40 to 60 yards of pace, whereas a winger will perhaps need to run farther during the game where he or anyone else gets an interception. More often than not, a winger has to finish any movement that's been created, and he probably needs to practise his running over a longer distance. The mid-field player needs a dynamic sort of running off the mark, whereas a winger would probably need to sustain his running over a longer period.

The moment to pass to a colleague in a better position

I think I get equal pleasure from making a break and from putting somebody else over for a try. I suppose it's within the team context that you don't mind who scores as long as you win the game. My role in mid-field is creative. There are not many times you can make a break and then run in 40 yards and score a try. Generally you've got to give a pass to somebody else.

I don't really regard myself as a physical centre, so I'm not often used as the battering ram to set up second-phase play in the middle of the field. I tend to feed off people. If you're small and you've got a big centre playing alongside you, he'll probably fulfil the battering-ram role and try to draw in perhaps the two centres, then let you have a pass.

I've done interval running in which you jog for 20 yards, stride and then sprint and then slow down again. You do it over a number of lengths of the pitch, and it does tend to produce the ability to go off the mark and away from a line of defence. It's all related to the game, and I think it's excellent practice and a good type of fitness training.

Finger-tip passing

I realize now, from playing outside half, how the centre likes the ball. I've tried to help the outside halves in Swansea to say that if we win the ball from the back of the line-out, say by a deflection, we straightaway try to use that ball. It's the best ball to have in the back line, and I try to incorporate this into the type of play that we use in Swansea.

It's very satisfying to be able to do fingertip passing, and I try to use it in the Swansea sessions to get the depth of alignment. We've been lining up far too flat, like a lot of sides. With deep alignment you can have a chance to look up from time to time to decide whether you want to take people on or still give the ball off. So passing quickly and also lying deeply are very important facets of play.

# 6 The Fly Half

## Assessment of the position *Carwyn James*

The fly half is also known as the outside half and the stand off, and is often referred to as *the pivot*. The words, 'pivot' in particular, point to the fact that the fly half is very much in control as far as the tactical play of the threequarter line is concerned. He is the general of the side, the tactician and, in the modern game, the caller of moves.

Historically, the strongest partnership in rugby football is the one between the fly half and the scrum half. They seem to come in pairs at international level and they develop an almost telepathic understanding. Without such an understanding, or merely to supplement it, signs are used to indicate whether the fly half wishes to go left or right. A language other than English is always useful: Arthur Summons, the brilliant Australian fly half, used to move his toe in either direction.

In the modern game, important as the back five and front five are, a creative middle five is *all*-important, with both halves working closely in both defence and attack with the back-row forwards. If the middle five are creatively strong, the side has a very good chance of winning its matches. Whether the side loses or wins possession, it is up to the back row and the halves either to win back possession or to use the possession gained wisely.

If I had to categorize, I would say that most fly halves are of average or below average build, with the Welsh, for instance, smallish, elusive, almost Iberian-looking, like Cliff Morgan or Phil Bennett. Into the other category fall the likes of Richard Sharp, Ricky Bartlett or even Albaladéjo: stand-offish, rangy and usually in the classical mould.

I should like to talk about some of the good fly halves I have seen. There is only one I remember before the war: W. T. H. (Willie) Davies, a contemporary of the master, Cliff Jones (a gushing, darting side-stepping type, in contrast to Davies). A former pupil of Gowerton Grammar School, Dav-

ies and his school scrum half, Haydn Tanner, both played for Swansea against Jack Manchester's 1935 All Blacks. Swansea beat the All Blacks. Willie Davies was a beautiful fly half – he was one of these gliding fly halves, a ghostlike figure who used to go quietly between the fly half and the opposing inside centre and suddenly he was through a gap which didn't exist. I feel that he had

Cliff Jones, generally regarded as one of the greatest fly halves of all time

what Barry John had, and that was imperceptible change of pace. And that is why I emphasize that the centres and the fly halves must look carefully at their striding – their length of stride which can be worked on. Start with the short pace for about five or six paces, then quietly lengthen the stride and lengthen again, like changing gears in a car. Start with short paces, lengthen through second, third and top gear and then into overdrive – the telling moment is when you go outside your opposite and inside the near centre. No gap is apparant but you are a gliding, ghostlike figure going through the gap with the opposition not really knowing what is happening. They are not aware of the striding of an opponent because the opponent holds the ball in front of him with both hands, perhaps moves the ball slightly because this distracts the opposition. Their eyes are on the ball and you take their eyes away from your feet. I always tell my players that if you want to tackle someone then don't be distracted. Keep your eyes on his feet, and then when you see what the feet

are doing you tackle low and get your man. Feet are so important to a front tackle.

Tanner, after the war, played with fly halves like Glyn Davies and Billy Cleaver. Quite a controversy raged because these two possessed contrasting technique and style. Glyn Davies was of the W. T. H. Davies type, the traditional classical Welsh prototype of a fly half. In opposition to him was Billy Cleaver, known as 'Billy the Kick', who was a superb kicker. He could put the ball on a sixpence and make it very difficult for his opponents, particularly the opposing full back, because he had played at full back himself and knew all the blind spots. Billy played to his wings (like Ken Jones, an Olympic sprinter), and they ran swiftly onto the ball. Cleaver had the full range of kicking at his command, the lengthy screw kick to touch, the diagonal, the lofted kick back into the box, the short punt over the mid-field triangle and the grubber. He was a model for any such aspiring fly half.

If you played with Glyn Davies you played a specific type of game, a running game, but if you

'Billy the Kick' Cleaver sells a dummy, starting the movement that brought Cardiff a try against the Harlequins at a deserted Twickenham in 1948

played with Cleaver you played a much tighter game, cutting out the possibility of mistakes. Billy was good at setting off his threes. I have a suspicion that centres preferred to play with a person like Cleaver because he was predictable. They knew precisely what was going to happen. But with a genius like Glyn Davies they were not sure. They did not know where and when they were to be given the ball, so they had to play off him; whereas with Billy they just played their natural game and they knew precisely when and how they would have the ball because any poor ball was kicked away.

A parallel in the modern game would be that Mark Ella is a Glyn Davies type, and Paul McLean is a Billy Cleaver type. So Bob Templeton, on his tour of this country, was in the very same predicament that the Welsh selectors were in in the forties and fifties.

In the fifties, the person who was dominant as a fly half in Wales was Cliff Morgan; in Ireland Jackie Kyle, another great player. In the mid sixties it was the era of Barry John and David Watkins of contasting styles. After them we had two fly halves, John Bevan and Phil Bennett, and the arguments started all over again. Phil Bennett was an attacker and a very good right-footed kicker, a sidestepping attacker who could tear the opposition defence into shreds. Now Wales have Gareth Davies, who is in the Glyn Davies/Barry John mould. But I must say that Gareth as yet has not matured to the extent we would have wished and we have yet to see the best of him.

In the thirties when Wales had Cliff Jones, Scotland produced Wilson Shaw. Ireland in the forties and fifties produced one of the greatest fly halves of all time, because he was a defensive player as well as an attacker – he had all the virtues – and that was Jackie Kyle. After him in Ireland came Micky English, who brought a new dimension to defensive play. He didn't really belong to the fly-half union because he was a tackler. He was one of those who loved to put great pressure on his opposing fly half. Until then fly halves had relied on their flankers to do their tackling for them and they had become coverers. Cliff Morgan was a classical coverer. You would always find him running behind his own threequarter line in attack or defence, in number 8 fashion, and quite often he would tackle a wing man on the overlap. These days, with the laws as they are and the offside line being different from what it was in the fifties, I think that fly halves should look after their op-

Barry John, pursued by Fergus Slattery

posite number. This is very important as far as any defence pattern is concerned in relation to the fly half.

Fly halves have a number of decisions to make at the beginning of a game.

1. As soon as possible they must give the feel of the ball to the rest of the threequarter line. This is important because a wing can go for twenty to twenty-five minutes without having the ball in his hands.

2. The fly half must always test the ability of the opposing full back with a rolling ball and with a high ball.

3. He must make up his mind whether he is going to take all the pressure himself, and if so he goes for the break, once, twice or three times, in the first ten to twenty minutes. By going for the break he virtually tells the opposing back row, 'You've got to keep an eye on me or I will

Phil Bennett, an attacker who could tear the opposition defence into shreds

break your defence and I am going to set up tries either for myself or for my back row or for my inside centre.' Or the fly half can say, 'Right I am going to give the ball to my three-quarters consistently, out-out-out all the time,' and lull the opposition into a false sense of security. Then, after a while, he sees his chance, breaks through and scores a try. I think that Ollie Campbell belongs to the second group because so often we see him play the quiet sort of game and then suddenly, when he realizes that the opposition is not quite as good as he thought, he goes for the try.

The fly half is really the pivot of the attack. Phil Bennett was known as the Welsh General. The difference in the game now is that until the last ten years or so fly halves never called the move before the ball came out. These days they are persistently calling the move before they get the ball. This, I feel, is the main reason why three-quarter play is so poor at the present time. The whole point is that I feel a fly half, when he gets the ball, must decide intuitively, instinctively, whether it is a good ball or a bad ball. A good ball means that he is on his toes; a bad ball means that he is on his heels. When he gets the ball he may decide, 'I am on my toes going forward – this is the moment to run at the opposition.' If he gets a poor pass and he is slightly back on his heels, this is the moment he has to decide to kick the ball to make it safe because it is not a ball that the threequarters can use. Calling the move before the ball emerges from the scrum or from the line-out, and going through the move irrespective of the quality of the ball, heightens the poor quality of threequarter play. Personally, I would prefer my fly halves and my threequarters not to think in terms of moves but to play off the fly half. This certainly is what happened with the 1971 Lions, and their play was quite beautiful to watch. Mike Gibson and John Dawes never called the moves beforehand. They just played off Barry John, and if Barry decided to run the ball then instinctively they just carried on.

What do we look for in a fly half? We look for a complete footballer. I like my fly halves to be two-footed. Jackie Kyle and Barry John certainly used both feet with accuracy. A two-sided player's dimension is so much wider. But when you know that a fly half is definitely one-sided his options are cut in half, and as far as the defence is concerned he is so much easier to counter. A fly half then should be a two-sided player, able to kick well. Line-kicking for the full back and the fly half is so important. Because of the dispensation law, the bounce kick into touch is invaluable – a new kick in rugby football which was mastered by Gareth Edwards. Campbell and Davies have spent a great deal of time concentrating on the bounce before the ball goes out of play.

I have always asked my fly halves to play a number of games at full back. Once you play at full back you begin to realize that there are certain blind spots on the field. If you play at full back you discover for yourself what the blind spots are, and then you are a much better tactical kicker when you return to play fly half.

I think that every fly half should also have the experience of playing in the centre position, because then he will realize that the timing of the pass to the centre is all-important. Too many fly halves run that yard or two too far, and when they know that they can't make the break themselves, they give the pass to their inside centre, and very

often it is a hospital pass. Because the pass has been delayed they set up the inside centre to be heavily tackled by his opposite number. Now a good fly half, in this situation, will not relay the ball to his centre. He will use another type of kick, which is an attacking kick: the grubber.

A grubber kick is a special technique and a fly half should be able to use this kick well. I am delighted to see that Ollie Campbell uses it. Another kick is the diagonal placed behind the opposing threequarter line and in front of the opposing full back with the ball bouncing as it goes towards the touchline – a ball that your own wing can run onto. This is a very important tactical kick. Another kick, which the Irish do very well, is the garryowen, the high kick, which can be pursued by the forwards or by the two centres. I think it is important to realize that while a fly half is in the process of kicking this ball, he is not able to follow up immediately; but his two centres should be. The first centre should arrive simultaneously with the ball and try to take it in the air from the opposing full back. In case something

Fly half kicking options

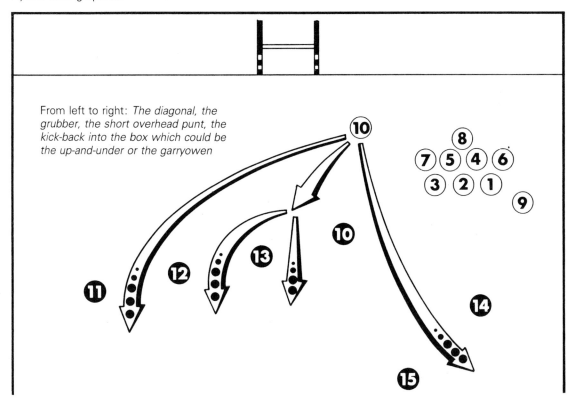

From left to right: *The diagonal, the grubber, the short overhead punt, the kick-back into the box which could be the up-and-under or the garryowen*

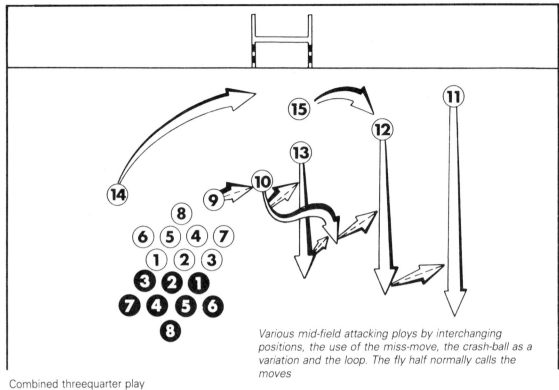

*Various mid-field attacking ploys by interchanging positions, the use of the miss-move, the crash-ball as a variation and the loop. The fly half normally calls the moves*

Combined threequarter play

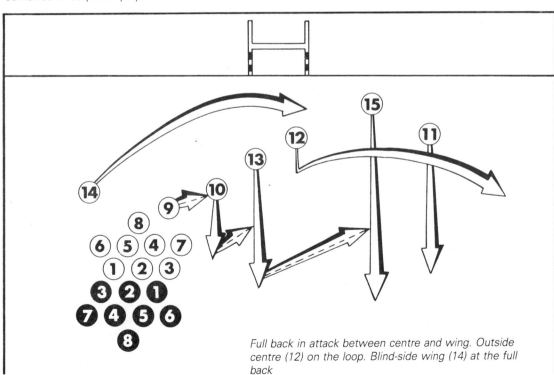

*Full back in attack between centre and wing. Outside centre (12) on the loop. Blind-side wing (14) at the full back*

goes wrong, the second centre should not be too close but backing up at a distance of at least 5 yards away, because if there is a mistake then he is in a better position to pick up a stray ball.

The garryowen

Drawing a man: this was the rage in rugby before the offside lines were changed, but we have a new game on our hands compared with what it was in the fifties and throughout the sixties. From the set piece the ball should now be relayed like lightning from the scrum half to the wing without anybody thinking about drawing a man. Once the ball reaches the wing rapidly, and he is tackled or whatever and the ball goes down, winning the ball from that particular platform is so important because now we have the second-phase possession. Such possession is the time that drawing a man is all-important, and when you've got your four-to-three or three-to-two or two-to-one situation, you must be capable of drawing your man. This is the part of mid-field play that must be practised well – how to draw a man and putting somebody free. After all, that is the essence of rugby, to pass the ball to somebody in a better position than you are in yourself. This emphasis on drawing a man is more relevant to second- and third-phase possession than it is to first-phase possession. It can mean the difference between scoring and not scoring a try.

There are individual skills as far as a fly half is concerned, such as side-stepping, swerving, the dummy and others, which the player himself must develop by continual practice.

# Introducing the player *Carwyn James*

Somewhat shy, Ollie Campbell shuns the focus of pen and lens, preferring to retire gracefully away from the limelight. He loves talking rugby, loves discussing the merits of fly halves of the past, and he frequently refers to the views of O.C. senior who provided the inspirational link with the other generations and who quietly became the most potent influence on the youngster's career.

Ollie looks and is Irish. He preserves that pale Dublin veneer unsoiled by the sun or by travel. Like an aristocratic parcel marked fragile, the goods inside are Harrods: proven, firm and genuine. Campbell's views are beliefs.

'Fly halves should tackle and I do,' he will tell you. That Barry John didn't is of no consequence. Mike Gibson did and that is of lasting consequence – Gibson, the man who moved and inspired him the most. Gibson, who by the power

of his tackling turned defence into attack and in attack was precise in his judgements. Gibson, a Protestant from the North, was the man to be admired by an aspiring young fly half who, like Tony O'Reilly, was enthusiastically taught by Catholic fathers at Belvedere.

Ollie Campbell now is sufficiently mature to have his own philosophy and sufficiently wise in the ways of the world to propound them eruditely but with more than a tinge of humility. Mature enough too to train on his own, to do the little things well. God willing, Campbell will continue to figure large in the annals of the men in green.

With the twinkle of a searching eye he over-praises the deeds of Tony Ward on the soccer field. While admiring his challenger he longs for peace away from the flow of words and more words which sometimes hurt.

# The player *Ollie Campbell*

I began, really, before I was eight – I used to play around in the back garden with my dad who got very interested in rugby. He really started off very late because he grew up with Gaelic football (he went to a Gaelic school), but when he left school and came to Dublin he got involved with a rugby crowd and became very interested in it then. So I was always playing around with him in the back garden, but I didn't start organized rugby until I was eight, in Belvedere College.

In school I would never really have watched Gaelic at all, but one of the best sides ever to play was the Dublin team of the mid to late seventies; and certainly when they came along and played a very, very good brand of Gaelic football I got very interested in it. When I was growing up during schooldays, though, I never really had much interest in it.

I was eight when I went to Belvedere School – the under-nines is the earliest team there, so I started straight away. There is no competitive rugby at that age – you play against various schools, but they are all friendlies. You don't actually play a competitive match until you are fourteen or fifteen. All the way from the time you start at eight up to fourteen or fifteen you're just playing friendlies, and you'd be playing twice a week for the whole season. You'd often play other sides maybe two, three or four times during the season, but it was all great fun and I must say I really enjoyed it.

I've had virtually no experience of playing in positions other than fly half and that is really something that I regret very much at this stage. I think I would have been a more rounded player and probably more appreciative of the other positions had I played in them. I started off in the under-nines as wing forward, believe it or not, and the following year I was moved to fly half. Apart from the three or four internationals in the centre, I have always played fly half.

I played one game at full back for my club in the mid seventies. I found it odd: I had been playing for so long at out half that I think the positionings and the feeling of playing at out half were in me, so I found it very difficult. I found myself actually drifting up to the out-half position during the game, which meant I had to concentrate very hard. I did enjoy it – it's a very different game and you've certainly more freedom when the ball comes to you from a kick or whatever than you have at out half. But the position I prefer is out half; even had I played in the other positions, I think I would always like to come back to play out half.

I would say that I appreciate centres more now than I did before I played in the centre. I appreciate their problems more, and I realize that the pressure which they are under just in the simple giving and taking of a pass is far more intense than at outside half. I never realized this until I played in the centre. I don't know whether it has made me a better player, but it has certainly made me more appreciative of the problems that a centre has.

Had I played full back – from the point of view of tactical kicking from the out-half position – I would probably be more aware of the Achilles heel maybe or the blind spots that the full back has. I think the time to experiment with different positions is when you are very young. I would say from the time you start at eight or nine to the time you're fourteen or fifteen is the time to experiment, and then to find whichever position you are best at, and then specialize. I think it's a bit late once you leave school to start picking and choosing and playing in various positions – I think that at that stage you should be fairly set on what is your best position.

My dad was a prop forward and I would say the one single skill he taught me was tackling. I can always remember him telling me to tackle low, to go in low, down by the knees preferably. I can remember doing that in the back garden time and time again, and I got to really enjoy tackling. It's not supposed to be something that out halves in general do – I must say it's something that I've never had much problem in doing and it's never really worried me. One of the things I get a great kick out of is making a good tackle, and that is the one single thing that I can remember learning from my dad.

The Irish fly half I remember as a great tackler is Mike Gibson – he was so good at everything. He never shunned tackles, he never was part of the union of non-tackling fly halves, so I idolized him. I can remember very clearly his first cap against England when Ireland won 18–5 at Twickenham. I don't have a great recall of a lot of past games, but I remember that one very, very clearly. I remember in the preview of the match someone mentioning Mike Gibson, and from that day just

Cambell's mentor, Mike Gibson, shadowed by Mervyn Davies

the name and his playing at out half, when I was playing in that position as well, caused me to follow his career avidly all my life – I was a great fan of his.

The first international I watched was when Ireland played against New Zealand in 1963; Mike English was playing that day, but I don't remember that game clearly. I've heard a lot about Mike English's character and his play, but I don't remember watching him play. (It's really only since Mike Gibson came along that I started remembering games.)

I was very young, probably five or six, when my dad first took me to see a match. I can remember him bringing me along to an Old Crocks match, and he was playing in it.

I think there are three basic requirements for a fly half. One would be good hands, number two

would be kicking (with both feet preferably) and number three would be running skills. Then I would say that concentration is very important; I think you must have an awareness of the team that you're playing in, an awareness of their strengths and weaknesses, and also of the opposition's strengths and weaknesses, an awareness of the match situation, the score, and so on. I think patience is one of the very important things to have – the sort of cat-and-mouse game that you play with the opposition is illustrated by the story told of Jackie Kyle. In Cliff Morgan's first game against Jackie Kyle, the game was going on and on and Jackie wasn't doing anything, so Cliff thought, 'There's nothing great about this fellow Kyle.' He relaxed and suddenly Jackie Kyle was through and gone. I don't know if you're born with that sort of patience. I think it's something to nurture. But I think it's certainly something an out half must have – he can't make a break all the time. During the whole game you are always trying to look for the opportunity when the gap will be there. So I think patience is very important.

What do I do with the ball early on in a game? It depends very much on the situation and the position on the field. Obviously, if it's in defence, I'll be most concerned with getting the ball to touch, not about length; and if it's in attack, if it's in mid-field, I would be thinking of perhaps putting the back three, the full back and the wings, under pressure straightaway. If they react well, then you have to look for another way of attack. If they fumble or make a mess of things, then you might be on to a good thing there for the game.

As early as I can in a game, I like to get the ball into as many pairs of hands as possible in the back line. I think it's very important, particularly for a winger, and particularly in internationals, because if they see a ball three or four times in a game they consider it a lot. I don't like going any more than two or three minutes without the ball in my hands, so I do like to get that ball along the threequarter line, just to give them a touch of the ball. From the forwards' point of view, basically what they want from a back line is for them to be able to get up from the set play when they have won the ball, or indeed from second phase, and go forward – they don't want to go back, so I am very aware of that. Obviously there are various ways of going forward – you can go forward by running or by kicking. Initially I like to get them going forward in the first period of the game so that they have confidence in me and they have confidence in my decision making.

If there is one person on the field that you want to test out as early as possible and see what stuff he's made of, it is the full back. The easiest of all the options open to you is to take a ball and put up a garryowen for him and see what he is made of. No matter how good a full back is, if the kick is high enough and in the proper position, it is very hard for him just to take a clean catch. It certainly does get the adrenaline going and it's an old Irish tactic, now accepted around the world. I would think the full back is the man who would be singled out or, if you feel that one of the wingers is particularly bad under a high ball, then certainly make a kick into the box rather than to the full back. If you have a JPR at full back, what's the point of testing him out? If you have a very weak

Good hands preparing for the screw kick to touch. Note the stillness and the concentration

winger on his right or left, then I would prefer to kick up through him, so he would be the man I would look at first.

If the full back is long-legged, then you can put in diagonal kicks. If he is a bit slow on the turn, you can put long diagonal kicks over the open-side wing's head and make him run, particularly if you've got fast centres and fast wingers who can put him under pressure as he's scurrying to get the ball. Just as he gets to it, he may be able to knock it into touch. So you may have gained that length of ground and it's still your throw-in.

Edwards and John are a partnership which comes to mind straight away because of the 1971 Lions whom I remember very clearly – we had the video of that at school and we watched it over and over again. Some people say it is the scrum half who dictates the pattern of a game, other people say it is the fly half. I think it's really a balance or a mixture of both. In some games it would have to be the scrum half, depending on how the game is flowing, and in other games it must be the fly half. I think Barry John has said in an interview that in some games it was he who was dictating the game and in other games he felt that it was Gareth who was doing it. Again, personalities must come into it – if you've a very strong personality in one or other position, then obviously that's the guy who would probably do the calling and dictate the pattern of the game. I think it is very important just to talk rugby, to understand your partner's attitude to the game, and just play. When I first played with Robbie McGrath I must say I was a bit concerned, but in fact we had no problems with each other because we talked before each game as to calls, what I wanted from him and what he wanted from me, the positions he wanted me to take up in defence and attack. I talked to him about the type of delivery I wanted, the odd flat ball and having some deep deliveries, and it was a question really of sympathy from me to him for his problems, and sympathy from him to me for my problems, and of helping each other out.

The weight of the pass is very important – it's difficult to take a hard ball, particularly if you want to attack yourself. I like a nice floating ball, not one that's going to loop but one that I can run onto and that I can see for a long time, one that's not going to take much effort just to hold, one that I know is simply floating there in front: I can just run on to it and actually look at gaps before

I even catch it. So I think the weight of the ball is very important, and it's something that I don't think scrum halves appreciate fully. Perhaps sometimes they just pass and as long as it goes to hand they think it's a good pass, but I don't feel that's enough.

For a long time I didn't vary the angle or where I took the ball. I don't know what started me thinking about it, but it seems a bit stereotyped if you take the same angle for a whole game. I would love to play against someone who does that because you're not going to have too many headaches. So I now take deeper balls, I take flatter balls, I take some short and maybe some longer: suddenly the defence (the wing forward, particularly) is not quite sure what's happening. The other thing is to take the same ball a number of times so that the wing forwards think that they have you, and then suddenly you take one differently. I think this is important, and it's something that out halves don't do enough. I think it's very important to vary the angles at which you run onto a scrum-half's pass and also the depth at which you take it.

Barry John ran like silk, he floated – it's a difficult quality to describe. I saw a television programme recently called 'The Maestro', revealing a quality you can't model yourself on, it's something you are born with. I don't know if that can be copied. It was poetry in motion and I haven't seen anybody else run like that before or since – it was beautiful to watch. I have the tape of 'The Maestro' at home and I've studied it, but I couldn't put my finger on it. I think the type of running that very few people have is this change of pace. Most people are very one-paced in that, even if they're fast, as soon as they get the ball, they are sprinting. I think that what is very hard to defend against is the guy who can do as Barry did, seemingly going at full pace and yet having more pace left. I know that Barry John when he was younger did a lot of practice on changing the length of his stride to change pace, and this gave the effect of ghostlike running.

My own personal training over the last few years has generally been on physical fitness, which I think has been a mistake for my position. About five years ago in the club we got this phys-

Fly half varying his angle of take

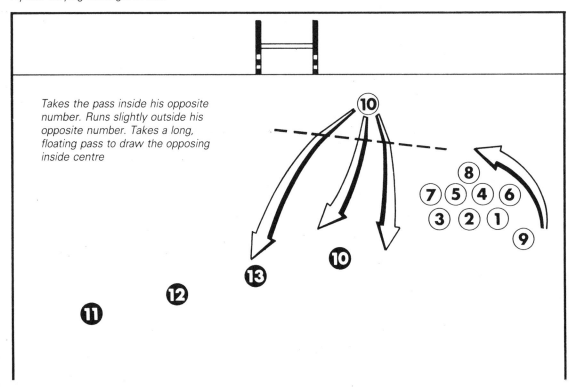

Takes the pass inside his opposite number. Runs slightly outside his opposite number. Takes a long, floating pass to draw the opposing inside centre

△ The break-through on the field comes from constant practice

ical training instructor who was to get us fit at the start of the year, so I spent most of my summer getting fit so that I would get through those physical sessions. I realize now that I should have spent all that time practising what Barry John used to practise – sidestepping and the shorter, sharper spurts which are really part of the out-half game. I've learned from my mistakes and, from now on, I intend to do a lot more track work with spikes – sprinting, change of pace, changing direction, that sort of thing. It is important that the training is applicable to your position, so if you're an 18-stone forward and you want to build yourself up, you maybe do weights or running if you want to get fit. If you're a light back and you want to put on a few pounds, obviously weight training again.

There's no such thing as an overall schedule for every rugby player. Each individual on a rugby team is very different and needs a different type of training. It's up to him to find out what he needs and to train accordingly. I would describe myself as transitional. I'm certainly not fast – I could do with a lot more speed. In fact, if I could be given more speed I would promise never to

Practising running skills ▽

kick a ball again! If I could be given the pace of a Cliff Morgan or even a Phil Bennett, I would swap it for kicking.

You must have a code of signals for the situations that recur over and over again, the situations that you know are going to happen and which do happen in 90 per cent of games – for example, when there is a line-out in your own 25 or a scrum underneath the opposition's posts. There are so many situations that do recur that I think you must have your signals. From our playing together, the scrum half would know what I was going to do in certain situations, and likewise I would know what he was going to do in certain situations. In every game there are situations which are unique to that game. There is a certain understanding that will come between halves from playing together for any length of time. Telepathic, maybe, is too strong a word, but I think an understanding certainly does develop when you play, and it's nice when you both react to an unusual situation in exactly the same way – that gives great satisfaction.

My signals are always verbal – I never give visual signals. The only visual one I give is if I want a ball straight back. Then I just point to my chest and the scrum half immediately knows. But apart from that they are all verbal. The one problem with using speaking signals, certainly at international level, is that the crowds are there and sometimes it's very hard for the scrum half to hear you or for the players outside you to hear your calls. I've never tried to decipher the signals of the opposition. You can often find out what the opposition are going to do by the positions that they take up. Again, it's very hard to hear signals, particularly in the bigger games, so if you just watch positions you often know what their intentions are.

If you haven't got a fly half and two centres who can take and give a pass at speed and run straight, then your attacking options are limited from the start (you see it at all rugby levels at the moment, from international right down). I think that the most important thing for back lines to understand is the question of angles of running, and again the question of straight running and not running across the field.

Calling the move before the fly half knows the quality of the ball is something that has always happened. Perhaps the difference now is that no matter what the possession is like, people often go through with the move, whereas years ago

they may have realized that this wasn't the ball for whatever move was called and would do something else. The difference now is that people go through with the call no matter what type of possession comes out, whereas before they had more flexibility and would realize that this was a very bad ball and call off the move. The calls must be made in the back line even before the ball goes into a scrum or is thrown into a line-out because the back line must have some idea of what is on. But I think the fault is going through with that call, no matter what the quality of the possession.

I don't worry very much about my opposing back rows. It may sound big-headed or conceited or whatever, but I've never gone out in a game and been concerned about a back row. I have been concerned about my opposition out half, and what he might do but, somehow, never about an opposing flanker.

I don't mind how quickly or how slowly the flanker comes out on me – if he comes out very quickly on me, I can take him out of the game if I hold onto the ball for a second and pass away to my centres. Even if he tackles me after the ball has gone I don't mind because I know that I've got the ball away and that the rest of the back line can do their work without him causing them problems.

My own back row is something that I haven't really concentrated on very much. Certainly I would be more aware, I think, of linking up with them if they came off the side of a scrum or, as Fergus Slattery often does, took a ball (a very flat ball) in the out-half position very close to a ruck or a maul. Fergus will often take it in the out-half position off Robbie McGrath, looking for a half-break, maybe running at the out half and looking for a half-break. I am very aware of being up beside him if he does get half through so that I can continue the attack there, but I don't often link up back inside with wing forwards. I think if I make a half-break, the ball should really go out to my centres rather than inside to my back row.

I don't really think it's any more difficult making the right decisions or taking the right options in front of a big crowd than in front of a small crowd. I read a game the same for my club as I would at international level. The fact that there happens to be 50,000 instead of fifty people there doesn't change the reading of the game itself. Pressure doesn't really make any difference.

It's always interesting when the first scrum

goes down, to know whether it's going to be a nice easy attacking game going forward or a very difficult one going back on my heels. I wait for the outcome of the first scrum just as keenly as the front rows do in any game.

I don't watch closely the play of the forwards. The only thing I'm interested in is the ball coming back on our side cleanly enough and often enough from the line-outs.

Until the ball has left the scrum half's hands, it is sometimes very hard to judge precisely when the ball is going to be in your hands. The golden rule is not to move until the scrum half has the ball in his hands.

I have played with three very good scrum halves in the Irish team – John Robbie, Colin Patterson and Robbie McGrath, and I can't think of one bad hospital pass that I've had from any of them. I've had a few at club level, and I don't like them any more than anyone else does, but at international level, thankfully, I have never had eight opposition forwards coming down on top of me when I've been given a pass.

Most of my games in the Irish jersey have basically been very stereotyped games, when I've done a lot of kicking just to keep the forwards going forward. My own personal game hasn't been what you would call expansive, so I've never really given the opposition back row that much cause for worry. So I wouldn't really see myself as a marked man. I would say I've concentrated on not giving away penalties rather than on any particular running skills. When the back rows are really keen to get at me, that suits me down to the ground because I can come off after a club game having done absolutely nothing, and people say, 'This man's supposed to be an international, but he didn't do very much today'; but I know that I've taken a wing forward out of the game for eighty minutes. That wing forward has done absolutely nothing – he may have covered me four or five times late or just as I've got the ball away, and he feels he's had a great game, but in fact our back line has played superbly because they haven't had a back row to deal with. So I think that at out half you don't have to do everything all

Practising the drop goal under pressure

the time. It's like management, you have to make sure things are done, but you don't necessarily have to do them yourself.

I spend a lot of time practising my kicking – all types of kicking. I spend most of my time on penalty kicks, but I have done a lot of work on my drop-kicking and on my punting as well. Diagonal kicking was my favourite and was the kick I employed perhaps 80 per cent of the time* up to about four years ago. At that time it was the kick that most out halves used, probably because of Barry John's influence. I feel now that it is a very difficult kick to master, and you have to hit the ball in exactly the right position. Wingers are so aware of it now that they hang back for it, so unless it goes to ground it can turn out to be a very bad kick. The grubber is a kick which seems to have gone out of fashion a lot over the years – it's a lovely little kick to use in attack. The one danger of it is that if I don't run up far enough to

The still head, the high follow-through of Campbell's classical line kicking

my out half and try it, the chances are that it's going to hit someone's legs and end up behind our centres rather than the opposition centres. So I think the secret of it is to go as far as you can and actually use your body as protection against your opposite number and just slide it through. Once it does get through, it's a very difficult ball to defend against.

The torpedo kick really is the basic kick. I haven't seen to this day a better kicker than Gareth Davies, who can torpedo-kick a ball 60 or 70 yards just with timing. Gareth is not a big man by any means, which proves the importance of timing with all kicking. The follow-through is probably the most important, the same as in golf where the bad shot is always the one you quit on. I think it's exactly the same with all types of kicking, whether it's punting, drop-kicking or place-kicking. I think the garryowen kick at the moment is being overplayed. It's a far more difficult kick than people think. It seems a very easy thing to do, but to put up a garryowen for a full back high enough and in exactly the right spot so that it's in the air long enough and yet not too far for your centres to get up underneath is difficult. It is the kick which is used now more than any other. I think it has come into play even more than before with the new tackle law because even if the full back catches the ball without making a mark – say it's outside the 22 where he can't mark – and he is tackled, he must let go. It has almost become a tactic because of that. So I think it is a very important kick. One kick that isn't used very much at all now is the box kick, or at least it's not used as much as it should be both to the right and left sides of the field. This is a far more exposed area than the area where the full back is standing. So these are all kicks that anyone playing at out half would need to master.

What determines the type of kick that you use in any situation is probably the position on the field as much as the situation that the game is in – whether you're behind or ahead, and wind conditions and so on. If you're on the attack and you're maybe 35 yards out on the left-hand side of the field (which would be the better side for me with my right foot), and if the full back has had a few bad moments and you want to test him out and keep the game tight, maybe that would be an occasion to put up a garryowen or one into the box. Again, if you bring it back to round about your own 10-yard line, perhaps there might be an

An instep, round-the-corner kicker, who practises often for a high percentage success rate

Good kicking action▷

opportunity there for a long diagonal kick because the opposite winger has to have an eye on his own man. Or again that might be an opportunity for a chip over the centres' heads, particularly if you're playing with the wind so that the full back has to stay back very far because you might kick long, either diagonally or a garryowen. I would say my greatest pleasure is actually running with the ball. I don't do it half enough, but beating a man, either by a dummy or a sidestep, really gives me a great feeling, and I think that, for a back anyway, man-beating is what it's all about.

In defence I don't consider my opposite out half as being anybody else's man but my own man. I don't expect my wing forwards to do all my tackling for me or to put him under pressure more than I do, although we should work as a unit in that regard. So, particularly when my opposite number is kicking out of defence, I like to put him under as much pressure as I can because if you do this it can mean as much as 10 or 15 yards off his kick.

The other important thing is to bring up the two centres. If the out half lies back, it leaves a very big hole there which the opposite out half can exploit, so it's very important to bring up the two centres – the three should go up together as one. When the opposing out half has passed the ball on, I would expect to be covering along behind the two centres; and if the full back comes in I really would expect to be there either to put him under pressure to kick or to tackle him if he decides to run.

I haven't over the years done much tackling practice, but I think young people, particularly, should do it. If you don't do it when you're young, there may be a certain fear once you get older. The time to realize there is no problem in tackling, to get the fear out of it, is when you are very young.

For me it is very important to be able to use both feet. I couldn't really imagine myself being happy going out onto the field if I didn't know that I could use my left foot. Certainly, in defensive situations, I know that if I have to I can use my left foot and I can use it quite well. I can use it in attack, I can put up a garryowen, a box kick, I can chip and I have actually dropped goals with my left foot.

Like everything, passing needs practice, and there are always going to be people who can pass better one way than the other. Having said that, I think it's very important that you can pass with equal facility, whether going from left to right or from right to left. That is a must for anyone who has designs on any standard of rugby.

I recognized this weakness in myself that I couldn't pass from left to right years ago. So I got down and I practised it like a scrum half would practise his weak side, and now if I'm throwing a long pass I prefer to do it on what was my weaker side.

# 7 The Scrum Half and Number 8

## Assessment of the positions *Carwyn James*

### The Scrum Half

The key position, the vital link between forwards and backs, is the scrum half. When the scrum half gets the ball from a scrummage he has eight forwards in front of him and six backs behind him. He has three options: run with the ball and put his own forwards onside; kick the ball ahead with the same required effect; pass the ball to his backs. In other words, a break, a kick or a pass. Before discussing each of the three, let us briefly ponder on the attributes needed by a scrum half.

The first, irrespective of physical bulk, is mental hardness, the ability to take knocks, acquiring the tremendous psychological advantage of being able to come up smiling when sponsored studs have trampled all over you.

Physical attributes are less definable because scrum halves come in all sizes but, like a well-oiled engine, they all need coordination, power in the upper body, agility, mental alertness and strong, strong wrists. Beginning at the third Christmas, every discerning Santa Claus should produce annually at least a dozen sponge balls for the use of each member of the male population of his parish. That sponge ball should wreak havoc and spin on wall, window, road and supermarket and should be worn out in a month. Imagine the value of having a rugby ball, even a plastic one, as a Christmas present, and the joy of pitting one's concentration and reflexes against an oval object rebounding in all directions from a tiresome wall.

### Passing

I must make the point, not for the first time, that our scrum halves in the UK are so badly taught at a tender age, or not taught at all, that by the time they are ready for first-class rugby they are almost

The young Gareth Edwards, pivot pass, blind to his opponents, and an unnecessary long back swing

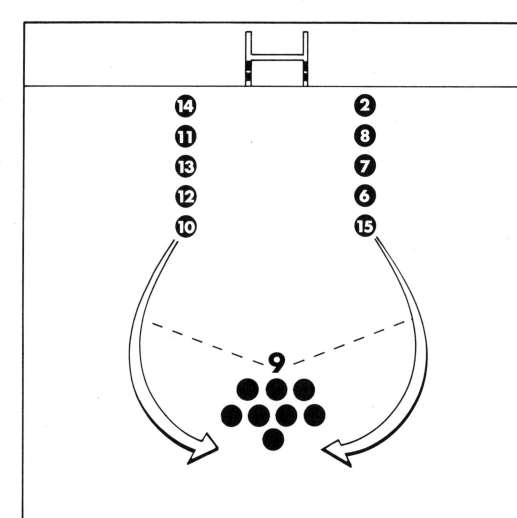

*Scrum half passing at speed. Test of strength and stamina. Four types: standing, pivot, dive, reverse. Coach calls: left standing, right pivot, right dive, left dive, left standing, right reverse, left reverse, etc.*

*1. At a slow pace concentrate on technique*
*2. At a much quicker pace concentrate on thinking response, accuracy, technique and eventually stamina. Recovering immediately from the dive pass is the killer. This is an invaluable practice for back-row forwards as well*

Chris Laidlaw, perfector of the spin pass

unteachable. Yet they have the other attributes which help them succeed.

Edwards, in fact, in his autobiography, *Gareth*, admitted that when he first played for Wales, passing was an embarrassment to him. A potentially great scrum half who couldn't pass. Despite our coaching courses we are still producing such scrum halves. Edwards became strongly indebted to Laidlaw's spin pass.

Let us first of all put our scrum half to the test. Slowly first and then under pressure. Four types of passing: standing, pivot, dive and reverse – going right and going left. All four passes are part of the total expertise which a scrum half needs. Wrist passing is superior to spin passing. Although I applaud Chris Laidlaw for perfecting the spin

pass and making a scrum half of G. O. Edwards, I repeat that every child now has discovered the easy way of passing at the expense of wrist passing. Even mid-field players spin pass to one another!

The spin pass is a more lengthy pass. A quick pass is a better pass than a long pass. Time is more important than length.

The best passer of a ball I ever saw was Ken Catchpole of Australia. From a line-out for instance he would take the ball on the perpendicular and without any backswing he would pass the ball like lightning a foot or two in front of his fly half at hip height.

Catchpole, Hipwell, Going, Loveridge and other Australian scrum halves are technically superb passers of the ball off the ground from scrummage and ruck.

◁ Pressure passing

Sid Going, a technically superb passer from off the ground

Haydn Tanner, who played for Wales before and after the war

Half-back partnership Onllwyn Brace and Cliff Morgan

From the dozens of photographs I have seen of the famous scrum halves of the forties and fifties, I suspect that they overdid the dive pass and too often they were guilty of a dive and a pivot pass. Passes don't come much worse than that. No wonder standing passers and reverse passers like Brace were too far ahead of their time to be appreciated.

In partnership the perceptive fly half appreciates the quick pass and varies his angles of taking the ball. In defence, the scrum half will give the ball to the fly half to kick if he is better placed.

Scrum-half passing

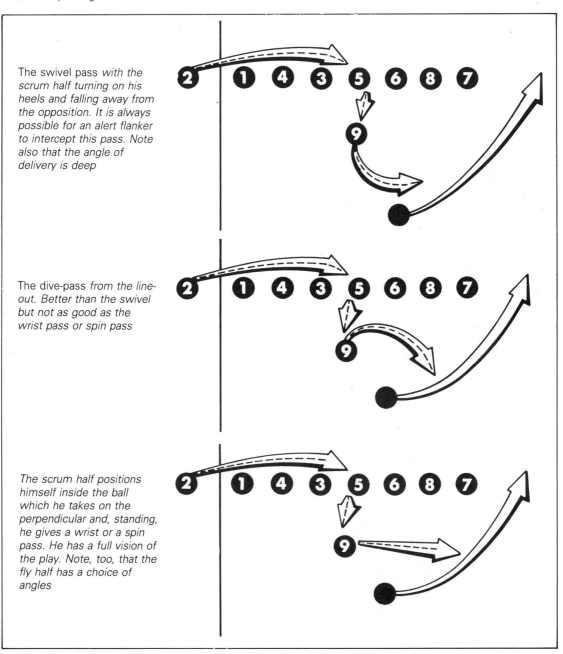

The swivel pass *with the scrum half turning on his heels and falling away from the opposition. It is always possible for an alert flanker to intercept this pass. Note also that the angle of delivery is deep*

The dive-pass *from the line-out. Better than the swivel but not as good as the wrist pass or spin pass*

*The scrum half positions himself inside the ball which he takes on the perpendicular and, standing, he gives a wrist or a spin pass. He has a full vision of the play. Note, too, that the fly half has a choice of angles*

# Kicking

A scrum half should be two-footed and a shrewd, tactical kicker. Before the introduction of the dispensation law, Clive Rowlands was the master of the line kick to touch and from scrummages, once he had spread himself by taking a couple of paces to the right, he would place a high ball back to the box for his left wing to run onto.

Gareth Edwards became the first to master the one ball bounce into touch from outside his 22.

# Breaking

I would agree with Dickie Jeeps, a tough, wiry scrum half and a former Triple Crown captain of England, that for the sake of his colleagues a scrum half should make one or two breaks in each half. Haydn Tanner, Roy Sutton of Swansea, Johnny Williams of England, Terry Holmes of Wales and Mark Douglas of Llanelli are all spoken of in awe as scrum halves who could break from the base of a scrummage, penetrate over the gain line and link with back-row colleagues.

The scrum-half position is probably the most demanding, but it can be the most rewarding as well.

# The Number 8

Ken Catchpole has this to say about learning his trade: 'I played centre at school for one season and learned the difference a scrum half can make to provide the centre with time and room in which to move. I also better understood the role and difficulties experienced by the stand-off. I believe every schoolboy scrum half should play stand-off or centre some time.'

Many players, of course, have heeded his advice, but somehow I can't see Dave Loveridge playing number 8. In the modern game, though, there is much to say about the number-8–scrum-half combination.

The modern game demands that a number 8 has sufficient weight to hold and to lock a scrum, and sufficient height to win possession at the tail of a line-out. In fact we are thinking of a Mervyn Davies, a Peter Dixon, a Roger Uttley or a Willie Duggan, all big, mobile men and all thoroughly conversant with the skills of the game.

Since he has to be a pretty perceptive reader of situations, he needs quickness over a short distance to get to a problem area. A number 8, like a scrum half, is never far from the action. He is less involved when the action ceases, but he has to be there or thereabouts. For that reason it must

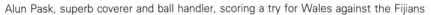

Alun Pask, superb coverer and ball handler, scoring a try for Wales against the Fijians

be a most frustrating position in which to play because it is far more demanding than rewarding. This was even more so in the traditional role employed by number 8s who were superb coverers and excellent users of the ball. Alun Pask is the prime example. Walter Spanghéro and Benoit Dauga, despite the fact that they were converted second-row players, were also adept at handling and running.

Mervyn Davies: transformed the number 8 position

I think Mervyn Davies transformed the position because he was a ball winner, a fetcher, always going forward, always challenging for the ball.

## Back-row defence at a scrum

Basically the number 8's job is second man round the scrum, filling a gap left by the breakaway flanker. If the opposition moves the ball wide, the number 8 will work out his angle of running, lining up each of the mid-field in turn and paying particular attention to the centre coming through on the crash ball following a scissors.

## Back-row defence at a line-out

If the ball is tapped back, the first reaction of the number 8 should be to pressurize the opposing scrum half, the other half of the pincer being the hooker. If the scrum half gets the ball away, the number 8 sets off on his covering run, lining up each of the opposing backs in turn.

## In attack

The number 8 is not given the clear support which the front and the middle jumpers expect. For that reason he tends to jump and deflect with the outside arm, a vertically falling tap for the peel, a more definite tap to the scrum half. I think that most number 8s feel a special responsibility for the health of a scrum half.

At a scrummage their guardian angel or protective role is even more apparent. If the scrum half doesn't like channel one (Gareth Edwards for instance didn't), then it is up to the number 8 to use channel two and place the ball and give it to the scrum half as and when he wants it. Channel three, to the right of the number 8, grants even more protection.

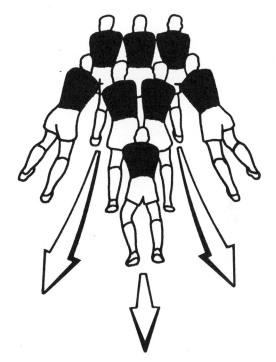

Channelling the ball at the scrummage: from left to right, channels 1, 2 and 3

The number 8 is in full control of this delivery. He will obviously vary the timing of the feed to make the opposition think. He also has many attacking options in relation to his scrum half. A telepathic understanding is absolutely essential since there will be two or three important attacking scrums in a game which may affect the result.

The number 8, in addition, must take the main responsibility for countering the disruptive wheeling of scrums which has become such a nuisance in the game as it is played today. Picking the ball up is one answer and starting a dribble is another.

Finally, a number 8 needs to be a strong tackler, fearless in the frontal tackle, the most difficult of them all. I have no doubt that a great number 8 affects considerably the play of a scrum half. I have heard Gareth Edwards paying glowing tributes to the genius of Mervyn Davies.

# Introducing the Scrum Half *Carwyn James*

After Dave Loveridge's All Black debut at Cardiff Arms Park, Welsh coach John Dawes addressed a telling remark to a neighbour: 'Tell me, when have we ever seen a weak New Zealand scrum half?'

Loveridge seemed to arrive gift-wrapped with all the technical skills in the book that day. Indeed, Cardiff Arms Park is a favourite ground for him, and it was here that he first donned the jersey against the Cardiff club and later made his Test debut against Wales when the opening fifteen minutes were so ferocious that the ground generated enough heat to cook the participants. Fre-

quently bundled off the ball, Loveridge's small figure stood out more as victim than instigator of the recovery of All Black composure, and it was not until Wales led by 9 points that the machine began to assert itself. Loveridge later confessed to Bob Howitt that he did not sleep the night before the match. But, typically on such an occasion, nerves or not, he has skills to fall back upon, and at the core of his play then and later, these skills add up to a formidable talent.

The first thing to notice about him is that he appears to lack physical stature. A late developer, so insignificant in primary school that he was

The number 8 in attack (black) and defence (white) on the blind side, working closely with the flankers. Note that the scrum half's (9's) role is not shown

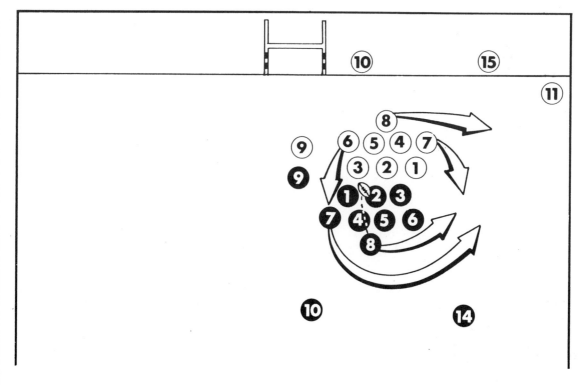

neglected by school coaches as a pipsqueak, he has been confounding them ever since. As Bob Howitt relates in *Rugby Greats*, Loveridge began his career with a lightweight side at the Inglewood club. There he must have learned that small is only beautiful with speed and it was as a shadow that he was most effective, so elusive as to be unstoppable.

At the heart of his play is his pass, the crucial hallmark of the ball supplier, and this pass of his begins low on the ground, quick, accurate, and with no appreciable backswing. It is his prime function as it should be with all scrum halves. The pass *is* the player in this position for nine tenths of the game, and nothing must hinder or delay it, not an inch, not a second, not a blade of grass! There must be a predictability to it, a total reliability and a conviction that anything lost is a black mark upon the character.

Loveridge himself says that good passing begins with the positioning of the feet, and it is no surprise to learn that he is also a cricketer of repute. Another of his qualities is his instinct, his knowledge of when to run himself because no scrum half can be too self-effacing. Like Sid Going before him, there is a certain foxiness, an ability to deceive his opponents, which makes him capable of that other essential attribute of all the great scrum halves, the capacity to be a bundle of trouble! It comes from reading the game, knowing where to place himself, and above all from his rapport with his forwards. Typically, Loveridge once sought to give reasons for his success after a good tour and picked out lock Andy Haden as the one man most responsible, describing him as the best taker of the line-out ball in the game. Haden was the Mercedes engine without which the *driver* could not race.

At the same time, Loveridge is an unobtrusive player, unshowy, brisk, efficient. He very seldom makes mistakes. You can see him talking to his forwards on occasion, and his two nicknames, 'Trapper' and 'Yapper', are part of him, but most important is the simple efficiency of that crisp, lightning pass. From the shadow of Mount Egmont in Taranaki an example has gone out to young players of a technocrat as near flawless as any in the game.

## The player *Dave Loveridge*

The scrum half's role has changed considerably during the time I've been playing rugby. The alterations in the laws which came into effect quite a few years ago, stopping us from kicking the ball out of the field from outside the 22, have turned the half back's role into one much more of passing. Twenty years ago we could simply kick the ball over the top of the forwards and out of the

Feeding the ball into the scrum: timing and angle are the key factors

Loveridge prefers the channel 3 ball because it takes the pressure off

field to gain ground, but that can't be done any more: half-back play has obviously changed and I think the whole game has altered considerably.

But it still remains true that at the scrum the scrum half's job is essentially that of feeding the ball in at the right time and angle for his hooker to hook it and then, at scrum and line-out – if he has a back move on – to clear it perfectly to the backs so as to allow them to attack. When the scrum half receives the ball, eight of his team – the forwards – are all offside, so he can put them onside by kicking forward either to touch or to his wingers. Equally he can hold onto the ball and run forwards. But perhaps more frequently he'll pass it to the next onside player, the fly half. The loss of even a split second in making a decision about what to do or in the pass itself can really spoil your backs' attack, so speed and accuracy are vital.

It is the number 8, of course, who passes the ball back to you, so it's very important to have a good working relationship with your number 8. I'm lucky in having Murray Mexted at that position and in having played a lot of rugby with Murray over the last few years, especially in Test matches. Imagine a team as a simple machine: the links between the working parts must be good

or faults will start to appear. I'm equally lucky enough to have a good number 8 in Taranaki, with whom I also have a very close liaison. We've played a lot together which has greatly helped my play and, I hope, helped the team. Of course, the number 8 sometimes picks up the ball and runs himself. Often this is a set move, but it's also important that the number 8 should know when a ball coming from the scrum isn't so good for the scrum half. If the number 8 automatically picks it up and takes the pressure off the scrum half at such a time, you have an example of perfect understanding between the two.

There are three channels by which the ball can emerge from the scrummage: I prefer a channel-three ball which has moved far enough to allow you to kick, run or pass to your backs without so much pressure on. Obviously, though, the type of ball you can afford to get away with depends on how the scrum is bunching up in front. If your scrum is going well and you're not being pressurized by the opposing scrum half, a channel-one or -two ball is not too bad. But in today's game you get pressurized by the opposing scrum half coming round and trying to upset play; then I think that a channel-three ball is safest and allows you to pass with more freedom. Most

The ideal ball from the scrum is on the ground – note also how Mexted's body positioning protects Loveridge from an opponent coming round the scrum

scrum halves do try to move round the scrum so as to upset play and put the pressure on – I certainly do.

For me, the ideal ball from the scrum arrives on the ground. I've found that to be the best position for passing it – especially if you use the flip pass, because you don't actually pick the ball up: it's moved by a quick flick of the wrists from the ground. Once the ball is in the hand, the whole pass is slowed down. I've done a great deal of work on the body position needed to pass a ball, and I suspect that body position is the secret of being able to use a quick wrist pass off the ground. If your body isn't in the right position and if you haven't got your weight evenly distributed, a spin pass or flip pass straight from the ground is much more difficult to execute. You have to work on this, taking into account where your feet are, how your body is positioned and how you actually move.

There seems to be some controversy about what might be the most time-saving pass. Different people have different opinions about the spin pass, for example; and the spin pass can also be

difficult to catch if not executed well. But it's fair to say that the longer the pass is, the more time it'll take. The dive pass can lose time and can also put you out of action for the second or two it takes to get up from the ground, as well as being a potentially tiring manoeuvre. But that is not to say that long or time-consuming passes are not extremely useful – they are. If the ball has gone loose and I have to move to it, I'll use a dive pass because I won't have time to steady myself for a flick pass. It can also be useful when the ground is greasy or when the ball comes back awkwardly. Of course, a dive pass increases the length of the pass and can also put you out of reach of the opposing forwards.

When passing I think it helps to face the opposition and to have a clear vision of them, though that isn't always possible. I certainly wouldn't make a habit of turning my back to the opposition though.

But whatever else you take into account, your choice of pass must depend upon what your fly half wants. Some fly halves may stand a long way away from their scrum halves and some may

Body positioning is the secret of good passing

The spin pass

stand close. The scrum half must know where the fly half is going to be. That's essential. He can then ensure that the ball arrives in the right place: say, a foot in front of the receiver's hips, so that he can catch it comfortably and use it immediately.

One tremendously useful experience is seeing yourself pass on film or TV. You don't realize how you're doing it until you see it like that. I think that in New Zealand all scrum halves pass in basically the same way, while in the British Isles and Europe they have a different style of passing. I suspect that younger people pick up such styles by watching players within their own countries; however, any style can be worked at. I don't see why a player can't pick up any particular style and see if it works for him. For example, the spin pass: Chris Laidlaw's play was based mainly around the spin pass – in fact that's probably where the spin pass comes from as New Zealanders remember it. They remember Sid Going as a runner with the ball, but I've always admired his passing too: I thought he was a good, quick passer.

Liaison between the scrum half and the fly half must be close, and in this liaison communication plays a large part. The fly half will try to help the scrum half and will call for the ball if he's in a better position. But, obviously, if you receive a bad ball it won't help if you pass it to someone who's in a worse position than yourself. Most scrum-half–fly-half combinations practise a great deal together. That way you develop your calls and come to know when the fly half wants the ball standing still or moving and when he wants it close, wide or flat. The essential factor is communication, and this becomes developed and natural with plenty of practice. Communication is also vital to your work with the number 8. Murray Mexted and I talk a lot before each scrum and so we know exactly what is going to happen with each ball. I think we rely more on verbal communication than on signals. Which one of us makes a decision in any particular case depends on the positions we are at in the paddock. One of us may say that a particular move is on and the other will either agree or offer an alternative.

In Test matches, where a vital game can be won or lost on just one or two mistakes, I like to have a fly half who will be at the right place at the right time doing the right thing. I think that fly half is very much a position where the player controls

play, and it's been very reassuring to have people like Doug Bruce (he finished for New Zealand in 1978) and Brian McKechnie who are safe – who are going to do the right thing. However, having said that, you can't play safe all the time and I certainly haven't. The beauty about adventurous play is having the confidence to do it – and, again, communication within the team is vital. The teams that I've played with over the last few years have had very good communication within them and that's been a huge asset. Also, we've had the confidence to do something when the players thought it was on. Mind you, I think that as far as the All Blacks are concerned our planning is more concerned with not giving anything away than with adventurous play – especially in Tests.

I've talked about the trio of scrum half, number 8 and fly half. The scrum half also has to liaise well with the forwards – the loose forwards and, especially, the flankers. That's important because they are supposed to be quick about the paddock and quick in setting up the ball for the forwards to win the game. A good understanding with the hooker is vital: obviously, you must work with him to ensure that you always win the ball at your own scrum. The two of you must practise put-ins together and you must ensure that your put-in technique doesn't vary during a game.

In a way, the scrum half is the pivot between the forwards and the backs. If the scrum half doesn't play well then the backs really suffer. However, I think that you can actually say that about most positions. If the forwards don't play well the scrum half won't play well, and if the fly half doesn't play well the centres won't play well. It's a chain reaction.

So far I've talked about passing from the scrum and line-out but there are, of course, the other options of running with the ball or kicking it. I might consider running with the ball two or three times in a game, perhaps because I'm better placed than the fly half in those particular circumstances. Most set moves have a call and these can involve the scrum half in running or kicking. For example, the number 8 might pack off the back of the scrum and feed the scrum half running or the scrum half might run on his own and link with the winger on the narrow side. Again, you might put up a box kick, or a high kick, behind the forwards, putting pressure on the opposing winger, or whoever is there, and allowing your own wingers and others to run on.

I said just now that most set moves have a call. Some use numbers, some use names – it doesn't matter as long as everybody is clear about what's to happen – and so you might have a number called when the ball is put in which is a call for a particular move. I think that most teams, and it's certainly true of the All Blacks, have either a planned move or a called move from every scrum and every line-out – though whether they always come off is a different matter. But I'd also say that I don't think any player knows where play is going to break down. To be effective in case of a breakdown you simply have to keep as close to the ball as possible all the time. That's what I've based my game on.

Positioning at both scrum and line-out is important. At the line-out I position myself fairly near the front – that's quite conventional. It allows you to have a full view of the line-out and to run onto the ball and clear it. It makes the pass to your backs a lot easier. However, in a game you can move to a position where you think a line-out ball is going to go to only to find that the ball is tapped and not controlled. You must then decide very quickly whether you can turn a bad ball into a good ball. You face a split-second decision as you say to yourself, 'Can I still move the ball away or shall I just run it out or kick it out?' The abilities to decide quickly and to compromise come into play there. And just as you can come under pressure at scrums so you can be pressurized at line-outs. Hookers with flankers can create a wedge which threatens to cut you off. During my career England's Peter Wheeler and Scotland's Colin Deans have been hookers who have caused me great problems by being quick off the front of the line-out. I'd say Peter Wheeler was master of the hookers.

I haven't spoken much about kicking. That again is something you must practise and practise, particularly if you fancy being another Gareth Edwards.

In defence a scrum half's role is also very important – and that, of course, applies to the rest of the team as well. At the scrum on the opposition's ball the scrum half must try to upset the opposition or at least prevent play getting past him on his side. I earlier talked about moving round the scrum: how effectively you put the pressure on by doing this depends on how well your scrum and the opposing scrum are performing. If the opposing scrum is performing well, it's difficult to pressurize their scrum half. If not, it's

obviously easier. I'd say that the scrum half who has worried me the most from the scrum has been France's Berbizier. He's quick in moving the ball and in moving round the scrum. I don't think that a scrum half on defence has a specific person to defend against as the backs do; for them it's more man-for-man. However, you must be able to make sure that an opponent doesn't run back at you or use the short side. If the ball is moved wide you follow the ball. Essentially you must be able to cover and to tackle.

It's difficult to say where one's skill comes from. I think I mainly picked up my skills along the way, though obviously I was influenced by some of the All Black players like Chris Laidlaw and Sid Going. I think that on the whole I have a natural talent that has fortunately been developed well. New Zealand rugby being renowned for forward play has helped. I learned a lot just by watching other players – notably Laidlaw and Going – and then I worked hard, hoping I would improve. But I can't really put my development down to one particular player. I was fortunate enough to have a good coach from my primary-school days and right through my secondary-school career.

Naturally, a scrum half must be fit. Agility and being able to move quickly and with coordination are important. To a certain degree you must be strong in the wrists, but I think it basically boils down to quickness of movement. That's probably why most scrum halves are smaller players, perhaps with powerful upper bodies. A scrum half must also have an agile, alert mind ready for snap decisions. The skills that I concentrate on most are passing, backing up, kicking and then tackling. If you look at those four skills then you're halfway there; and you must keep on looking at them. Some say a scrum half takes a lot of punishment but I don't think it's as much as the forwards get. Mind you, your level of punishment depends upon how well the forwards are playing – what kind of ball you're getting from them.

But I don't think anyone goes into the game worrying about how much punishment he's going to get. As far as I'm concerned, the game of rugby is essentially one of comradeship between players. That's probably one of the major things that keeps rugby players playing: that feeling of comradeship when you play. To get that you must enjoy the game and you must enjoy playing alongside other players – your own side, the people you play against . . . the people you meet.

# Introducing the Number 8 *Carwyn James*

Shaw, Mexted and Mourie are highly regarded in a land which has continually produced back-row forwards of the highest quality.

As a young lad, Murray Mexted watched the third Test between the Lions and the All Blacks at Wellington in 1971 when Mervyn Davies and Brian Lochore, recalled from retirement to play at lock, were in opposition. As number 8s Davies and Lochore had differing styles, Davies always close to the ball, Lochore more of a coverer and a traditionalist. But the young Mexted would have hardly been aware of such sophistications.

The influences on his game came later – none more so than that of another Wellingtonian, Andy Leslie, an All Black captain of some standing. And when Leslie was ready for retirement, Mexted was so well versed in the arts of a difficult position that his name soon easily carried the geographical data: Tawa, Wellington, New Zealand.

The name of Mexted means more in Tawa, a small township some fifteen miles north of Wellington. Dad was and is the king of the place, an All Black loose forward who played against the 1950 Lions, a respected councillor, an elder statesman, an owner of a garage and a store which sells almost anything that a community needs. So entrenched are the Mexteds in Tawa that Murray always had dreams of travelling to distant places in other continents.

When Leslie quietly phased himself out following the All Blacks tour of South Africa in 1976, Mexted was almost ready to take over. He soon established himself as a provincial player and made his debut in the two unofficial Tests played against Hugo Porta's Pumas in 1979. Dave Loveridge was the captain and the two loosies were Kenny Stewart and Murray Mexted.

In the meantime, however, some of Murray's dreams had been realized. For six months in 1977 he played number 8 for Agen, a respected First Division side who became the champions of France in 1982, and he kept out Dominique Erbani, a most promising player who opposed Mexted at Toulouse and Paris when the All Blacks toured France in the autumn of 1981. In July 1982, Erbani and Serge Blanco were the two French representatives in the Five Nations team chosen to open Ellis Park, Johannesburg.

Although Mexted had spent a couple of months in Durban at the start of the 1982 rugby season, the call to return home to play against the touring Wallabies had to be answered. He played in all three Tests in a series which the All Blacks won 2–1.

Murray Mexted has the qualities of leadership which will soon be recognized. He could well follow Graham Mourie as another great New Zealand captain.

# The player *Murray Mexted*

I started, actually, in the backs when I was at primary school at less than thirteen years of age. Of course, most people in New Zealand start at five or six years of age and I think since I was twelve or thirteen I have played either number 8 or as a flanker. My father was a number 8 also, so I grew up looking at the game of the number 8 forward. Every time I watch a game, I watch the number 8s – you can't help but do that; it's instinct and it's interesting, and I've taken it from there. Probably the first number 8 I watched and studied as a player was Brian Lochore.

The corner flagging game is an interesting game and it's a game I grew up with from a young age. I never changed that game until three or four years

ago. In fact, it wasn't until I made the All Black team that my style changed. I had always heard the phrase 'cover, cover, cover' as a number 8, but the game today has changed considerably. We feel, in the All Black team, that if you can get two players to the ball before the opposition, then you are going to retain possession. So from set phases the two closest forwards to the ball are actually the open-side flanker and the number 8. Today the number 8's role of covering has changed – he is supporting the flanker, and the blind-side flanker takes over the old role of the number 8 in cooperation with the winger; they work together as a pair. Our idea today is to get the first player to the breakdown and release the

Brian Lochore

winger or some other forwards, hold the ball there and then move it wide again. And then from second phase we might have third phase, and if we achieve possession from a phase-three ball, we are going to score. An old All Black move is where the number 8 forward detaches and backs into the opposing half back and the open-side flanker – in other words, he takes out two men completely. The blind-side flanker comes around the base of the scrum and, if I have taken out my two men, I can easily feed it to the blind-side flanker who should have an unopposed path to the goal line. It is normally done within 5 or 6 yards of the goal line.

I think there is definitely an understanding between the scrum half and the number 8 – it is a very important part of the game. It is not actually a verbal understanding, it is just an understanding of what you are going to do in a certain situation. It is a matter of rapport between the two players.

I have been fortunate at club level – I have had an understanding with my half back for years now, because my half back for Wellington Club was the same as for Wellington Province. Also, since I have been playing for the All Black team, I have played with Dave Loveridge on almost every occasion. We have now played fourteen consecutive Test matches together, so we have been able to achieve this understanding at this level – it is the sort of situation which I am sure doesn't arise too often.

To me, Loveridge is by far the best half back in the world. He is a half back who makes a line-out forward look good and makes a bad line-out forward also look good. Dave Loveridge can make the players ahead of him look good because he can distribute and release almost any ball he is given under almost any situation. He can be given a terrible ball at the line-out and he can free it rapidly to his first five eighth. It is an art, and it is an ability that he has and he seems to be a lot better than any half back I have played against. He doesn't need a backswing, he seems to have a great wrist movement and power from a limited area of movement. He will take a ball on the ground and fire it from that spot. He will take it above his head, fire it with two hands, he will flick it behind his back – he is complete in my opinion. I have seen him release the ball in so many tight situations when it appeared that a second's gap and he would have been covered. I feel he may have a little backswing, but I would be surprised.

ball and give it to the second player. In other words, Mourie's whole object is not to stop play and set up another ruck but to continue play. That is what we are trying to develop, and I think we have been reasonably successful over the last couple of years. He is freeing the ball, moving it on to me, and I am taking it forward, and by that stage I should have an open-side lock with me or perhaps the other flanker.

I think it is easier for a back line to operate from second-phase play. From first-phase play it is man-to-man, every angle is covered and it is very hard to create an opening, a scoring situation. We often use the blind side to set up secondary-phase play – in other words, we drag in a half back, a

Mexted talking of Loveridge: 'He can distribute almost any ball he's given under almost any situation'

From a scrum, the ball normally comes between the flanker and the loose-head lock. On occasions it comes out between both locks. In New Zealand rugby nowadays we prefer the ball to come between the flanker and the loose-head lock for a simple reason: it is easier for the hooker. The hooker can strike at the ball at a more advanced position. The channel is far more open and, provided your scrum is solid, the number 8 can use the ball far more easily without it being obstructed or trapped prior to the ball being released from the scrum itself. I would say almost every scrum is predetermined before the ball goes in. Occasionally, it is left to my discretion; if a ball comes out quickly enough for me to be able to do something individually, then I have a free rein to do that. It may only happen once or twice in a game.

The calls for the backs are made from the backs, from the first five eighth or the second five eighth. They are overruled by scrum calls. The decision is normally made by the captain, whether it's Graham Mourie or Andy Dalton, but always the forward move overrides the back call. Before the ball goes into the scrum, Dave Loveridge will tell me the number of the move – we know the complete range of back moves as well as forward moves. They are all worked on in training and around the bar. A lot of our moves are worked out by sitting down and talking about them. We don't train a lot

of them while we are away on tour, for obvious reasons – because opposition teams watch training runs. We don't do any of our tap penalty moves that we're going to use in a game on tour – we do them prior to leaving New Zealand. We might run through them casually once or twice during the tour, but each player is supposed to have the ability to remember and perform those moves when called upon.

There are many attributes required for every position. For a number 8 today it seems desirable that he is tall enough to become a jumper at the back of the line-out. I would say that he must *want* to get the ball more than *be able* to get the ball – to me it's a mental thing – 'positive mental approach' we call it. You must have the ability to apply yourself completely to the task. In other words, if you're a line-out jumper, you've got to want to get that ball, it's as simple as that. When the ball is thrown to you in the line-out, you have to say to yourself, 'I want this ball,' and if you don't have that approach then you're not going to get the ball. There are many line-out forwards in the world who are short by international standards but who continue to get an amazing amount of ball, and this is because of the mental approach.

Mervyn Davies was not a great influence on me because I didn't see a lot of his games. Growing up in New Zealand, we don't see enough rugby

Channel 1: the quickest ball

on television (of the Five Nations, for example). We have only a limited coverage, which is sad since it's our national sport. One of the reasons, of course, is that in New Zealand we are a country of participants, not a country of spectators. So they are keeping a lot of the rugby off TV so that those people who are available to watch games will go along and pay for their tickets. Of course, we only have three million people in our country.

I don't think it is a disadvantage to be a tall number 8 – I think you can be *too* tall and, for sure, you can definitely be too heavy. On a number of occasions I've marked number 8s who have been 16½ or 17 stone and 6 foot 5 inches: by the time half time comes they are well behind the play. It makes it very difficult for a man that big to be the second man to the ball in our style of rugby; I appreciate that it varies around the world. If you've got the height then you probably shouldn't be too heavy. Height is a definite advantage, unless playing in the same team you have a flanker who may be 6 foot 5 inches, as in the French team today. They have a flanker who is 6 foot 5 inches and he jumps at the back of the line-out, so it hasn't been necessary to have a tall number 8.

Probably one of the better number 8s whom I've played against in the last couple of years has

The number 8's options: channel 2 where the ball goes between his legs or channel 3 where he directs the ball to the right with his foot

Mexted maintains that jumping requires a positive mental approach

been Mark Loane, the Australian number 8. Mind you, the Australian game of rugby is very different from our game. Morné du Plessis from South Africa would obviously have to be rated as one of the top number 8s, but he is retired at the moment. Roger Uttley was the best number 8 I'd played against up to 1979, without a doubt. I played against him in the North of England and I thought he was magnificent – he was so commanding at the back of the line-out and he was playing with Dixon and Neary who on the day had the better of Graham Mourie and myself and Ken Stewart.

The relationship between the number 8 and the scrum half is very important to the success of the team as a unit. We're the hinge where the ball is distributed from the forwards to the backs, so it's vital that there is a complete understanding there, and that there is no hesitation.

My first priority is to be aware of where my open-side flanker is. It's a great advantage to know what sort of game your open-side flanker plays, as with Graham Mourie – I have to be aware of where he is on the field so that if he gets to the breakdown and he turns, I'm the guy who receives the pass. From a defensive situation in a line-out I also have to be very close to him, and this varies depending upon the position on the field. Sometimes it's a matter of my anticipating what I feel the opposition half back or fly half is going to do, and I will make a decision spontaneously, whether I go a little bit deeper than normal or whether I attack.

We have a look at the opposition before a game and our defensive pattern is worked out. If we desire the opposition to play the game close to our forwards, then we'll have a situation from a line-out where the last man in the line-out runs wide of the first five eighth, and I run inside the first five eighth, the whole aim being of course to turn the first man inside.

We have never used one, two and three channels in New Zealand rugby as far as I'm aware. The ball I give to my half back is supposed to be the same ball every time, irrespective of whether I'm positioned between the flanker and the lock or between the two locks. The ball has still got to be in exactly the same place every time for my half back. That is, the ball comes through, I guide it with my right leg (I travel with my left leg, I guide the ball with my right leg) across to the right-hand side of the scrum about equal with the right-hand lock's feet, and then my left leg stays in the same place which is a deterrent for the opposing half back to obstruct my half back. In other words, the left side of my body is protection for my half back and the ball is moved by the right side of my body to the right-hand extreme.

It would be the first priority for any number 8 to protect his half back; that's actually my job. In the line-out, the player in front of me is supposed to look after me, and consequently the same thing applies to me – the person I am responsible for is my half back. He is responsible for his whole back line and unless he has freedom of movement, the line won't operate; in other words, my first priority would be to protect my half back to enable him to have freedom of movement to feed his back line. If I'm jumping second from the end, the end man in the line-out is no assistance at all – he must drop back – but the man in front of me, in the style of the game that we play, is supposed to stop any obstruction from any player apart from the man that I am directly marking. We play it so that each man is responsible for the man he opposes in the line-out, which is different from the Welsh and British situation. Mark Shaw does that for me – he is a blind-side flanker, he plays at 6 in the line-out (5 if you count the hooker off). He does it particularly well, better than anyone I've played with.

At Swansea in 1981 there was a great understanding between a small number of players. For this particular try, I positioned myself between the lock and the flanker because of the necessity of freeing the ball as quickly as possible to my half back, who was going to run on the short side. If the ball was freed quickly enough, it would enable them to beat the blind-side flanker, meaning the only opposition we would have between the scrum and the goal line would be the blind-side winger and the full-back support. The ball came through sweetly, I fed Dave, he beat the flanker, he drew the winger and fed back inside to his supporting loose forward. Play was taken on, it went through about two or three pairs of hands, and Mark Shaw (the blind-side flanker) dived over reasonably unopposed with maybe two All Blacks in support (I know it was me and probably Dave Loveridge).

It's very flexible in training. Sometimes the delivery of the ball is held up within the scrum. If the ball comes out slowly and I feed the half back, he is tackled by the flanker; if that's the case, and then I run outside him and he feeds me outside, I try and take out the winger and feed it back into Mark Shaw. If he gets away quickly, he beats the flanker completely; all he has to do is draw the winger and pass back to me running on the inside. I've also got Mark Shaw and our winger on the outside, so it's a terrific thing. We do it on both sides, we do it left and right of the scrum, we do it with me passing to Dave or Dave passing to me.

We probably have about ten different moves from the base of the scrum. Obviously in each game you don't get into situations to use the ten – we may use three or four at the most during the eighty minutes. It depends on the scrum, the position on the field and the style of the game that's being played. The first move that we do is very basic – I feed the half back running on the short tight-head side of the scrum. The other move is exactly the reverse – I leave the scrum early, Dave Loveridge feeds me on the short side of the scrum, running hard. I'm supposed to make contact and feed back to Dave or feed to Mark Shaw inside or my winger outside. Number three is when the short side of the field is on the left-hand side and I feed Dave running on the short side again. I take out the half back, the half back goes for me, Dave is left running and all he has to do is draw the winger, and our winger outside him is

Mexted makes a characteristic break

unopposed. We scored a classic try in the second Test against Scotland in Auckland doing that move – it worked perfectly. The same move to the right-hand side of the scrum where I feed Dave Loveridge, he takes out the flanker, runs in close, and feeds outside to me.

Another move is where I feed directly to the first five eighth and Dave runs the short side, left-hand side maybe, and I feed to the right-hand side. The straightforward number 8 detaching is when the ball is released very quickly and is often not called beforehand – it's not a premeditated move, but something that's used at the discretion of the number 8. Another move that we use in New Zealand is when the number 8 detaches from the scrum and backs into the opposing half back and flanker, and feeds his tight-head flanker coming round the base of the scrum. The number 8 effectively takes out two players, perhaps an opposition first five eighth or an opposition wing (and the tight-head flanker is left unopposed). I call the move when I pick up the ball, which gives me about one and a half seconds to get my body positioned correctly so that the tight-head flanker can come round and take it in a driving position. The most I would take would be a yard. On some occasions, the flanker is held up: I remember in the first Test against the Springboks at Lancaster Park we called that move, I detached and backed into the half back and the flanker, and our flanker didn't arrive – he had slipped over on his way. Fortunately, I could turn and drive from that position, our forwards went over us and we won the ball from the second phase, but that's an unusual situation.

Five years ago, the kind of game the number 8 played was based almost solely on anticipation of where the ball would land or where the ball would end up – in other words, he ran to where he thought the ball would be in five or ten seconds' time. So it was possible for a number 8 to go through a whole game and cover an immense amount of ground but not actually do a great deal; he was more of a safety device with the corner flagging, taking the kick which didn't find touch, the secondary tackle that was missed by the first line. Today the game has changed according to our style; the number 8 no longer anticipates where the ball is going to land. He is more pre-occupied with supporting his open-side flanker, so in other words the number 8 should be involved in more play than he was five years ago.

# 8 The Flanker

## Assessment of the position *Carwyn James*

Now for the role of the flanker. He used to be known as the wing forward – and that was expressive enough, for the flanker has to be pretty quick. The other qualities needed are strength of body and limb, hardness of mind, willingness to go into the tackle – which will frequently demand considerable courage – and the presence of mind to make the ball readily available to colleagues.

We usually think in terms of flankers as 'open side' and 'blind side'. This was the traditional pairing, with the quicker of the two men on the open side; that is, in both defence and attack he had the larger part of the pitch to cover. His partner was usually a kind of policeman on the blind – or 'narrow' – side of the play: his activity started there, after which he had a support role on the open side.

Things changed a lot during the seventies, after the Welsh Rugby Union brought out a definitive paper on back-row play (to which I was pleased to contribute). They went very firmly for the concept of 'left and right' – that is, flankers packed on their allotted side at every scrummage and did not change sides depending on the position of the set piece. Wales (amazingly in my opinion) were still persisting with this system as the eighties got under way – though at the line-out they used the fly-by-night, the quick flanker on the tail and the other, not-so-quick, man in front of the number 8 forward.

It surprised me to find that South African coach Nelie Smith also took the view, adamantly, that it is asking too much of a flanker to be on the open side of all scrummages. Yet the Springboks of 1980 who beat Beaumont's Lions team had Rob Louw as a flanker, a very, very quick man who exemplified to me the nature of the breakaway type of game – I would have put him on the open side at every scrummage because he was capable of getting rapidly to the point of breakdown. But the South Africans persisted in playing Louw on the right side and a big man called Stoffberg (a lock or number 8 for Northern Transvaal) on the left side.

Personally I do not go along with this system, though I agree that in the Home International Championship it has proved popular. With my British Lions side of 1971 I felt that it would not work well. John Taylor, a classical breakaway type of flanker, had to be on the open side at all times as far as I was concerned. On the blind side I picked big men built more like number 8 forwards, such as Derek Quinnell, Peter Dixon and later Roger Uttley, capable of giving protection at the line-out to the jumping forwards. I must say that they each, especially Quinnell, did extremely well in opposition to leading All Blacks like Brian Lochore and Ian Kirkpatrick. The British Lions team of 1974 under Syd Millar carried on with this policy in South Africa.

So much for the types of men involved. Let us look more closely now at the kind of tasks they have to fulfil. These were affected by a change in the offside law made in 1962.

Before that time, provided they remained behind the ball, wing forwards (as they were still called) could break away from the scrum in a forward direction. The new law said that they had to withdraw behind the rearmost foot of the last player in their own scrummage before going forward once the ball had emerged from the set piece.

Just to digress briefly, this change affected back play in an unexpected way. Before 1962 the breakaway flanker was more or less shaking hands with his quarry, the fly half, which meant that the latter's reaction had to be instinctive. The new law gave the fly half more time and space in which to think and plan – he now calls moves before the ball leaves the scrummage, and the back division goes doggedly through these moves irrespective of whether the position is good or bad. All this, in

Open-sided and blind-side flankers: John Taylor, the breakaway type, and Peter Dixon, built more like a number 8

my view, adds up to one reason why threequarter play has suffered of late.

At the same time – and with the same motive, that of liberating the backs from unfair pressure from opposing back rows – the International Board altered the line-out law, also pushing backs (with the exception of scrum halves) farther from the forwards of the other team. In later years limitations were put on the length of the line-out and its duration so that the great breakaway flankers of the late seventies like Jean-Pierre Rives and Fergus Slattery had to adhere to two offside laws (that for maul and ruck, incidentally, has remained broadly the same as that for the scrummage). Clearly this has a bearing on the angles at which the breakaway flanker can run off the set pieces.

His first target is the fly half, trying to tackle him in possession (rarely possible) or make him part harmlessly with the ball, if possible forcing him to run across field and cramp the backs outside him. Once the ball is delivered to the centre, the flanker changes his angle and attempts to get

inside him, and so on – going across as far as he can and perhaps even reaching the wing. In other words, unless he tackles one or the other, he functions as a sheepdog, and he shepherds the opposing threequarters across field.

This means that it is important for a fly half giving a pass to 'fall away' – that is, for one stride he is virtually moving parallel to the touchline and thereby checks the progress of the flanker, effectively putting him out of the game.

One might pause here to note that sometimes a breakaway flanker will attempt to neutralize an inexperienced fly half by conniving with his co-flanker or, as often as not, his number 8. What happens is that the breakaway tempts the fly half to try an inside break by appearing to overrun him. Instead of finding himself in hoped-for space, however, the ball carrier is enveloped by the second back-row player, who knew exactly what was going to happen.

Whether, therefore, the breakaway decides to stay at a line-out and help his team mates complete the job of winning possession, or runs backwards to take a long throw, or makes straight for the fly half as the opposition win possession, he needs acute awareness of what other forwards are doing. He can be sure that the opposing scrum half is being looked after by his hooker team mate (on the narrow side) or by the number 8 forward going through the line. The latter, since the revolution in number 8 play pioneered by Mervyn Davies, works in very close liaison with the breakaway because he is usually the second man to the breakdown and must immediately supplement the work of the flanker.

In attack, back rows can work out potent combined moves from the base of the scrummages. The more common form of packing down is 3–4–1, and you will find the number 8 picking up the ball and making a break – usually away from the side where the ball is put in – doing a half turn and slipping it to a flanker, after which the flanker turns and gives possession to his co-flanker and so the team is going forward. There are variants on this progression: New Zealand, for instance, found that an occasional reversion to 3–3–2 gave more flexibility.

All in all, however, both attackers and defenders must be on the alert for back-row moves, which are an integral part of any team's attacking potential. For example, they are one of the best ways

Fergus Slattery

Back-row defence at the scrummage

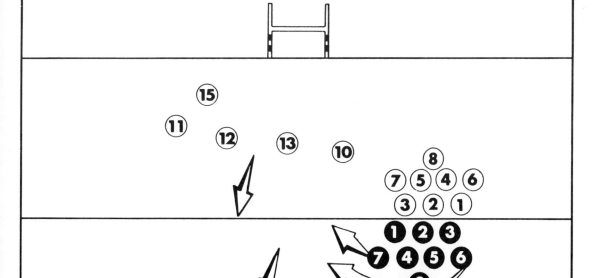

of occasionally taking pressure off your half backs and mid-field players.

A couple more points: we have made the point that the breakaway flanker should be first to the breakdown from scrummage and line-out. This means that he is frequently completely committed to the resulting maul or ruck, and his subsequent role changes somewhat. So, if he is caught at the bottom of a ruck and is therefore last to the next one that forms, he can legitimately resume his normal scrummage or line-out function, standing out a metre or two.

Let's conclude with ways a flanker gives immediate practical support to team mates. He may become involved in a peel at the front of a line-out. That is, if the ball is secured by the number 2 jumper of his own team, then it's possible that the flanker will come around and take possession from the catcher or from a supporting prop.

Then there is the help he can give the mid-field player – and let me just pause to observe how in the modern game the two positions have a degree of interchangeability about them. Certainly there have been centres in recent years who would have made very good flankers – for example, strong powerful players like Steve Fenwick and Ray Gravell, who not only possess the necessary physique but also have the aptitude of threequarters for handling the ball.

But, put very simply, the help a flanker can give threequarters amounts to this: once the ball has been successfully moved from scrummage or line-out, he must get himself into the kind of position in which he can accept a pass – whether the centre accepts a tackle or simply draws a man. A classic exponent of this kind of constructive support play was John Taylor and, until he slowed down late in his career, so was Jean-Pierre Rives.

Back-row defence

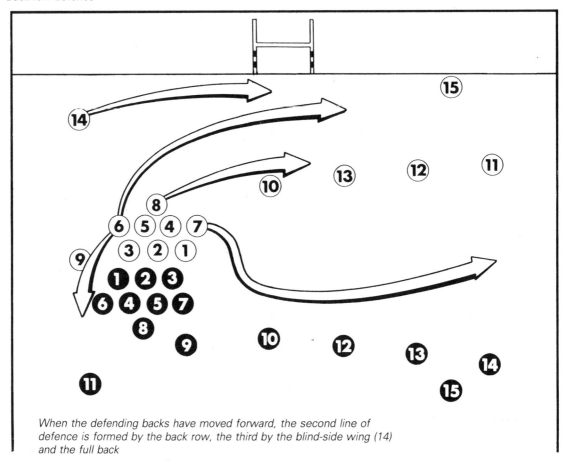

*When the defending backs have moved forward, the second line of defence is formed by the back row, the third by the blind-side wing (14) and the full back*

# Introducing the player *Carwyn James*

Jean-Pierre Rives, with a Toulouse tan and a mop of blond hair worn a little too long, came to the fore for France with Skrela and Bastiat. Skrela in the mould of Greyling and Dai Morris, Rives the Jan Ellis or the John Taylor type, and Bastiat cutting a figure more like Mervyn Davies than Tommy Bedford. They all came in threes and each was the better for it.

Early on in his career Rives came under the influence of the fluent French forward style full of panache, full of confidence and creatively stimulating. The flick pass over the shoulder was surely taken by A to his right or B to the left, the firm, supporting base of the imaginary triangle.

It was a sad day when the unadventurous and kicking approach of such players as Fouroux and Romeu took over. France became dull and uninteresting, and although they were still capable of winning more than their share of internationals, they rarely won in style. When Rives was appointed captain he made positive efforts to revert to the French way of playing, and following defeats in New Zealand his method was rewarded with a memorable Test victory. At heart Jean-Pierre is a disciple of the Barbarian approach and it was no surprise when he founded the French Barbarians.

But his own game at club level for Toulouse and for France has been hard and uncompromising. At club level French rugby can be the most brutal in the world. It is a tough school. Rives, despite, or perhaps because of, his film star looks, is as tough as any. He is unquestionably the uncrowned king of Toulouse, extremely kind and patient with a host of admirers.

Rives is quick to the loose ball. Fearlessly he will pounce on it in close competition with equally fearless adversaries. The years have taken their toll. In 1981 I watched him play at Brisbane, Sydney and Pretoria as well as in Europe. On each occasion he was injured and there were times when he took the field in considerable pain.

1982 was not a good season for France in the Five Nations tournament. Poor selection meant three defeats, but Rives's men, better selected on this occasion, bounced back to lick Ireland, the winners of the Triple Crown. The game badly needs the presence of colourful, likable personalities like Jean-Pierre Rives, who never give less, whatever their talents, than their all.

# The player *Jean-Pierre Rives*

I started playing rugby when I was fifteen years old and since then I have only ever really played as a flanker. However, when I was a cadet we used to play seven- or eight-a-side rugby, and then I would play in the threequarter line; I even played a couple of matches as centre.

The main reasons which determined the fact that I now play flanker were possibly my build, my way of playing rugby, and the wishes of my coach. Also a certain temperament is required for this position. As for build, I am one of the smaller flankers today on the field, both at international and at club level. There are lads who are much bigger. It's not an advantage being relatively small, but whether it's an inconvenience, perhaps, at the line-out is difficult to judge.

Stamina, energy, tackling, defence and attack are all required qualities, all of foremost importance, and indeed you should try to fulfil all of these functions. You should do this to the best of your ability for the full duration of the match – if you run as long as possible and as quickly as possible, then you have fulfilled your role on the field. Every position requires a specific effort with possibly specific training, and therefore the qualities which become specific through that training should evolve over time.

Determination and aggression are perhaps two qualities which are identical and are fundamental requirements of all rugby men from the word go. Rugby is a contact sport and accordingly requires much aggression. Equally, a physical presence manifests itself in determination.

Every position in rugby is of interest. Perhaps I would have liked to have played fly half or centre, which are two very different positions, but more likely fly half. It requires clear-headedness and many other qualities. It is, of course, a much more specific position than flanker; you are at the crossroads of the game; you must make good deci-

sions rapidly. I don't know what it is that makes me a flanker. The most important quality of a flanker is to be near the ball as often as possible. You have to know and anticipate where to intervene quickly; to back up in either a defensive situation or an attacking one, but as quickly as possible.

In the ten years that I have been playing rugby, my game has evolved for better or for worse, and I certainly don't play today as I did when I was eighteen. Your staying power increases and you achieve greater stamina – I don't know exactly how to define the problem, but it is just different. It also varies with the team you are playing with, the ground on which you are playing, and whether you are going forwards or backwards.

Rugby is a game of contact; it is physical; but it is not a dangerous game provided you remain within your own particular category. So long as children stay within their own categories there is very little risk involved. Problems arise when ten-year-olds start playing with fifteen-year-olds. I don't believe that people get injured more easily or more readily at flanker than at any other position.

As to my own preparation, I train a lot and in many different ways. I try as much as possible (and I believe this to be the best training) to train to put myself into the same conditions as one finds in a match. That is to say I must run a lot, fall over, get up, accelerate, but above all run a lot for as long and as quickly as possible. I don't think you should avoid training by yourself – you should get yourself ready on a physical level: this is something personal. However, afterwards you must get yourself into similar conditions to those of a game – you mustn't go off on a false base. It requires a lot of rigour and discipline to train by yourself – on a physical level, that is.

Rugby hasn't escaped the fact that any game undergoes a certain amount of evolution and progression, and I think that rugby players train better and longer and in a much more systematic way than they did once.

As for weights, I've only used them since my accident, but what I do mostly is running. I run a lot. However, weight training, supervised by people who know what they're doing and who are competent, can certainly bring benefit to the rugby player.

I don't think that the positions of flanker and centre are interchangeable. For a centre you need qualities which are specific to that position, and these are different from those required for a flanker. However, it is fashionable to take people from the flanker position and put them in the centre. There is a fundamental difference in the necessary qualities required for each position also and training is different – in training one must work hard on certain plays and movements so that these become automatic, and for that one must play in only one position, a fixed position, in order to have the appropriate automatic reactions.

There is a difference between the left flanker and the right flanker. The first difference is method. There are some lads who are two-sided, but it's not the same game, particularly in defence. I prefer playing on the left. I can play on the right, but I feel better on the left, possibly just through habit.

Rives in running mood

There are very few teams who use the open and blind system. Only the All Blacks use a constant open and blind method. It's possibly an advantage – it's certainly an interesting exercise. If you have a flanker who is better at covering, then it's probably better to leave him on the open side so that he can intervene in either attack or defence, but it's not something which is done in Europe. It's perhaps an experiment worth trying.

The move I like to play, and the one I've played for a long time, is the one in which the flanker puts himself between the scrum half and the fly half in attack. Such moves interest me, even though I am playing in more of a defensive style at the moment. I think this is because, after five or six years of playing for France and for my own club, our game has become more and more defensively minded.

As regards a wheeling scrum, a flanker should try above all to distance himself. Of course, it depends which way the scrum is wheeling and whether he's playing on the left or on the right. If it's his own pack who are wheeling, it's not so much of a problem. If it's the other pack who are wheeling when you are on the left, you must stay and remain bound in; when you are on the right you must split away in order to remain facing the ball because a scrum will always turn from right to the left. Therefore, if it's the opposition

who have the ball, you must stay as near as possible to the ball in order to frustrate the opposition scrum half. But the right-hand flanker splits away and stays in his original position so that he is able to counteract any attack which may come towards him. Wheeling a scrum can do one of two things: from a positive point of view, by turning a scrum you set yourself up for an attack or open things up for the scrum half; but if the scrum wheels when you are going backwards, then you have to act negatively. So it depends on who's got the ball and who is wheeling.

At a set scrum, there are two different positions for a flanker. Either you push straight onto the prop (3–4–1), which is the more traditional way and the most used, or you push on the second row (3–2–3). When I'm in the 3–4–1 situation, I'm pushing on the prop with my right arm bound into the second row. The other players do not bind onto me because they would get in the way.

When a scrum is going backwards, ideally the flanker should be helping in the counter-pushing as long as the ball is in the scrum and then intervene as soon as the ball goes out of the scrum. The only problem is when the ball goes out behind the number 8.

In a scrum, the ball comes out favourably for my team when it comes out on the right-hand side of the scrum. This protects the ball and the

Rives about to pack down behind the prop in the traditional 3–4–1 formation, as France goes in against Wales

scrum half can take it or give his pass in ideal conditions. If the ball is coming out on my side (the left-hand side) for any unfortunate reason, I try to prevent it from coming right out, send it off to the right-hand side, and channel it through. But if the ball has come out, then you must grab it, protect it and save it to give it to a forward in a better position or to the scrum half who can free it from the situation.

Rives practises breaking from the scrum by using a goal post to simulate the position in the scrum

As a flanker I have a duty to screen my scrum half. There is a law that you must always be part of the scrum, but you can still protect the scrum half effectively. When the ball is heeled by the opposition, from the moment the ball has come out, defence takes on one of several systems. It's an individual but also a collective effort. First of all: the defence on the scrum half. Here you de-fend against the person who gets the ball first (that is to say either the scrum half or the number 8). Alternatively you may defend directly against the opponent who gets the ball second; and if you move off onto the second player, you must have full faith in your number 8 in order to cover the inside, which you are leaving open. Personally, I think it's more valuable to defend against the first opponent to get the ball. You should intervene generally as soon as possible.

The points about the best form of defence are to avoid causing any infraction of the rules, most importantly never to lose sight of the ball, and to intervene as the ball goes out and not on the person who is already going forward with the ball. Therefore you must intervene in relation to where

the ball is and not to where the player with the ball is. You must never lose sight of the ball.

In the context of a scrum, whether attacking or defending, you must push. The only difference there can be in the scrum with regard to your position depends on whether you are defending or attacking. You are either pushing on the prop in the 3–4–1 formation or you are binding and pushing on the second row from where you can possibly attack a little bit better because it is easier to go round the scrum. From this position you can set off a little bit farther back in order to attack.

The flanker's role at a line-out is twofold. There are flankers who jump, and therefore their role is as jumpers and catchers of the ball. If your side loses the ball, you take on the role of defender.

Rives keeps a watchful eye on the scrum half before stalking the fly half

Shoulder strength is vital to the flanker

The positioning of the flanker should be such that he can be the first to arrive at breakdowns

Sometimes I take the place of the scrum half at the line-out – it's something which is not often done in the British Isles. We do it in France perhaps because we're just used to doing it. If we are using the throw-in where the ball goes right over the line-out, and there is any form of contact. As a forward I am more robust than perhaps the scrum half to carry out the manoeuvre.

For a ruck, the flanker is generally the player who should arrive first in a backing-up role, to help the player who is holding the ball. The flanker backs up either by taking the ball or by pushing on the ball holder, binding in with him. Similarly the role of the flanker at a maul is to be the first to back up.

As regards the successive positions and positioning of the flanker in a ruck, often he will take on the role of prop as he is the first to arrive. You must try to be the first to arrive and the first to leave. If a flanker arrives late at a ruck he has one of two possibilities. Either he joins in the ruck, if the ball has not come out yet, or he stays on the outside and plays the part of the first attacker, then passes the ball down the line or just remains in the first wave of attack.

The central element is almost certainly always to be as near the ball as possible.

The most important things with regard to tackling are to get down low and to avoid absorbing a tackle. Arrive at the same speed as your opponent, wrap yourself round his waist and then lower yourself and let yourself slide down the legs and arrive at his ankles, squeezing his legs hard: even force him backwards if possible. There is a specific training for tackling and really the only effective way of training and improving your tackling is to tackle.

I feel there is less and less difference between the requirements of a British flanker and a French flanker because the game of the flanker has changed in the last few years and become more international, if not universal.

I've never really trained seriously with regard to kicking. Certainly there are people among the loose forwards who are kickers, but nowadays we very rarely see a loose forward who uses the boot.

The fact that I don't jump at line-outs probably enables me to intervene and move more quickly in either defence or attack.

Having taken on the captaincy, at the beginning I had a lot of problems because captaincy is a particular function which has to be learned. I'm

The flanker must be fearless, hard and uncompromising

still learning. This obviously affected my role as a player, but it affects me less now – a lot less. Now it's more a question of pressures and the identification of many things and it's perhaps a bit of a struggle sometimes, but it's continuing to get better all the time. If I only had to take account of my own requirements and my own problems, I might achieve a better performance; for in only looking after one's own problems one concentrates more on the individual and personal level, and I would almost certainly play a better game. I have had a relatively long career despite the game and despite the little incidents, perhaps because I am able to recover very quickly. I also train a lot, and above all I really like rugby. More and more I have learned, particularly towards the end, how to pace myself and how to be patient.

I'll stop playing top-class rugby some time – when, I still don't know. Certainly, I've more behind me now than I have in front. I just know that one of these days it will be over: I am very conscious of this fact.

I believe rugby is a team sport, and by the same token the game of the loose forwards can be and should be an inner team game because there are three boys who each have a specific role but who together form a unit. One finds players who are complete within themselves and I think it is important to play with a complementary trio of loose forwards.

Playing with Jean-Claude Skrela and Jean-Pierre Bastiat, who were great players, really was very pleasant. As a combination we were very good, although I still play with fine forwards like Joinel.

# 9 The Second Row

## Assessment of the position *Carwyn James*

Locks like Colin Meads, Frik du Preez, Benoit Dauga and the Spanghéro brothers have revolutionized forward play. The concept of second row or locks merely shoving in the engine room or the power house and jumping for the ball in the line-outs is no more. The lock's mobility in the loose and his power play in the loose scrums are of paramount importance.

Locks, to state the obvious, come in twos. The one complements the other. Rees Stephens, the prototype of the rugged, powerful type, complemented the agility of Roy John; R. H. Williams was a foil to Russell Robins; and so was John Currie to David Marques, Allan Martin to Geoff Wheel, and Bill Beaumont to a lesser extent complemented Maurice Colclough.

The jumping of the locks
R. H. Williams and Russell Robins with Courtenay Meredith

David Marques head and shoulders above the rest

# The scrummage

Whether they pack left or right, all of them have to be strong enough and fit enough to scrummage throughout the full period of eighty minutes. Locking their own scrum and exerting an eight-man shove on their opponents' ball is the modern pattern with which all second-row forwards are conversant. An absolutely straight back, the head tilting slightly back, one leg slightly bent, the other forward and half bent, a comfortable position ready for the shove with the straightening of the legs and the eye always on the ball.

It is a skilful operation to channel the ball without hindrance and afford the scrum half maximum protection. Whether the ball is held or not is a question of tactics usually governed by the middle of the back, the number 8.

Wheeling as a constructive ploy, alas, is a forgotten art. As a disruption, however, it is the bane of the referee in the modern game because it leads to such a mess with players of both sides easily finding themselves in offside positions. So penalty follows penalty from a set piece meant to provide the quick, usable ball. The more discerning packs know how to counter the disruptive wheel: the left side of the scrum will draw their opponents' tight head towards them, the right-hand side will drive forward and the whole front row, aided by their locks, will shuffle slightly from left to right. The ultimate balance can be provided by the flankers working in harmony with their front five.

# The line-out

The line-out, more than ever, is the problem child of rugby football. How dearly I wish we could go back to the late forties and early fifties to see the ballet-like jumping and the dexterous two-handed catching of Roy John, who was protected from the opposition by his own forwards legally driving a wedge. The double-banking days of the early sixties were equally productive but less aesthetic.

Today's line-outs are a shambles, a lottery wherein the referee can usually take his pick if he wishes to penalize either side. Historical evidence alone could solve this unnecessary problem.

The best line-out jumper is the thrower. Throwing in used to keep the wing threequarters em-

The relationship between thrower and jumper: the ball here has been thrown to where only Delme Thomas can reach it

ployed, and so each team had two throwers. For a little over a decade the role (the world over) has been taken over by the hooker. Fashions catch on quickly.

The thrower's job, so David Marques once said, is comparable to a cricket fielder's task of throwing in at speed to hit the top of the stumps. The hooker must throw the ball at the correct speed and flight to the position where the jumper wants it. Jumpers vary in their needs. Some like the ball to be thrown up so that they can catch it on the way down, while others prefer the quick ball on a somewhat flat trajectory which means that only

the well-timed and highest jump can take it.

It is well to practise the dart throw which conceals the thrower's intention from the opposition. A slight spin and the ball will keep its direction and it is more easily caught than the over-arm bowling action.

Usually the thrower has three options, to number 2, 4 or 6. He must recognize the style of each, whether, for instance, one tends to step slightly forward before timing his jump. Jumping off the ground, not merely raising arms, is all important. So is catching the ball with both hands. A deflection should be a variant and not the rule.

The catcher has the option of taking and giving the ball in one movement which, when managed, is the best possession of all. It isn't always possible, and that is why the support play of the other forwards is all-important. With such support, line-outs are often turned into mauls, and certain teams, like Australia in recent times, have placed the ball on the ground and driven over in a rucking formation.

Locks need to practise a lot with the hooker. The timing of the jump is all-important. Improvement in jumping will only come from strengthening the legs, and the thighs in particular, by all kinds of exercises, like running up steep slopes, steps or stairs, and squatting followed by a leap with outstretched arms. Squatting and touching the crossbar is a favourite exercise with lock forwards.

Paying particular attention to the body position is the most important factor in rucking – leading with one shoulder in the drive with the upper part of the body as near parallel to the ground as possible.

The key factor in mauling is to look for the ball all the time. Upper-body strength, as demonstrated by Geoff Wheel for instance, is the essence of ripping the ball away from your opponents.

In the modern game, in the manner of the Daugas, the Spanghéros and the Meadses, the lock forward needs to be mobile, extremely fit to do all the chores, and to be a competent ball handler as well. It is a far more interesting and worthwhile job in the modern game. The day of the donkey is over.

# Introducing the player *Carwyn James*

The record books will have it that William Blackledge Beaumont of Fylde played on thirty-one occasions for his country, more than any other England lock, that he captained them seventeen times, as well as leading the Lions in South Africa in 1980. He served his apprenticeship for that highest of honours when he was called out as a replacement to New Zealand in 1977.

Bill Beaumont, to me, personifies what is good in the coaching manual. At 6 foot 3 inches and 16 stone he wasn't the hugest of men but he probably had the hugest heart. Somehow, when I think of Billy, more so than any other rugby man, the platitudes seem right – 'the true spirit of the game', 'a 100-per-center plus', 'a real gentleman', 'he played within the laws', 'a fine ambassador'.

He was, and is, all of these. I now hear the last line of that Gilbert and Sullivan stanza, 'For he iiiii-s an Eeeenglish man.' So much so that when England beat Wales by three penalties to two tries at Twickenham and went on to win the Triple Crown and the Grand Slam, the whole of England was ready for a cult figure which Fleet Street readily presented to the most nationalistic of nations.

Even girls like Jean Rook were knitting cuddly teddy-bear-type articles around a lovable but embarrassed personality. Yet through the unfair euphoria they had woven, Billy, the workhorse, got on with the job to plough a lonely furrow. More so than the journalists who failed to appreciate that in the late seventies it wasn't that England had reached a high but that rugby football at home had reached a pretty disastrous low.

Beneath that soft, bulldog exterior lurks the harder version of a man of decision. Beneath the Englishman lurks the Lancastrian, a man of the North where they play their rugby that little bit tougher and with a touch of humour. That the North, for the second time, could beat the All Blacks and that within a week England couldn't must have hurt.

Beaumont's game was one of total commitment. He played it like the manual; he shoved hard even in the last scrum of the match; at the line-out he would lunge rather than leap at number

2; at the loose scrums he knew no danger; and, I suspect, the occasional wayward boot took advantage of an innocence which expected fair play from all those who call themselves rugger men. It was his undoing, but it was fitting that his last game was played for Lancashire.

At the end of the 1980 tour, at Johannesburg airport, I asked Bill for his autograph. Suitably and with a smile he responded: 'I thought you would be the last person on earth to ask me for my autograph.' I know that he appreciated that my criticisms had been levelled more at the system than the man. After all, he had reached far greater heights in his playing career.

It grieves me that because W. B. Beaumont has now written his memoirs and makes appearances on the television, he will not be allowed any more to plough back his knowledge and experience to the game. For the likes of him and other superstars, which the game and sponsorship created, the International Board needs to shed its mantle of anachronism.

---

# The player *Bill Beaumont*

I started playing rugby at the age of nine and I progressed through my schoolboy career never playing second row at all – I used to play full back or stand-off. I think when you start playing rugby at school, the master in charge usually looks at you and if you're slow and fat he will put you in the forwards, and if you're thin and fast you'll go in the backs. At that point, I was thin and fast. It was only really when I got to the age of seventeen, when I went down to the Fylde Rugby Club and they said, 'Oh well, you've got no chance of playing anywhere else except in the forwards,' that I ended up in the second row.

Looking at second-row players from the past, there are a number who have influenced me. Colin Meads is certainly one and Willie John McBride has to be another. They played very much the kind of game I always tried to play. They were front of the line-out jumpers.

Of course, guys like Peter Whiting, Andy Haden and Frik du Preez were great middle of the line-out jumpers, fine line-out catchers. More recently, I'd be looking at players like Allan Martin and Geoff Wheel from Wales and Nigel Horton and Maurice Colclough from England.

As a lock, you've got to have certain physical attributes. Physical size makes a great deal of difference to what position you're going to play – obviously you can't be 12 stone to play in the second row and equally you can't be 17½ stone to play effectively on the wing.

There are two different kinds of locks: one, the mauling type of forward, the other an out-and-out line-out man. So you have two different sizes. At international level the average weight is about 17 stone; 6 feet 4 inches is about the minimum height really for the front of the line-out and 6 feet 5 inches or 6 feet 6 inches for the middle of the line-out.

Maurice Colclough and I used to share responsibilities – I was the front of the line-out guy and I would do all the messy sort of work (not that Maurice wouldn't do it, but I was perhaps better at it). For instance, if the ball was on the ground, I would clean that up and I was perhaps a bit better handler of the ball than Maurice was; whereas he is really a far better line-out jumper than I could ever dream of being. Maurice and I used to swap over; we played a lot of rugby together and obviously we knew each other's roles.

There is no substitute for experience, and for the front five forwards this normally comes in your late twenties or early thirties. Most great players are still going well into their thirties. Experience comes by knowing what's happening – the law of the jungle as it were; you know what's going on and basically, like any good player, you're in the right place at the right time. I found at the end of my career that perhaps I wasn't as tired after a game because I knew the little short cuts.

I know a lot of people call the locks 'donkeys' or 'workhorses', and certainly it's not the most glamorous of lives. Normally you're pushing your head in a little hole all the time and some days you don't see a lot of daylight. So I suppose it's a fair expression – I always used to say to the threequarters behind us that we are the donkeys and we need the carrot, and the carrot is the ball, and it's got to go in front of us. You don't see a donkey going back for a carrot!

The front five basically decide who's going to

Beaumont's front five about to go down against France. Points worth noting are the concentration and the binding. Beaumont, the nearer lock, grips the prop's waistband through his legs. His partnering lock has his arm as far round Bill as possible and is gripping Bill's waistband

win the game. Obviously, if you're winning all the balls, then nine times out of ten you're going to win the game. So the front five have a great bearing on how the game is played and how the backs or the back row are going to play the game. That's how important they are.

It doesn't matter if you've got backs full of world beaters, you've still got to have a front five that is, at the worst, adequate; anything less than that and you're really going to be struggling.

The two locks obviously have an important part in the scrum. Of course, you've got to have a good front row; I mean if you've got a weak front

row it doesn't matter if you're King Kong, you're not going to be able to hold them up and get a good push through. So from that point of view, the front row largely dictate how good the second rows are – and that's OK from our point of view. I always find it very pleasant pushing behind guys like Graham Price because you always know that he's dominating his opposite number, and that you've always been going forward into everything. So the two locks basically do what their name implies – they lock the scrum. They are really supporting the front row, whether it's your own ball and you're trying to push the opposition or

Beaumont, here, is the right-hand lock in this Lancashire scrummage. Straight leg, straight back and feet apart mark him out. It is doubtful whether an inch of daylight reaches the ground through this solid, tightly bound pack

whether they are trying to drive you and you're just locking it.

I always used to play behind the tight-head. I preferred pushing off my right shoulder and Maurice Colclough always used to prefer to play on the loose-head; so it always worked out well. I always felt that going behind the tight-head was harder because the way the scrum is balanced means that more weight comes through on you; your body position in the scrum really determines the amount of push you can put in. Obviously you've got to be strong in the shoulders to keep tight on the prop in front of you, which is so important. I always used to keep my legs straight for pushing in the scrum, and it's perhaps only to drive that I would drop my knees and then lift up. Dipping, bending and lifting are what scrummaging is all

about and so in practice I'd do a lot of squat thrusts to strengthen my thighs, which is where you take the weight. Also, if you keep your back straight, all the weight comes straight through your body and you don't move; but if your back is bent, then obviously you'll bend upwards and so get no push forward.

Foot positions are very important too. I used to try and get both feet flat if I could, which meant as many studs as possible in the ground. This is very important for gripping on soft ground, although on hard ground it doesn't matter as much because your studs will hold anyway. So I used to try to splay my feet; if I couldn't do it with both feet I would always do it with one, normally my right foot, so that I'd got all the studs in. It meant that I could push with much greater power. I always used to have my feet slightly apart – never together – because obviously the scrum is moving and you might have to take a little bit of extra weight on one leg or the other, which you couldn't do if your feet were both together. The one thing that you don't want to do in your scrum is to move your feet. A good scrum is locked down and nobody moves – they are all solid, all tight. A bad scrum is when they're all moving their feet around. We would normally try for channel two or three; we'd get the hooker to knock it down to the second row behind the loose-head, who would just push it across, or we would just push over the ball. Obviously on channel one, we'd keep a little bit tighter on the right-hand second row so the ball can come straight out in a channel; but it largely depends on the hooker – he is the important one to decide where the ball is going.

The snap shove is basically all eight of you pushing together in the scrum. As the ball comes in, the scrum half says, 'Ball now.' On 'ball', you drop your knees and on 'now', you just straighten, so it's just dipping and lifting; perhaps all you need is 3 or 4 inches – you don't need any more than that – 3 or 4 inches just to push over the ball and get the opposition going backwards.

As far as wheeling goes, probably a team of schoolboys could wheel against an international pack. Normally it's very easy to wheel. If you want to do it properly, your tight-head stays static and your loose-head pushes up, and once it's twisted you all push. Wheeling is very easy to do but hard to stop. The way to stop it is as their loose-head prop moves round, your tight-head prop on the side with the ball should bring his right shoulder in and push on the hooker, so you start pushing it up that way. It's quite effective because if you find that the scrum moves round like that, then all the opposition's tight-head players are out of the game, and then you straighten it and push; they're all stuck on the side of the scrum and you can just keep pushing.

Your binding has to be right too. I used to grip between the legs of the prop on his waistband and try and move my arm as far round towards the hooker as possible, to keep it tight. As for the bind with the other second row, I'd be a liar if I said I did it on the shorts every time because you don't in a game – you tend to do it on the shirt. With guys like Colclough, who is 18 stone, it was really hard sometimes in the heat of the game to get your arm round. So normally I'd just grip as

tightly as I could onto his shirt; but the best position would be on the waistband and pocket of his shorts.

I always used to find that my hands and arms would be really aching after a scrummage session or after an international game. It's so important that you have strong forearms in rugby because quite often you're either gripping the ball in the rucks and mauls or you're in the scrummages, and that's all forearm and hands.

The best way to practise scrummaging is with a pack against you – there's no substitute for that. There's no point in scrummaging against a pack of less weight because you get nothing out of it. Only use the scrummaging machine if you haven't got another eight forwards of equal stature to scrummage against. Scrummaging machines are OK, but you've got to make it hard – it's great for practising an eight-man push on the opposition's ball but very hard to practise your own ball.

Once the ball is out of the scrum and the scrum half has passed it, you should be looking to move. Normally, you know the ball's gone as soon as the number 8 pulls away. Same with the front row – they realize the second row are going; so that's how it is, a sort of chain. Obviously, on the opposition's ball, your scrum half says, 'Ball left' or 'Ball right', and it's gone, and you know then to go because you can feel the wing forward move off your side. It's quite easy to get out of a scrum quickly – but I wouldn't recommend it really, because I think quite often you can wear down the opposition and push them that little bit more, even though you've got the ball. But obviously it does hinder you if you want to get to the breakdown quickly.

Another vital area for the lock is the line-out. I always stayed at 2 in the line-out – I'd get lost if I went anywhere else! – simply because I couldn't compete against top-class jumpers in the middle. So I realized my limitations and stayed in the front line. Number 2 in the line-out really has to be a little bit sharper than the guy in the middle because the ball is often bobbing around. A number 4 jumper has to be more of an athlete – he has to be a little bit more athletic than the number 2 jumper because he's got to get up and secure that ball. He is a true jumper, which you don't have to be at the front of the line because you are relying on other things – there's a bit more hustle and bustle; whereas at number 4 you have to get up there on your own.

The hard, fast throw taken with both hands at the front of the line-out

There are two types of throw; normally most players have two variations of the throw – a lob throw or a hard, fast throw. But you find more and more that props are starting to cut out the fast ball, so jumpers now are having to revert to the lob. It doesn't matter if you're 6 feet or 6 feet 4 inches; your timing is the important thing. The most vital guy in the line-out is the one throwing the ball in – it's important that you must practise your timing with the hooker and this is something I'd done for years with Peter Wheeler. We'd been on two or three tours together and played thirty-odd games for England, and so I knew his timing and his signals and he knew where I wanted the ball to be. The jumper must give the signals to the hooker. Sometimes, of course, the hooker might say no if he didn't want to throw that ball. The kind of ball he throws is dependent on where you are on the field. Obviously on your own line you

wouldn't want a hard, fast ball going in because it's a little bit easier to spoil and the ball could be flying anywhere. You'd look for a lob which is a bit more controlled. So really it's the part of the field where you are which controls what kind of ball he's going to give you.

The other players who are vital to a line-out jumper are the support players. In my position at the front of the line-out standing at number 2, it was the prop standing at number 3 in the line-out who would perhaps give me a bit of help – he might give me a slight lift, something which is illegal. But he knew exactly where the ball was coming, so he could block the opposition from barging me, and thereby let me have a clear jump.

It's always cleaner if you catch the ball, but sometimes the back line want a fast tapped ball because they can then move the ball away quickly. It's quite hard to get a two-handed catch and so you'd often tap the ball to somebody farther down the line, usually from number 2 onto number 4. He can take the ball in and then feed it to the scrum half; so really you have the advantages of a two-handed catch but you can slow things down.

I would often use the peel as a tactic at the line-out – either round the back or round the front. If you're peeling round the front then the number 2 jumper is catching the ball. If you're peeling round the back, the prop will often take the ball. I used to do it lots of times for Fran Cotton – he would take the ball, commit the opposing wing forward at the end of the line-out and put the ball up to me, hopefully with a free run.

On the opposition's throw-in you try to sort out the line-out signals that they're using, to see if you can figure out where the ball is going; obviously you're looking at your opposite number. I always used to try to get shoulder to shoulder with the guy in front of me. Sometimes, if I had a good prop who would cut out the low ball at the front, I would stand slightly behind him because I knew that he wasn't going to be able to get a clean catch on taking a low fast ball. If he did catch it, I just used to try to spoil him, pull an arm down or barge into him or something, which is probably highly illegal. If he took a lob ball behind me, then obviously I was trying to mess him up there, if he'd sort of outfoxed me. So really you're looking at each other and wondering what kind of ball is going to come in, and I think on the oppos-

The clean but sometimes difficult two-handed catch

The tap: Beaumont feeds the ball from the line-out having had it tapped to him by Maurice Colclough

ition's ball I largely used to try to spoil it rather than win it out and out, because if you spoil it and give them a bad ball, then you are putting them under pressure. You're not supposed to touch him until he's touched the ball but it's almost impossible not to. The line-out is a bit of a grey area – a referee could penalize everyone if he wanted to. I think the best thing to do would be to legalize lifting, and that would mean that you'd get a cleaner ball. But I think if you didn't have line-outs you end up like rugby league.

You have to have an understanding with your scrum half at line-out – especially if you're deflecting the ball. Most scrum halves don't mind as long as the ball's going open. If the ball's going back towards the 5-yard area, they're dead then, they've got no chance. I always find that having worked with a couple of scrum halves for a number of years, you know where they're going to be. A ruck is when you go into a tackle and you are tackled and you go onto the ground, and you put the ball on the ground. Then the players coming

over you just ignore the ball and go over you, and basically they leave the ball for the scrum half without it touching another boot or what have you. If you look at a very good rucking side, then nobody touches the ball, they just go straight over the opposition and leave the ball for the scrum half to come up and move away. It's important in the ruck that when you are being tackled, you are tackled on your own terms, making sure that your body is between the opposition and the ball. If you fall the other way, your side can't ruck it out.

You can only ruck the ball going forward – you can't ruck the ball going backwards because it is very difficult for your players to get behind you: You have to maul it when you are going backwards – you have to stay on your feet because you're waiting for time. You don't perhaps need as much time when you go into the ruck and so it's important to keep driving and then, when you feel the ruck is stopping, just go down and leave the ball; or keep driving low and as you're going down just put the ball on the ground; the rest of

Having been isolated with the ball, Beaumont must look for support or form a ruck. It is important that he keeps his body between the opposition and the ball

the players are driving in behind you and the ball is left there. When you hit a ruck, hit it low, and really, if you can, try to grab hold of one of your team mates and look for a space and just hit it low and keep pumping and driving your legs. You are then driving the opposition back and also with your head you are looking down so that you can see where the ball is as well as where you are treading.

In scrum-half style Beaumont feeds from a ruck situation

I'd like to see the ruck law changed really. At the moment players aren't too sure what to do; if you're going into a tackle I can't see any harm in your playing the ball slightly on the ground, because you're still trying to keep the ball in play. I don't mean handing the ball back but just at least letting players go in and get the ball out – at least you're keeping the game in motion whereas at the moment you get these pile-ups and grey areas and players don't know how to react to them.

As regards mauling, there are differing techniques, but the most important person in the maul is the one who's got the ball. What I would normally try to do, if I went to the tackle and I was going to maul, would be to use either my left or my right shoulder to hit the opposition and always

carry the ball farthest away from the opposition. As I hit them I would keep driving if I could, and then just turn with my back to the opposition, and make certain that the next man into the maul took the ball off me. He would take the ball off me and the rest of the team would have the same body positions as if it was a ruck, and would just keep driving – driving in exactly the same body positions as we've talked about in the ruck. It's important that you keep pumping your legs as well in the maul.

The second-row player has to do a lot of running and so you need a great deal of stamina. You are constantly running from a scrum to a ruck, or from a ruck to a line-out, or from one ruck to another ruck, or from a ruck to a maul. You are going as fast as you can, though you're not sprinting all the time. Of course, the pace is very different in an international game than in a club game.

Beaumont closely in support as a maul is formed. Turning his back to the opposition, the ball carrier Maurice Colclough will be ideally placed for Beaumont to take the ball

Most of my stamina work would be running – road running (four or five miles every day), striding, and some sprinting (though it probably wouldn't look like sprinting to most people). When you look at the lock forward's game, you realize just how important stamina is because one minute you are at the bottom of a ruck and you know that you've got to get to the next one just as quickly as you can.

Catching the ball from kick-off is another of the lock's responsibilities. If you concentrate on anything else apart from the ball, then you'll never catch it. You have to cut out the opposition – you know that they're coming, you know that they're going to clobber you. I always used to shout, 'My ball' and get up early for it if I could – get up and stamp your authority on it because there's nothing better to start the game than to call for a kick-off, get it, make a couple of yards; you've got one over your opposite number then. I would always try to catch it if I could – and always with two hands. There's no future in trying to tap it back.

I always used to stand where most props stand – on the 10-yard line – because I felt that if the ball had gone slightly behind me I could still call for the ball but I was moving back with the opposition. If you're waiting static for the ball, the opposition can do you a fair bit of damage, but if you move back with the ball and go up for it, you are moving with the tackle.

At the start of the game you just want to get a solid catch, a good platform to give your scrum half time to put the pass to the stand-off to kick it away. You can work various things – you might have a driving ball if you're dominating the game

Ball handling is a skill which is often not attributed to second-row players. But the modern game demands it: all forwards must be able to handle the ball well

or you might pop up a pass for a forward coming short; but usually you leave it for the scrum half to make the decision. Normally I used just to concentrate on catching the ball.

I think some people believe that second-row players are not good handlers of the ball but the game is becoming more and more mobile and you can't afford to have guys that can't handle the ball. You've only got to look at players like Meads, Graham Price, Fran Cotton; outstanding players, running with the ball. There are times when you have to make ground and go forward and you've got to know how to take a tackle; you've got to know how to give a pass. I always used to pride myself on my hands – I'd be very upset if I dropped a ball.

I used to love it if I could run at a back – Steve Smith often used to give me a pop-up pass to run onto. It was a bit embarrassing when they tackled me and I'd lose the ball, but that was great for us, you know, to get the ball and run at these little backs.

I think my handling owes something to the influence of rugby league. I think the handling skills in rugby league are tremendous; we used to play it in training because it's hard training and makes you tackle. Certainly pre-season I play a lot of it (with rugby union players, I might add) and it did influence the handling in a way – the way that you might give a ball or take it, or try to commit a couple of men, and so really it did have quite a big influence as I think it does with all northern players.

There have been a lot of successful captains playing in the second row. Most people say you can't captain a side from the second row; you don't know what's going on around you. Sometimes that might be a good thing. I suppose scrum half is an ideal place to captain a side from because he's aware of what is going on in front and behind; I've always been influenced by guys like McBride and Meads who have captained sides by example. They haven't been the most skilful players in the world, but they've always been leading from the front. I think this is what lifts players up and I've always tried to be honest with them – I've never asked them to do something that I wouldn't do.

Really, the captain and coach should be as close as a captain and any of his players – I've been really close to Mike Davis, the current England coach, who played second row. His philosophy

Big Bill Beaumont is a formidable sight when running at a much smaller centre. Ball-carrying forwards can be powerful and invaluable attackers

about the game was exactly the same as mine, and I think that all good sides have a captain and coach who are close. Basically, the coach has to put things over on the training field and he can only do this with the help of the captain.

Apart from the captain, there are several players who are important to the lock. The main one is the scrum half. He determines (with the stand-off) how the backs are going to play the game. He determines with the forwards what kind of ball he wants – whether you're going to ruck it or you're going to maul it, and obviously he might say, 'Leave the ball' or 'Ruck it, ruck it'; he might see a gap and want the ball quickly, and obviously the

forwards can't see that. So it is very important that the scrum half is always chirping away at the forwards – I always used to let my scrum half talk a lot when I was captain because basically they are confidence players, they want the ball always, so let them have it. Really it is vital that they are contributing something. You don't want a scrum half who keeps quiet; you want one who is saying something relevant. I can't dictate the game from where I play it – I rely on good players to make those decisions for me in vital positions. Then there's the prop behind you in the line-out and the prop in front of you in the scrum. Obviously your second-row partner is important too and you need

Ultimately, all rugby relies on the basics, for the second row as much as anybody else. A good tackle round the legs is just such a basic skill

to have a good understanding with him, as indeed you do with the hooker who throws the ball in at the line-out.

I've always played rugby to win – not win at all costs, but within the laws. There's a real difference between club and international rugby; there is far greater pressure in every scrum and every line-out ball because you're playing against better players. When you get tackled in an international, it's that much harder because the guy tackling is that much stronger and harder. Vice versa, when you are tackling somebody, it perhaps hurts you that little bit more, but the guy's running faster than he normally would. However, the basic things you try to do never alter; the simple things done well really are what rugby is all about, and

that's the right thing for a second row. If you do the simple things well, you'll win the game. Whether it's at international or club level, it's still the same technique.

I don't know of a side who can win without a good scrummage and line-out. Every player thinks his position is vital and I'm no exception. The second row is important to the team in a number of ways; they have to get possession at line-out; they have to support the props and the hooker by locking the scrum; and of course they have to make an important contribution at rucks and mauls. Teams who win more ball than the opposition invariably win games. Normally, it's the forwards who determine who will win the game – it's the backs who determine by how many.

# 10 The Front Row

## Assessment of the position *Carwyn James*

For an analysis of the position, nowhere on the rugby field is experience of playing as necessary as in the front row of the scrummage. Graham Price has packed down a thousand times in a thousand scrummages, so he knows all the intricate goings-on and the carefully guarded secrets of the front-row union. I leave him to tell his own tale, and for those who enjoy discussing the job of the tight-head and the loose-head prop, I would draw their attention to a couple of most revealing essays written by Ian McLauchlan and Ray Macloughlin in *The Lions Speak*.

I would, however, like to dwell a little on the role of the hooker in the modern game. Gone are the days of the small, light, swinging hooker. Today he needs strong, shoving shoulders and he has to be burly enough to withstand the roughest, toughest test of forward play. He should be almost as big as his props in a game which demands a powerful scrummaging hooker.

His greatest asset, however, is the quick strike, the keen reflex action which propels his right instep, preferable to the near foot, towards the tunnel to strike the perpendicular ball as it touches the ground. One of the problems facing the hooker is finding the means whereby he can practise his specialized skill. He always needs the presence of another player and preferably his club scrum half with whom he needs constant practice to perfect the timing of the strike. As a signal for his scrum half to put the ball in, the hooker usually uses his left hand. Most hookers prefer the overarm to the underarm method of binding because it gives a tighter scrum and places the body more over the centre of the tunnel.

Hooking the ball on the tight-head is a difficult task. Bryn Meredith of Newport, thirty appearances for Wales and a Lion in 1955 and 1959, has this to say about striking against the head: 'The best advice I can give is to go for the ball every time.'

Meredith, arguably the best hooker of all time, would not offer such advice these days, simply because forward packs are geared towards an eight-man shove, which is meant to slow down their opponents' heel, and occasionally they may even retrieve the ball by pushing them off it. It is only when a pack doesn't go for the eight-man shove that a hooker should strike for the ball against the head.

Hookers unquestionably live in a world of their own in a set scrum, the world of a two-man battle with assistance coming from the props. At the end of a game, they are only partially concerned with the match score, preferring to think in terms of three to one or five to one, which is the tight-head count.

There was a time when hookers had to be good jumpers at the front of the line-out, and they would also guard the no-man's area between the thrower and the 5-metre line. They would also take it upon themselves, if their side lost the

A close understanding between the hooker and his scrum half is essential. Timing is improved by frequent practice together

line-out ball, to rough up the opposing scrum half, a potent part of a pincer movement, aimed to put the opposing number 9 off his game, a duty well done by Ireland's skipper, Ciaran Fitzgerald, in their 1982 Triple Crown triumph.

A particular breed of front row: the Japanese, small of physique, pack tight and low

Hookers, by virtue of the fact that they are the throwers-in from touch, are not conversant any more with line-out techniques, except of course observing the method used by each one of their jumpers.

As a breed, current international hookers like Peter Wheeler, Colin Deans and Alan Phillips are quite pacey and Jeff Herdman of Swansea has scored many a brilliant try in support of his threequarters.

I must, however, sound a warning note to all hookers. Because they are last out of the scrummage and the farthest away from a developing line movement, there has been a tendency for some of them to stand off from the mauls and the rucks. Traditionally, hookers have always been in the thick of the action and a number have been forceful leaders. In fact, Karl Mullen was the captain of the 1950 Lions, Ronnie Dawson the captain in 1959 and Eric Evans was a famous skipper of England in the fifties.

Hookers are remembered mainly for their job in the scrummages, which means that they are usually as good as their props. Bobby Windsor, who for years packed in between Charlie Faulkner and Graham Price, would probably agree.

# Introducing the player *Carwyn James*

Props are a people apart. They are born to a proud freemasonry or a front-row union which allows membership to none but those painfully initiated to serve a sentence for life, preserving the code of behaviour of a game within a game.

To the prop, the score is more likely to be 4–1 than 12–6, the result which appears in the press. 4–1 is the tight-head count or the number of strikes which the hooker makes against the head or on the other side's put-in at the scrummage. Being a prop, somehow, is like working underground, a hard graft, a dangerous craft and, after the toil, like unto like share the refreshments in chosen isolation.

There was a time when hookers were honest men. They did the job that God ordained they should do; that is, they struck for the ball in the scrum. It isn't so any more. We now have the sophistication of the eight-man shove. Graham Price, thirty winters old, 6 feet, less an inch, and 15 stone give or take a pound or two, was born

into this kind of sophistication intensified by the game, and sometimes by the infamy of belonging to the Pontypool front row, immortalized in song by the Welsh minstrel, Max Boyce.

'Up-and-under here we go' combines a lyrical lilt with the stamping of feet as the Pontypool pack, the best club pack in the world, bear down on the poor unfortunate who awaits the reappearance of the high ball from out of the gloom at Pontypool Park on a dark and drizzly winter night.

Charlie Faulkner, Bobby Windsor and Graham Price, from loose- to tight-head in their order of packing and propping: Windsor, the hooker, will yield not an inch to any forward unit. Rather than surrender, they will force a standing or an aerial combat. They love playing the tight game, driving into the rucks and rolling at the mauls.

Graham Price, the most capped of Welsh props, has overtaken Denzil Williams, another man of Gwent, and with thirty-eight consecutive appearances to his name, as well as Lions tours of New

Graham Price

Zealand and South Africa, it looks as if he will create many more records.

Price is the prodigy of Prosser, himself a rugged lock and a prop for Wales and the British Lions. Even if he finds the sophistication of back play unmoving, even boring, and even if the rumour that Lord Lucan was believed to be playing on the Pontypool wing was true, no one can take it away from him that Ray Prosser has produced some of the best forward displays ever seen, reminiscent of the All Blacks at their best.

Skilled in the art of propping, Price made a memorable debut in Paris in 1975. With five new caps, Wales hammered the French in a game remembered by most for Price's try. From a movement started inside the Welsh 22, Price, at the end of the game, had the fitness to pursue the likes of J. J. Williams in a hack-chase-and-hack counter to gather the final bounce and fall-over for a most rewarding try.

I leave the technique to a proud member of the front-row union and will offer only a few considered observations, with much humility, on the thinking behind it all.

# The player *Graham Price*

Every player thinks his position is the most important on the field – that's natural. But I can honestly say that every team talk that I've had at international level or club level always started up front. This is probably the catchphrase – 'It always starts up front' – which is an indication that if you haven't got the basic platform to build on, then all the rest of the game is going to fall apart.

I think a lot of the work we do goes unnoticed, really. We're in the thick of the action, normally buried at the bottom of a ruck or maul or deep in the heart of the scrummage. We're not reputedly the quickest of players but, on the other hand, we are expected to scrummage our hearts out *and* run about the field. Possibly, well I would say definitely, it's the hardest physically of all the positions but you're still required to do a bit in the loose.

To start off with, you've got to be naturally strong – you've got to have something to build upon. If you're the right physique, you're not too tall, you're fairly stocky and broad, and generally speaking you've got a strong back. You obviously use weights and other methods for building up your strength as you go along, but this natural strength is very important.

For a prop forward, the back strength is important, so the exercises used and the weight training involved would be to increase the back strength; but squats and dead lifts are the exercises which I used at one time. They don't improve all the muscle groups necessary for scrummaging so the actual scrummage training is probably *the* most important – it takes a long time for a prop to develop his strength; this is probably why a prop

doesn't really come into his own until he's in his late twenties. He reaches a peak after a while, and once he's reached that peak he can stay at the top for quite a number of years.

As a schoolboy, you tend to notice the flashy things and you like to see players hammering the ball there were quite a few props around in my schooldays who were good in the loose. I'm not saying that they were the be-all and end-all in the scrummage because the scrummage wasn't considered to be that important at that time; the eight-man shove wasn't used. Players like Barry Llewelyn were good handlers in the loose – this is the sort of thing which you notice as a schoolboy. As time goes on, you start playing first-class rugby – I was lucky enough to have a very good coach in Ray Prosser and he put us on the right track. The scrummage is the most important part of the prop's job and, as such, he's got to develop his play along those lines. As Prosser would say himself, he doesn't give a damn what you do outside the scrummage; you can go and sit in the stand with him if you like, as long as the scrummage goes well.

Probably the country with a reputation for the scrummage – they concentrated on this quite a lot – was South Africa. You always hear about these very large Springbok props like Moff Myburg, really strong men; they concentrate on the scrummage, they let the rest of the team worry about the loose play, but once the scrummage foundation is set, then it's something they can build on.

It's very important to be this sort of build – stocky, not too tall, because you find that the tall

Graham Price and the Pontypool front row. Always a formidable sight

prop who's a bit stringy does tend to get bent a bit in the scrum. It's important to keep your back fairly straight in order to have a good scrummage. Being a bit on the short side does help in getting underneath the opposing prop when you do attempt the eight-man drive.

The loose-head prop at the present time has got a totally different job to do from the tight-head. At one time the props used to get down, they used to lean on one another, and it was a case of 'If you leave me alone I'll leave you alone'; but at the present day the loose-head prop has got to be tremendously strong, possibly stronger in the back than the tight-head because he gets the whole weight of the tight-head bearing on him plus the forward shove that the opposing pack is exerting. He's got to enable the hooker to get a good sight of the ball so he can strike the ball

cleanly and, of course, he's got to keep fairly high up off the ground so that the ball comes into the scrummage anyway. The tight-head prop will probably get more weight coming on him from a horizontal direction. This is why it's more advantageous for a tight-head prop to scrummage lower than a loose-head prop.

It wasn't until I was about fifteen years old that I settled into a position (I just used to enjoy playing – I used to enjoy putting the ball under my arm and having a run). At one time I was playing centre for my school side and prop for the local district union, but after my experience as prop I realized that this was probably the best position for me. I was a naturally strong youngster but having experienced other positions, I found that I had a few bonus skills to offer as well as the scrummaging and the donkey work.

I think handling is one of the basic skills, along with tackling. It is a game of physical contact and tackling is the basic skill for *all* rugby players. It is also a running and passing game, so handling is the next most important. Then you settle down in your own individual position – you've got to develop the skills for that position. Then, after that, if you've got a certain quality, you try to bring it out – as my coach would say, 'Find out whether you've got it, and then do it as well as you can.'

Through having this experience of playing in the back division, I've got a better turn of speed than a normal prop would have. My hands are fairly good – I can give and take a pass – and I like to keep fit. This is one of the things in which I do take a pride. I'm out training most nights and during the summer I don't take the opportunity of having a rest like a number of players. I use this in the same way as an athlete or a runner would use the winter, as a means of building up stamina.

The method I use is to do a lot of hill and mountain running. Obviously, you come to a stage where you're only plodding up the hills, but even this, as long as your legs are hurting and your pulse rate is increasing, is bound to be doing you some good. The stamina is not built up through, say, a summer's training – but is built up over a number of years because you've not only got to be able to run but you've also got to be able to take the bumps. There are many things which happen in games which you can't simulate in normal fitness training sessions. This is why the match fitness aspect is so important. The thing which a prop has to do, which you probably wouldn't be able to do in a training session, an individual fitness session that is, is to be able to accept all the bumps. When I first started playing I used to come off the field and I would be really shattered. During the latter years I've been able to take it in my stride and I've had no problems.

A typical Graham Price maul

I haven't noticed myself getting slower. One of the things by which I judge my speed is chasing the kick-offs, and I'm still up catching the man in possession, still up tapping the ball sometimes. Perhaps it doesn't show in every match – the situation has got to be right for me to do it – but I do try to chase these kicks. A prop doesn't normally find himself on an overlap like a winger would because he is generally in the thick of it. Every time a prop gets the ball he's normally got about half a dozen opposing forwards jumping on top of him.

Once you're out of the scrum (as I said, you form the basis of a good scrum with everybody else pushing on you – you've got to be fairly strong in the scrum for them to push on you), what you rely on then is coming to the ruck and the maul with the platform for you to push on. The roles are reversed really. I like to think that the first two or three men to a ruck or maul, usually the back row from a set piece, would play the same sort of role that the front row would play at a scrummage; so obviously we try to get to the breakdown as quickly as possible because if we're last out of the scrum, we're last to the ruck or maul. We've still got a job to do, we still drive in, push the ruck as hard as possible and attempt to win the ball.

In loose play, it's every man for himself as far as the front row is concerned. The nearest we've come to having a defensive responsibility is at the line-out where we attempt to protect the ball catcher by taking our opposite number out of the game. I suppose you would call it legalized obstruction – I think it's catered for in the rules: as long as the person who is protected has already caught the ball, then we're allowed to bind on him and stop the opposition from pouring through the line-out.

If it's our ball, it's my responsibility as far as I'm concerned to stop my opposite number from coming through the line-out onto, say, a badly tapped ball.

The line-out peel is an attacking ploy which is used quite extensively at Pontypool and by the Welsh team. This involves the ball being thrown to the back of hhe line-out and probably the number 8 or one of the flankers tapping the ball down to one of the props, or sometimes the second row, peeling round from the front of the line-out. I normally take this for Pontypool and Wales. There are a number of aims in doing it, such as

Price playing for British Lions against Baa-Baas in 1977, moves in to protect his line-out jumper

taking the back row out of the game by forcing them to step out and tackle me, from which I can set up a maul or a ruck. Or I can take out the first man who comes to tackle me and pop the ball up for a supporting player or, if the situation is right, I can perhaps run around the back of the line-out myself if the marking is weak, and have a chance of running at the backs, making the backs tackle me, which takes *them* out of the game. If we win the ruck, then it means that their backs have one man fewer to mark ours.

At the scrummage, on the opposition's put-in, we will always use an eight-man shove: we try to disrupt the opposition's ball so that the ball is jumbled about and they can't win the ball cleanly. As a result, their backs are stepping backwards, they are not in a good position from which to attack, and the best thing they can do is kick the ball away.

The best man to decide when to shove is the flanker on the side where the ball is being put in. He normally shouts a couple of 'readys' before the 'now' to let us get set for the put-in. He'll wait until the scrum half arrives at the scrum with the ball; the scrum half will then bring the ball down to the scrum; then we get our two 'readys', and as the ball comes into the scrum we get the 'now' and everybody straightens his legs and drives back, lifting the front row. We try to disrupt that way.

There are a number of other ways which I don't believe are as good – they might have the desired effect, such as wheeling a scrum, but I always believe in wearing the opposition down. Probably the best way that a forward can do this is by driving in the scrum, making them work. It stops the front row and the second row running about; the back row have got to stay down and work a bit harder; the second rows towards the end of the game can't jump so high in the line-out. In quite a few games that we've won at Pontypool, and for Wales in fact, the scrummaging has had the effect of winning us the game in the last ten or fifteen minutes: by sheer pressure, by wearing down the opposition. Once they start to get tired, their concentration goes, and they can't cover the field so well to blot out a certain attack.

Probably the most important binding technique for the forwards is to make sure that there is no give between players. They should be bound tightly, gripping hold of the jersey, so that when the opposition do attempt to wheel them or push them backwards, no splitting-up of the players occurs. As far as individual binding is concerned, it's a case of each to his own. As long as it has the desired effect, then all well and good. The second rows have a choice – they can either bind under the arms of their partner, taking a tight grip of the jersey, or sometimes they take a grip of the top of the partner's shorts; both are good methods. In the front row, the hooker will bind over the top of the arms of his prop forwards. This prevents him from being pushed backwards from the centre line of the scrum. There used to be a technique (it's not widely used now – in fact, I don't know of any of the top hookers who use it) of binding underneath the arms of his prop forwards, which means that when the opposition do exert a shove, he is not really going to be supported that well by his props – the props can take the weight but the hooker does tend to be pushed back that fraction which is important when it comes to striking for the ball.

The foot position of a prop forward is important – he must have a fairly wide base so that he has a stable footing. The loose-head prop will probably keep his legs a bit wider than the tight-head prop

The best binding for the front row: hooker's arms bind over the top of the props' shoulders

because he's got to start off the channel for the hooker to hook the ball through. Sometimes, with Charlie Faulkner (Charlie was an exceptional player, one of the strongest loose-heads that Wales have ever had), his stance would be so wide that the hooker's feet would actually be inside Charlie's feet. I think this is a fairly commonly used technique. The tight-head prop has a bit more weight on him from the horizontal direction, so he's got to scrummage lower, his feet probably have to be farther backwards and he's got to have this wide stance, but not nearly as wide as the loose-head prop. Usually the props would have their outside foot a bit in front of the inside foot – this is to provide a bit of stability with regard to the downward direction – and the loose-head prop must have something to work off in order to keep his back up to give the hooker a good sight of the ball. For the tight-head prop, it's more advantageous to be in a low position, so he's got to rely on the loose-head to do a fair bit of his work. There's a certain amount of pride and self-respect with regard to propping and you always expect your opposite number to do his share; e.g. when the tight-head prop is bearing down, it's not to the loose-head's advantage to allow him to pull him down – he's got to keep up, so there's a stalemate.

First of all, you've got to be bound tightly. If the opposition use the eight-man shove and you suddenly split, then the whole foundation of the scrum has gone. This is one of the humiliating parts of the scrummage if it does happen to you. Fortunately, at Pontypool, we do take a great pride in our scrummaging and this very rarely happens unless we've got a very weakened side out. It is important for the tight-head prop to scrummage lower – it forces the opposing loose-head prop to use his strength in an upward direction in order to combat this, which means that he hasn't got the same strength to push in a horizontal direction. The loose-head prop has an advantage in scrummaging in a higher position than the tight-head, so the loose-head prop tries to lift up that little bit. The feet have got to be back in what we call a digging position, or what the textbooks call a locking position. Everybody else behind has to be in a similar sort of position – obviously they rely on the front row to form the basis of the scrum, but they must get their feet back in a good position to resist the shove as well, and then you just rely on your footing.

At Pontypool, and for Wales generally, we never use the hooker striking against the head, which means that we've got all eight forwards attempting to push the opposition backwards. Only occasionally have I known a hooker, an opposition hooker that is, striking against the head all the time, and that is when they've got a weak pack

Hooker channels the ball through the legs of the loose-head; this is why the loose-head needs a wide stance

Front row foot position: Loose-head – feet wide apart, front foot forward; tight-head – feet closer together, both back

where they've got no chance of disrupting you, so they just take their chance on taking a few strikes against the head.

This is one of the things you've got to get used to over the years. Young players coming in find a big difference nowadays. When I first started playing, the props used to take the attitude, 'If you leave me alone, I'll leave you alone,' and the hookers used to strike against the head – it wasn't so hard – but over the years this eight-man shove has come in and it may be a bit more difficult for the young players because of all this bumping. When you drive into a scrum, you generally pick your spot to go in. Your heads interlock, so you're not really having the weight on your neck or the top of your head – you find that the weight all goes through your shoulders. It's not as jarring as most people think – it does hurt a bit if you get caught awkwardly, but for an experienced prop forward this is no problem unless you are charging in from about 5 yards, when it obviously is dangerous. But the referees nowadays will not allow the front rows to get together before the scrum half has arrived with the ball, so you find that the scrums go in now from just about a yard apart which does take all the buffeting out of it.

The game is a bit too fast nowadays for a side to contain a number of thugs. I can't really remember the last time I had a second row send in a punch on me. Intimidation does go on, but it doesn't happen that much now. I am against it – the game's all about skill, not about thuggery. You learn to accept that it goes on – if you weren't prepared to accept it then you probably wouldn't play in the front row.

At a line-out I always stand facing the thrower-in, but sometimes the first jumper will take a low hard ball and I'm able to cut this off by jumping – purely on a reflex action – and catching the ball. The number of second rows who use this technique now is diminishing, so it doesn't come off as often as it used to, but still the threat is there and it's important to try to cut off this source of possession. The next job I've got is to try to disrupt. If the opposing second rows do tap the ball back badly so it's not straight to the scrum half, then the opportunity is there to break through the line-out and perhaps hack the ball up the field or drop on the ball and set up a ruck, or sometimes pick up the ball and feed someone else if I can't run on myself.

In Ray Prosser we have a superb coach, probably the best forward coach in the British Isles. He's a perfectionist, if you like. We can play a game in which we scrummaged well, perhaps we were wheeled or pushed back in one scrum, but when we have the next training session it's not all the other scrums which he remembers but the one scrum in which we were disrupted. This is the right attitude – we've got to aim for as near perfection as possible. Obviously, perfection is impossible to achieve, but the better you can perform the better for the side.

I'm not a great believer in the scrummaging machine, not for a front row. For everybody behind the front row it's beneficial because it's just a matter of binding on behind the front row and pushing; but as far as the front row is concerned, there are more techniques than just lying in the scrummaging machine and pushing. There's a lot of bending and twisting and a lot of things which happen in a scrummage which you cannot simulate on the scrum machine.

We've got a fairly intensive programme of rugby in Wales – probably on average two matches a week. So with a training session as well, you find you do enough scrummage practice; you don't need any more.

I can't say that I've ever come off the field and thought, 'I didn't do this particular skill well.' You have your lapses for a period; the scrummage does tend to go off if you're not concentrating as much on it as you ought to. . . . This is for the coach to spot and tell you. Concentration is important. At international level a lapse in concentration for one scrum could mean a score, as when we played against Ireland in 1982. Perhaps two or three players had a lapse of concentration at one particular scrum and we wheeled, they won a ball against the head, and they scored from it. As far as weaknesses are concerned, I don't think I've ever thought, 'I'm not good at that so I should try to put it right.' When I was a lot younger and first started playing for Pontypool, I used to go out on the field and I used to say, 'I'm not going to bother with the loose play, it's to our advantage to get the tight play right, so I'm going to concentrate on getting all the tight phases right.' This was when I was a young up-and-coming player and I used to think, 'Right, every ruck I'm going to pile into, every maul I'm going to pile into, every scrum I've got to push as hard as I can and get the technique right, every line-out I've got to block properly and try to disrupt as well as I can, and I'll do that no matter what.' Nowadays, when you play a match, you've got to read each situation. If you come to a ruck and you can see that the ball is just about to come out (if you are at the bottom of the previous ruck, you are late coming to the ruck), then

2 vs 1 scrummaging practice: excellent for neck and shoulder strength

perhaps you might stand out; but in those days we just used to pile in regardless.

I'm a tight forward, a specialist in the tight phases of the game, so this is my job. But obviously, if the ball is coming out and I can see the scrum half going blind, then it's advantageous to have an extra defender on the blind side. So you read the situation and act accordingly. Preferably, I'll pile into the ruck.

You couldn't go flat out for eighty minutes, that's just not on. At line-outs you get a chance for a breather – if you get there first, it means that you've got to wait for the others to arrive and you can catch your breath then. If the hooker takes his time to make sure the throw is a good one, you've got an extra breather. You have a chance during an injury, but apart from that you've just got to take everything as it comes.

Why do I play? It's a good life: at the top level you've got a chance to visit a lot of countries which you wouldn't be able to go to under your own steam. I've been lucky enough to go to South Africa a few times, Australia a couple of times, to New Zealand, Fiji and the United States. These are places which I could never otherwise afford to visit. I enjoy being with the boys – generally speaking, the rugby boys are characters. It's an amateur game – we play it purely and simply for the enjoyment of it. You find that all the boys will stick together; it's part and parcel of the game.

# 11 Interviews

*Carwyn James talks to Bob Templeton
and Tom Kiernan*

## Bob Templeton

Bob Templeton, the coach of the 1981 Wallabies in Great Britain, provides the answers to Carwyn James's questions.

*Q. Fred Allen said that the philosophy of the game for him was resolving complexities into simplicities, because rugby is a highly complex game, and it is up to the coach to make it as simple as possible for the players and for everybody else concerned. What is your main philosophy on coaching, Bob?*
**A.** Rugby is a highly complex game because you have lots of pressures. As a Wallaby squad we train many times every week and we do a lot of unopposed training. That's marvellous but, when you're asked to play the game, you've got fifteen people who are competing against you, coming at you and putting you under an enormous amount of pressure, so a coach has to isolate various segments of the game and put them into a match form, so that players react properly in a match situation.

*Q. If you could look at those segments, Bob, perhaps we could start with the skills of the forwards. Scrummaging to start with?*
**A.** Yes, scrummaging is obviously the main platform on which you start the game and if your scrummage is right, and you're scrummaging your own ball, you have security of possession. Should you win your own ball well you can create so much better, and you ruck and maul so much better, and that factor has a tremendous influence on your line-out play as well. So scrummaging really is a unit; it's a very important segment in starting or restarting the game and providing a proper platform for attacks you are able to mount through your threequarters.

*Q. A coach has to be a person who can diagnose good, bad and ill. What do you look for in a good scrummage?*

**A.** In a good scrummage I look for tightness, I look for a good low scrummage that can hold and retain a static ball, so that you don't wheel and that you don't go backwards. In other words, that you can deliver the ball how and when you want it to your scrum half. I think that any ball, and I'm certain backs will agree with me, that is held in a scrummage after about four seconds, if they're going to attack with it, is not much use to us; I believe we have to work on providing a reasonably quick quality ball, provided from the strike to be released within one to three seconds so that your backs can do something with it.

*Q. Which channel do you prefer?*
**A.** Some scrum halves can cope with the channel-one ball provided it is hooked quickly, and is flicked away. John Hipwell is extremely accomplished at that type of ball, a beautiful ball, I believe, for backs to use on attack. The safest ball obviously is channel three, but being a little slow, it allows the opposing backs time to assess what is happening.

*Q. What about the opposition ball?*
**A.** The aim is to make their ball as bad as possible so that your backs can put the opposition under as much pressure as possible. What we're trying to do there is wheel or disrupt them, to throw them off line, push them to delay the ball in the scrummage and to pin their back row. In other words, you're not just going to lie on a scrummage and make an easy ball for them; you're going to drive them backwards and move their backs on the back foot when they're receiving the ball, and make them that little bit slower.

*Q. Do you tell your hooker to strike for the ball occasionally?*
**A.** No, I don't believe that hookers should come off and say, 'Well, I won the heads two to one.'

The wheel as a disruptive force: here the wheel has resulted in a loose ball, preventing any possibility of a quick, clean ball to the backs

I would rather that we worked on the basis of how effectively we destroyed the quality of their possession, or disrupted their possession. That to me is more important than winning a head. For example, if the opposition has twenty put-ins and we can say we mucked up nine of them, I think that's marvellous.

*Q. Is there a marked difference between scrum-maging on hard surfaces and soft surfaces?*
**A.** With our scrummaging deficiencies on the hard ground, where your feet don't tend to move about as much, we can get away with a lot of the inefficiency, but once you come on to the softer ground, where your feet tend to move, your scrummaging has really got to be excellent. We have worked very hard on this particular area, and I think now that our scrum is starting to improve, but it's been a slow process. Nothing succeeds like hard work, it's just a question of application.

*Q. Bob, you mentioned wheeling as a disruptive force, what about the wheel as a creative force?*
**A.** I don't think we've thought enough about the wheel as a creative force, particularly when you're

going to use a back-row move which can be very effective if it's done with control. Using the back row going into a clockwise wheel can be very effective because you've thrown the opposing back row right out of the defensive line, and it gives your attacking back row quite a decided advantage.

*Q. The All Blacks use the 3–3–2 formation very often when they've got a back-row move up their sleeve; do you use the same formation occasionally?*
**A.** No, not really, but 3–3–2 is quite effective in the wheel where you shift the number 8 across, packing between the left-hand flank and the left-hand lock, and the right-hand flanker comes across and packs in the number-8 spot. That to me is very effective, and it accentuates the wheel.

*Q. Do you feel that the new law introduced for September 1981 has done away with collapsed scrummages, which it was intended to do?*
**A.** I don't really know whether the law has made a great difference to the collapsing of the scrum. I'm sure that it has made the tight-head terribly

vulnerable now, the way they're asking him to pack. Probably what it's done has made every player conscious of not taking the scrum down because we're all aware of not giving penalties away, so everyone's really trying to stay up. I don't think the law is completely successful but, I repeat, it has made the tight-head much more vulnerable. In fact, the referees should be looking a lot more at the loose-heads, at what they're doing, rather than at what the tight-head is doing.

*Q. You mentioned earlier on that if you have a good scrummaging pack it helps other phases. Do you think that countries in the southern hemisphere, particularly New Zealand and Australia, ruck much better than teams from the northern hemisphere?*
**A.** Yes, I do, probably because of the attitude of player and referees. We obviously play a lot against New Zealand provincial sides, and against the All Blacks, and there's an acceptance that if players go down to the ground, and they are on the ball or they are near the ball, we will drive or step over them, which to me is quite acceptable. I don't believe anyone is going to get hurt by going over the top. Kicking a forward has no part in the game, but raking back when a player is supposed to release and roll away or make an attempt to roll away from the ball is perfectly acceptable.

*Q. What do you think is the essence of rucking?*
**A.** The essence of rucking really is primarily that those first two or three players drive past the ball. I call it 'in, over and out' and I believe those first two or three have got to – as I call it – create a vacuum, they've got to go right past, right past the player with the ball on the ground, and to do that you've got to have a scrummaging body position. When you're going in over the top, many players tend to step over, which lifts their shoulders, and they get a very poor body position; those first two or three players have really got to hurl themselves in over, and if they walk on someone as they are going over, whether it be their own players or the opposition's, we accept that fact. But the body height and the binding are both terribly important on entry into that ruck situation, because we don't want our players falling on the ground. If they go on the ground, how the hell can we drive forward? So, it is very much a game of staying on your feet and thrusting in a forward direction.

*Q. Rucking on hard surfaces obviously must be more difficult than on soft surfaces?*
**A.** Yes, it is. For example, in Australia, obviously, we tend to maul much more because the ground is usually extremely hard, and obviously the ball is much more fiery; it tends to bounce around and naturally it is in our hands more. But, by the same token, we tend to do what we call hand rucking, that is, taking the ball, driving forward and laying the ball and leaving it behind us. I think that is a beautiful ball for backs to operate on and I believe a lot of maulings become static situations where the ball is held up and held in too long. I'm not a great believer in the rolling maul because I think that's bad ball for your backs. I believe you've got to go forward. I believe it's far better to deliver the ball too quickly than too slowly, because if it comes quickly, and I'm sure backs will agree with me, the gaps are still there for them. If it is held in too long, the defence realigns and you're back to a static situation again.

*Q. I notice that quite often from the line-out you develop a maul situation. In other words you have created an immediate secondary platform from primary possession.*
**A.** Yes, well, perhaps that's come from the ball being deflected. We want to try to keep the ball off the floor and give our scrum half a good position from which to operate, and with our sweepers we try to collect the ball before the scrum half gets it, particularly if it drops in what I call the 2-foot area where we try to create and set up play.

*Q. The line-out has been referred to as a lottery and as the illegitimate child of rugby football. How do you view the line-out at the present moment?*
**A.** I call it a dockyard brawl. Really, I'd hate to see the line-out go out of the game. It's got lots of problems. I just hope that the legislators leave the law alone, let us settle down and work on the line-out. Perhaps it might be better to go back sometime to double banking, which was used in the early sixties quite effectively. But the way the law is framed now, I'd hate to see other changes come in because referees have got so much to look for that you could blow up at every line-out. I think the laws of the game should be left as they are, and let's develop the game from there. It was probably the interpretation of the laws which over a period of time caused changes to be made. I

think the interpretations were not strong enough to prevent those pile-ups and the collapsing of scrums.

**Q.** *I notice that your lads deflect quite a lot. Do you spend a lot of time practising deflection?*
**A.** I don't like the word deflection, I like the word guiding. Yes, we do. If we can both jump the same height, you are always going to beat me if you go up with one hand; you're going to get that little bit higher and win the ball. That is a fact of life. We'd all like to be able to catch the ball with two hands, but what we're trying to do is to push the ball to another man in the line-out who is conscious of it coming to him, so that he can gather it.

**Q.** *I notice that Steve Williams uses his outside arm quite a lot, whereas, obviously, he'd get far more height if he was using the inside.*

As Peter McLean proves in the 1981 match between Australia and Pontypool, a one-handed deflection with the inside arm is the way to gain a line-out ball against an opponent who can jump to an equal height

**A.** The line-out jumper should use his inside hand; I believe that he should hold that inside arm up before the ball is even coming into the line-out. If he is holding it down low, it's quite easy for someone to prevent him from getting the inside hand up and I'm a great believer in having that hand held high so that, if there is any obstruction, perhaps the referee will pick that up.

**Q.** *Which is the best ball for you in the line-out, 2, 4 or 6?*
**A.** Well, on attack, the best ball is the back of the line-out, where you're obviously restricting their back row; you're tying them up, you're containing them for that vital second or so where your backs are going to have less pressure. They're going to have enough pressure from the opposing backs, but they've at least got 20 metres to manoeuvre in. But if you're containing the opposition back row by throwing to the back of the line-out, well, you've contained them fractionally, so to me that's the best ball.

**Q.** *Are you a great believer in peeling at the front of the line?*
**A.** I think peeling at the front of the line is pretty potent 10 to 15 metres from the opposition line, provided the drive goes where you can pull the back row in. It works in other areas, but 10 to 15 metres from the line I think is very good.

**Q.** *Rugby football obviously starts with defence, Bob. May I have your philosophies on defence?*
**A.** A lot of coaching is done on attack, when your own side has the ball, but you have the ball perhaps for only 50 per cent of the time and the other 50 per cent you're trying to put the opposition under pressure. Now, pressure, or defence, works first on contesting, you know, contesting in the scrum, contesting in the line-out, contesting the ruck and maul, contesting the ball on the floor and in the air. It's contesting, trying to make a direct tackle. And the next is covering. You have to create a contest in a certain area, forcing or making the direct tackle, or causing decisions to be made hurriedly and I encourage players, even though they may not make the tackle, to realize that it is important to deny time and space to the opposition. In other words, we cause decisions to be made hurriedly and, we hope, badly. And then the next important thing to me is making certain that while our players are going forward, contesting

Fifty per cent of a team's work is in defence. This means putting the opposition under pressure by continually contesting the ball

and forcing, we've also got people covering our second line, which is very important. Those are the basic principles we work on when we talk about defence. The other thing is just tackle, tackle, tackle.

*Q. Would you agree that your back row is the first line of defence, your middle line of defence is the mid-field and then, the way you operate with wings as semi-full backs, you've got a third line of defence?*

**A.** In and around the scrummage, each man must know his particular duties. The same when switches are employed. He should be picked up if he's going laterally across the field. In other words, he's going wide to create space. If we're coming, we're holding our line. Our centre should take him, and the five eighth should be checking when taking the man coming back and likewise the flanker. The only danger there, of course, is the outside break. If we're holding our line, we should be able to cover any particular type of

switch. Again, we work a lot on people kicking to us. We like to counter from that sort of situation, and I think if you can get the back three working together, there are all sorts of possibilities which you can develop from that sort of situation. But the back three really are very important, particularly against a side who are going to kick against you.

*Q. I have noticed that your mid-field trio have the facility of virtually shepherding the opposition across to the touchline.*

**A.** Well, Carwyn, yes. I believe that our boys have got a lot of pace. I don't think that, collectively, there is a back line in Britain that can match us for pace. And I believe that we're being allowed to a certain extent to shuffle off like the Lions did in 1971 in New Zealand, where you felt you could cover, and we're being helped by bad alignment, by the bad attacking alignment of the opposing teams that are playing against us. We feel that a lot of their attacking is done running towards the side line. We really feel we can hustle them across the field.

*Q. Are your half back and your first five floaters in defence?*
A. Yes, you know, another theory I've got is that a half back or a scrum half, in many situations, can beat the back row to a breakdown. I always say that the scrum half should have his nose on the end of the ball, whether it be in attack or defence. Ken Catchpole was a great exponent of that.

*Q. You mention Kenny Catchpole, one of the most brilliant scrum halves I ever saw. What was Ken's secret and the secret of half backs as you call them in the southern hemisphere, because their technique seems to me so much better than the technique of scrum halves in Britain?*
A. Ken was a marvellous reflex player, his reaction to ball out at line-out, ball out at scrummage, to ball out at ruck and maul was tremendous. And Ken could never tell you why he did things, he did them instinctively. I call him a spontaneous player who did things completely by reflex. He worked not so much on a long pass but on a very quick and accurate pass, and I think to me that really is the essence of good scrum-half play; you can build length onto that. Basically I think that was Ken's philosophy and also he was very quick around the ground. He didn't dive pass much, he tried to stay on his feet. Sometimes when you're playing under certain conditions, you have to dive pass, but basically we try to get our scrum halves to stay on their feet, so that they can play a supporting role; and I believe they can beat, certainly, your own back-row forwards to the point of breakdown, and I believe we've got a chance of beating the opposition back-row forwards as well.

*Q. What about the youngsters in Australia, do they use a spin pass, or are they content to use the wrists like Ken Catchpole?*
A. Well, there are a lot of youngsters using the spin pass. We even see the centres doing the spin pass now, which to me is terrible because I think it slows down the movement of the ball. I discourage my centres from spin passing. We have a couple of them in Australia. I believe the ball should be caught and transferred as smooth as silk. The ball never stops, it goes on an endless chain. In spin passing you've got to adjust the ball and that takes time and yards, so I discourage it, but it is happening.

*Q. So, technique really is the thing that matters in passing generally?*
A. Yes. Technique allied with what you're trying to achieve. If you're giving to a scrum half, passing to his right, it is much better if he gets the ball really a little bit to his left so that he can transfer the ball in one movement.

*Q. Paul McLean is a player who can play under pressure. You've got a number of young players in your team who don't play too well under pressure. How long do you think it takes?*
A. Well, I think those young players probably have learned a tremendous amount from this tour, and they have had to learn to absorb pressure, and also to take pressure off their forwards. Early in the tour we were lying too flat. We were not only taking pressure from the opposition but we were putting a hell of a lot of pressure on ourselves because we were trying to clear the ball. If it wasn't quick and accurate, we were in all sorts of bother. We tend to lie back just that little bit deeper now, draw people onto us. Move the ball, as I've said. We've got pace, and if we can get people coming straight at us in defence rather than going across, we've got space still to work on.

*Q. Would you say, Bob, that the kind of rugby that those young Australian schoolboys played in 1978 is not possible at senior international level?*
A. Well, it is possible, certainly, but what you've got to remember is that when you play international rugby, it's a game of intense and continual pressure, and the things you're able to do at the level of schoolboy-type rugby are not possible. Continual pressure on backs and forwards, so the backs have got to be able to relieve the pressure on their forwards, and you know, it's much more difficult to play that type of game continually at international level.

*Q. I love the phrase 'as smooth as silk' for moving the ball quickly from scrum half to wing. Would you say that that was the basic, traditional Australian method of threequarter play?*

**A.** Yes, being able to move the ball quickly with accuracy and speed, and making certain the backs are running on the right line, is certainly the traditional way of Australian rugby.

**Q.** *Did you ever go through Ian MacRae and the Joggie Jansen phase of crash-ball in mid-field?*
**A.** Yes, we've had a centre in Geoff Shaw in recent years who is a blockbusting type of centre who has certainly served us well. I suppose it all gets down to the type of game you're going to play and the type of players that you have. I mean, if we're going to move the ball 'as smooth as silk', as I say, and if you haven't got those passers in your line, well we are going to be in awful trouble. So, I suppose it's a question of really trying to play the game with what you've got available.

**Q.** *Would you tell me, Bob, the advantages of playing inside and outside centres, or second five and a bona fide centre?*
**A.** I have an open mind on whether you play left and right centre or inside and outside centre. It depends on the type of players you've got. Normally, the inside centre, as we term him, or what the New Zealanders term a second five eighth, is a player of very good judgement, and that means judgement not only in being able to pass and when to pass and so forth, but a tactical kicker, generally a strong man who can take the ball to the opposition and who is strong defensively, because to me the point of contact from scrummaging, if something happens, is going to be the inside centre or second five. Generally the outside centre is very much a beautiful server and timer of the ball to his wings. He should be able to turn an opposing winger's head by virtue of acceleration into the half gap. Playing left and right has two obvious advantages: an understanding with the wing he is playing with, and it may cause confusion in the opposition who suddenly find that they are marking someone different.

**Q.** *Would you say that Hawker and O'Connor form an ideal combination?*
**A.** Yes, I believe Hawker is a strong player. He's got a sure tactical boot on him, and he's a very strong defensive player. O'Connor is a fine attacking player, brilliant on his feet, although you haven't seen the best of him. And he, probably, is one of our best backs. So to me they work well

with one another and work off one another extremely well.

**Q.** *I noticed that against Swansea, when you missed out a threequarter, the missed player did the loop well, and supported the wing or the full back.*
**A.** Once a player is missed out he should try to find space where he can get into support again. He must play a supporting role.

**Q.** *Roger Gould, from full back, varies his angles of entry into the threequarter line. Do you feel that that is important?*
**A.** Yes, I do. There are times when the man entering has got a couple of roles to play. If he's coming in to penetrate, he's got to vary his angle of entry. If he's coming in to play the extra-man role, where he wants to turn the winger and pull the winger onto him, obviously he's going to take a different line.

**Q.** *Talking about covering, do you feel that the Mervyn Davies-type role of a number 8 is now more relevant to the modern game than the old method of corner flagging?*
**A.** Yes, I believe that the number 8 now has got to play very much closer to the ball, and I think that the number 8 of the old type who corner flagged incessantly could go through the game without even touching the ball, without even bringing off a tackle. You know, I believe now that you've got to play so much shallower in your line, and you've got to, I call it, keep in contact with your backs, because I think a number 8 really plays very much a role with his half backs and his inside backs. A supporting role there both in attack and in defence is vital.

**Q.** *So would you say that the old corner-flagging role of the number 8 has now been transferred to the halves and the blind-side wing?*
**A.** Well, yes, I would prefer to say that the corner-flagging role is now played by the blind-side wing, who does a lot of covering work and who can also pick up any cross-kicks.

**Q.** *What about the use of the short or the narrow side?*
**A.** The use of the short side is very much under-used by a lot of teams and particularly by Australia. They are great avenues for getting over the gain

line and gaining ground, which is a very important principle of play, but I think it has been under-used. Gradually now we're starting to use that particular facet of play much more.

*Q. What are the qualities you look for in a captain?*
**A.** I think the captain has got to have a great understanding with the coach, knowing what the coach wants to do and what the coach believes the team can attain, and knowing what you're going to do in certain circumstances. In other words, the coach should talk a lot with his captain about how the game is going to be played, what's going to happen in all sorts of circumstances, what you're trying to achieve. It's a very important role – once they go on the field, well, as I say to the captain, 'The battle is yours, I've done all I can.' Your captain should then be able to handle the situations and if the coach hasn't done that with him, then the coach should accept a lot of the blame and not blame the captain.

*Q. Your dressing-room technique, Bob?*
**A.** Well, I'm not a shouter and a raver. I believe in a very quiet approach. I like talking to my team before we go to the ground. I don't believe in long team talks because you should do your prepara-tion on the training paddock and then in your talks merely recap what you want to do. I'm also a great believer in pride, pride of the individual, pride of what the team wants to do, that second best is certainly not good enough – only the best all the time. You know, setting standards; and I be-lieve each individual has got to set himself a stan-dard which he wants to attain and maintain, that's very important. I'm a great believer in that pride business and not so much national pride but a pride in what you want to do yourself.

Well, I'm a great believer in an individual and also in the team having tremendous pride in their performance – as we say, second best is not good enough. I believe rugby football is like a way of life, if you're going to do something, be it in work or play, you're going to do it the best you can every day of the week. And I've got no truck with anyone that goes out and is prepared to have a second-class performance. To me winning is everything really, but winning by achieving a stan-dard of excellence. The only time I will accept defeat is when we've played well, when we've played to our full capabilities and we've been beaten. Grudgingly, I will accept that we were

beaten by a better side. But I hate accepting de-feat when we haven't performed anywhere near our best.

*Q. Pride also means discipline, Bob?*
**A.** Yes, very much so. And discipline is not 'No, sir, yes, sir,' but it's maintaining order, not panick-ing but sticking to the task in hand. That's where I've been a little irate in certain matches here which we've lost and in which we've been run very close. No matter what flair they have, all players must try to work within the framework. I don't want to stifle players, but they must work within the framework of what the overall team is going to achieve. Otherwise, if you've got six players trying to do something and nine others trying to do something else, you're going to achieve nothing – so discipline is very important.

*Q. And imagination?*
**A.** You've got to have imagination, you've got to be innovative, you've got to be able to be creative, you've got to think. And that's the wonderful thing about rugby football – there are many ways to play the game and there are always new things that you're going to learn about the game, particu-larly as a coach. We can all learn from one another, and it's terribly interesting to watch other teams, to talk to other rugby players and to get their ideas, and there might be one point that you pick up which can be very helpful to you. Fortunately I'm still learning; and I will continue to learn. I've learned a tremendous amount on this tour and I hope I'll be a little bit wiser and maybe a little bit better as a coach at the end of the tour.

*Q. Do you believe in getting retaliation in first?*
**A.** No, I don't. Certainly a side shouldn't be intim-idated. In other words, I think that it's a man's game. There's no doubt about it, you've got to be able to take the knocks and you've got to be able to give the knocks and accept that. But I don't believe in getting your retaliation in first. Certainly not. It's a game which teaches you many things. It's a great test of character, of being able to maintain your cool and not getting distracted from what you're doing.

One or two of my young players can get dis-tracted, and they've been spoken to severely be-cause I think that while they're being distracted they're not playing the ball, and the ball is all-im-portant as far as I'm concerned.

# Tom Kiernan

Tom Kiernan, coach of the 1981–82 Triple Crown winning Irish team, replies to Carwyn James. ·

*Q. Well, Tom, it must have been a most memorable season?*
**A.** After the disappointment of the previous year it was very pleasant to win the Triple Crown, particularly after such a long period and with so many players who have given Ireland such great service. I think, in a coaching position, one has to take a realistic and an honest view of the team's performance, and I was quite convinced that we would be as difficult to beat as any of the other international teams in the Championship.

*Q. What would you say was the high point of the season?*
**A.** The second half against Wales or at least the last fifty minutes against Wales, where we displayed a lot of the qualities that teams capable of winning a Triple Crown must show.

*Q. I suppose, Tom, we've all been influenced to a certain extent by some of the teams that we've seen in the past. What great teams from different parts of the world influenced you?*
**A.** In the early sixties the South African teams, particularly the team of 1961 for their forward power and the relentlessness of their tight forward play. The New Zealand team of 1963 and 1967, again, by the power of their forward play, but particularly of their loose forwards, coupled with probably the best New Zealand threequarter line that I've seen; then I thought a lot of the rugby was mediocre up to the Welsh team which emerged at the end of 1969 and which carried them through the 1970s. The Welsh forward power never quite matched the relentless forward power of the South Africans or the New Zealanders, but it was more than adequate. It was very good forward play rather than power, and they possessed as many skills, but they weren't as single-minded, and the reason they weren't as single-minded was because they had so many threequarters who were quite capable of playing wonderful rugby. If you were to ask me what team would be my ideal, it would be the Welsh team of the 1970s.

*Q. Would you say therefore that this power really is the key to success for any rugby side?*
**A.** Power has been the key to success of the New Zealand and the South African teams. I wouldn't necessarily say it had been the key to Welsh success, but it certainly can be a dominating factor because again it's harder to create than defend; if you lack power in the pack, despite what strengths you might have in the threequarters, it's very easy for another side to dominate you, and it makes it far more difficult than when you have great power in the pack with perhaps an average threequarter line.

*Q. Have any coaches influenced your coaching style?*
**A.** Well, I followed Noel Murphy, who was my club mate in Cork. We probably have different ideas on some aspects of the game, but we've known each other a long time. Of course, before Noel, we had Roly Meates and Syd Miller, and prior to that Ronnie Dawson. All these individuals were part of a very small circle in Ireland – and I think there is a general agreement on the requirements for Irish international teams amongst the whole lot of us.

*Q. Would you say that there's a vast difference between coaching a first-class team and coaching a national side?*
**A.** With a national team, you're coaching for four matches a year – so it's essentially a short-term task. In coaching a club side, you have about thirty to thirty-five matches in a season, with a build-up at the end of the year to a club competition. So you're able to have a far greater influence upon the manner in which the players might play and in their selection. At club level, you have a close association with your players which you might not get with an international team.

*Q. What is your main philosophy of coaching?*
**A.** My philosophy of rugby per se is that I should like to see the skills of the game displayed in a more appropriate manner by those who possess them, and to see players maximizing their individual talents. In the context of international rugby, I've got to take a shorter term view and my philosophy is dictated by the circumstances in which I find myself. I suppose the priority must be to try

Tom Kiernan

to win international matches – after all, they re-emphasize the strengths or weaknesses in one's own country and there is the question of national pride at stake. I also have a little idealism that I want to win and also play good rugby at the same time. One has to be realistic in trying to reach these two ideals and one also has to take into account the resources at one's disposal; but, broadly speaking, I would love to achieve in rugby what I feel was achieved by the Welsh teams in the 1970s.

*Q. Do you think, Tom, that perhaps coaching has become a bit stilted – that we may have lost our way as far as coaching the individual is concerned? Does this apply in Ireland?*
**A.** Most of us think and believe that training sessions are an absolute bore but they are a necessary evil and, in the international context, one assumes that the players have the basic skills and requirements and, although they must practise them and sharpen their skills up, one tends to believe they have it and one is more interested in coordinating them. But I would agree with you that perhaps at a lower level coaches are becoming a little stereotyped in their methods, although in the home countries I don't see many alternatives with the standard of our pitches and the conditions under which we play with so much rain and that sort of thing. We tend to be greatly influenced by the elements.

*Q. Do you feel that your job as a coach is to lay down certain patterns and then it's up to the players themselves to work out the moves and the little details of the game?*
**A.** That is the way I approach it – other people may have different views. Essentially what one does as a coach on a national side is to ensure that the players are physically fit, and particularly in anticipation of the international season where you have a long run in, you can ensure this to a great extent. Having achieved that, it becomes a matter of assisting the players, expressing your views to them, coordinating different ideas and trying to help them with your observations of the opposition; but, more than anything else, probably trying to give them an identity as a national team. Here it can't be overemphasized how important it is that you have a strong continuity in a national side and the ability to have selectors who are capable of withstanding criticism of the side

where you believe that there were no alternatives available.

*Q. When you are coaching at the highest level, would you say it's important that one constantly reminds players of the habits, the fundamentals, the basics of the game?*
**A.** I think the most important aspect is *how* you remind them and I, in fact, don't know whether I've had any success in that area or not. I think it's a most controversial area, and one has to be very careful in dealing with players of that calibre in suggesting to them that they may not be doing something quite as they should be, or that they may simply have forgotten some aspects of the play.

*Q. How do you react to the prima donnas of the team?*
**A.** I was with Barry John in South Africa in 1968 when he was a very young man at the beginning of his career and certainly he played some marvellous rugby up to the time of his injury in the first Test. But I always treat these people the same as the other players in the team and I think this is the way that they like to be treated. It's partly in the imagination of the press and the critics that they become prima donnas because, you know, rugby is a great leveller, and one day you may hit the heights and all the kicks may go through and the next day you may have to carry all the stick when one drifts outside the upright. Amongst the players there are a few prima donnas and one tends to take them as one does the other players. It's essential that players are able to express their own individual flair and imagination and, as I've said many times, there is no one way to play rugby football – it depends on the strengths and weaknesses of your team and the opposition. But one hopes that the differences between one's own team and the opposition at the end of the day is that little bit of flair or genius, or whatever you like to call it, that a particular player is capable of realizing at a particular moment.

*Q. I'm fascinated by the way people sit round a table picking a side. How do you eventually pick a player?*
**A.** Well, there is another factor that comes into this and that is the strength of the opposition. I know that I'm very conscious, when selecting a side at representative level, of trying to find out

who the opposition might be because, as you say, some people have strength in the scrum but may not be so versatile in loose play. It's a question of trying to have the ability and foresight to see who might be the most appropriate players in the circumstances, provided of course that you have the alternatives.

*Q. Is it always possible to get the ideal balance you're looking for?*
**A.** Yes, indeed, you're struggling for it – I'm sure I seek perfection in that area, but you are always struggling and sometimes I don't think there is any harm in struggling because the feeling is abroad that one's pack might be inferior to another pack. This is when the intangibles come in and the heart begins to pound and you see the true character of the players.

*Q. Would you concur with the view that a coach is only as good as the players he has available to him?*
**A.** That is certainly a great influence on the coach's success or failure rate but I also believe that the coach himself must take a certain amount of the responsibility. Perhaps it's a combination of both the players who are available and the coach himself.

*Q. What do you understand teamwork to mean in the context of rugby?*
**A.** One of the objectives of a coach in representative rugby is to try to bring the players together in a short period of time into something like a club atmosphere and to try to create a team in which each player knows what is required of him and indeed what the other players might be trying to achieve. Within a broad framework we try to get the team to play with what is considered to be their strength, and on the weaknesses of the opposition. If one can achieve that in a representative side, one has achieved as much as a coach can do off the field.

*Q. Would you say that teamwork all comes back to a question of having the basic skills?*
**A.** There are a lot of qualities required of rugby players and, of course, of rugby players in different positions. In any of the key positions – the three-quarter line, half back, full back and perhaps hooker – they need to be fairly skilful. But there is room in rugby for the people who are not pos-

sessed with great skill, who haven't got the ability to be very dexterous in their movements but who have big hearts and who will fight to the end in the adverse circumstances in which most rugby teams find themselves at various times

*Q. What facets of teamwork would you say, looking now at the unit skills and possibly the unit skills of the forwards, are the most important?*
**A.** It is very difficult to divorce one from the other, but the ability to concentrate on obtaining the ball is the most important quality of forwards, as I see it. I'm not talking here in the context of whether I have powerful scrummagers or whether I have good leapers in the line-out; I'm talking about maximizing the eight forwards together and their ability to get the ball under pressure and make it available to my threequarters as often as possible and to know when to do it and how to do it.

*Q. What do you feel should be the relationship between the coach and the captain?*
**A.** In international football both coach and captain are there for perhaps short periods of time, but they must have a close relationship. The coach must have full confidence in the captain, confidence in his ability to lead the players on the field, to make correct decisions during the course of the game. He expects him to be able to assess the opposition and to make various positional changes as well as liaising with key players like the out-half about the kind of game they should be playing.

*Q. What are your memories of your time as captain, Tom? How do you feel captaincy has changed since the introduction of the coaching system?*
**A.** I captained Ireland for a number of years before the appointment of a coach, which was in fact in 1970 when Ronnie Dawson was appointed. But we had toured in South Africa in 1968 and you might remember that this was really the second tour in which a coach was appointed to the Lions, the first one being the 1966 tour to New Zealand. We were very determined before that tour to South Africa that we were going to make the system work because we believed it was right and it was difficult before that time to determine the exact responsibilities of the captain and coach. Through the offices of the home unions and through my own discussions with Ronnie and

An important facet of forward play is the ability to get the ball under pressure and to make it available to the threequarters as often as possible

David Brooks, we didn't have any problems whatsoever on the whole tour. Indeed, my whole philosophy during the years after that when Ronnie was coach of Ireland and I was captain was that the coach had a great input in the preparation of the team, principally because the captain didn't have the time – he wasn't watching his colleagues in other matches, he wasn't selecting the team and consequently he was meeting them on the weekend of a match in which his priorities were motivating them for a particular event. So from the point of view of selection and preparation the coach had a lot to offer, and also from the organizational point of view. Now Ronnie Dawson never interfered with my priorities on the pitch and my responsibilities, and we would merely discuss games after they had taken place in order to iron out any problems which he might have seen. But I was fortunate in that I had the utmost confidence in him and it was a pleasant situation to be in, in those intervening years. Since then, of course, it is more or less taken as the norm that you have a coach, but again, in the international context, as a coach one has to be conscious of the fact that the captain at the 'heel of the hunt' on the day has to take the decisions as he sees them according to the tempo of the team and how he feels about the opposition. I haven't had any difficulties in wearing that hat with the captains I've coached with.

*Q. Do you think that in Irish rugby there has been a carryover from one captain to another?*
**A.** Ireland have been extremely fortunate in having a person of Ciaran Fitzgerald's ability to take over the leadership from Fergus Slattery, whom I considered a marvellous captain. I think Ciaran assumed the responsibility tremendously well, though of course he had great support on the field from Slattery; more than any other thing the combination was instrumental in Ireland's success.

*Q. How long does it take to cultivate a player to become a good captain?*
**A.** I think the example of last year is that it doesn't take any time at all. Ciaran Fitzgerald just went into the job as if he had been there for years. In a realistic sense I suppose it depends on the individual – you can certainly nurture a captain and allow him to grow into maturity with the job over a period of time, but I would have thought that in his second year as captain of a representative or national side the captain should be in a position of total command of the team.

Ciaran Fitzgerald and Fergus Slattery: instrumental in Ireland's 1982 Triple Crown success

**Q.** *Is there room in a team for a captain and a pack leader?*
**A.** I've never been in those circumstances because I think that the essential qualities of a pack leader tend also to be quite similar to those of a captain in most cases. But I would prefer to get the opinion of the captain before I, as a coach, would make that decision, again particularly in an international context as distinct from a club context.

**Q.** *If the captain is a forward, to what extent can he rely completely on one of his backs to be in charge of tactics?*
**A.** Usually in international back lines you have some person who has been around for a period of time and who has the maturity to accept the responsibility. It's preferable if that person is in a key position in the back line, and I would imagine that in most international teams you get this sort of situation. I've seen it, particularly in English teams, over, let's say, the last ten or fifteen years where they lacked somebody with a dominating personality of the likes of Dickie Jeeps at the base of the scrum, and I think it was one of the reasons why England's resources weren't maximized during that period.

**Q.** *The kicker is now very important to the international team, because of the increasing importance of penalties. How do you view this?*
**A.** From the coach's point of view, one of the great imponderables in looking after a national side is that there are now circumstances totally outside your control, and indeed outside the players' control, in which a penalty kick at goal results

in matches being won by specialist kickers. Recent statistics have shown a far greater number of penalty kicks at goal in the last number of years than there were fifteen or twenty years ago, and this is a worrying trend because it's now becoming a bit of a lottery. One is very much at the whim of the referee's interpretation, and, of course, when you change referees every fortnight during an international campaign, you meet different circumstances. So I would say it is one area that will have to be looked at, and whether it means the introduction of an indirect free kick, which has serious implications, or whether it comes back to the referee's interpretation of the laws, remains open to question.

*Q. Would you say that rugby has, to a large extent in the last couple of years, developed into a pressure game, putting the opposition under stress?*
**A.** I haven't seen any great change in rugby in my experience at international level. I always found myself under tremendous pressure both in playing and in coaching representative rugby or indeed international rugby. I think we tend to see this from the strengths of our own particular countries. In Ireland we've rarely been dominant over a period of seasons – we've always struggled to win two or three matches a year and consequently we have relied on putting pressure on the opposition more than perhaps Wales or, to a lesser extent, France, who have the greater ability to create their scoring opportunities through their own skill and numerical strength.

*Q. Moving on now to look at particular aspects of teamwork, let's start with the scrummage – what are your views on scrummaging?*
**A.** Scrummaging is an integral part of rugby football, but it has to be controlled to some extent, and I think perhaps it has been controlled. You may have seen an improvement this year – a lessening of the number of scrums collapsing. But I do think that rugby is a physical game and is as much dependent on power and mobility as perhaps on skill. To emphasize my point earlier on, different types of people can play the game – people with different heights, weights, speeds, whatever. I like the thought of a set scrummage in rugby. I do not like the persistent wheeling of the scrum, I do not like the delays in setting up the scrum, but there are other issues which should be corrected.

*Q. There are different views about the type of ball one should win from a scrummage – which do you prefer from your boys?*
**A.** If the scrummage is from left to right, I would imagine most scrum halves would like the channel-three ball, but if the scrum was from right to left, if it can be manipulated by your number 8, then either a channel-two ball or a pass from the number 8 to the scrum half perhaps is appropriate. But it depends on the circumstances, and it depends on the pressure which the opposing pack is able to put on your scrummage.

*Q. I think there's a feeling amongst certain members of the International Board that some legislation should be introduced to do away with this disruptive wheeling that we've seen so much of in the last two or three seasons. Would you go along with that?*
**A.** This is worthy of great debate because it's another spoiling method. You mean now that the team without the ball is wheeling the other scrum in towards the touchline. It's worthy of debate all right. Some teams have tended to counteract it better than others but I would be very interested in a debate amongst the senior players of the national sides. In training on the Thursday before the game we don't have too many – we certainly have ten or twelve scrums – but I would consider it to be the essence of the training session, more or less an exercise in getting people together again and beginning the motivated process and the coordinating of the put-in and so forth. Certainly, perhaps in the session before an international, one would tend to emphasize scrummaging to a great extent and I usually tend to leave that to the pack leader who also tends to be the captain.

*Q. Do you think the new law has done away wit' collapsing scrums as intended?*
**A.** It would be premature for me to judge that because I wasn't really concerned with that aspect of the play last year. What I would say is that it seemed to me that there were fewer collapses, and I believe that particular law is probably worthy of continuing for another season or two.

*Q. Now, what about ruck and maul? I sense occasionally that, as an Irishman, you like the ball at your feet and that by nature possibly, in compari-*

son with the New Zealanders, you may prefer the ruck rather than the maul. Am I right?

**A.** I think the ruck is more appropriate to the Irish because I think the Irish packs have not tended to be as big and broad as the overseas packs, particularly in my own experience and on our tour to South Africa. The Springboks have some huge forwards who were just not mobile enough to get down into rucking as we know it, and we certainly dominated the loose rucking in South Africa. I think the Irish are better going forward at speed coming into loose play rather than trying to maul the ball from tight play.

*Q. Would you say that the·line-out is still a bit of a lottery?*

**A.** It's still too easy to play a good line-out specialist out of the game or at least to cause him a certain amount of obstruction which isn't penalized. I suppose the ideal ball is to number 6, but there is very little difference if you get an ideal ball either at 4 or 6. I am in favour of peeling either at the front or the back for perhaps different reasons. I tend to visualize peeling at the front of the line-out more or less from defensive positions where one is more or less trying to control the ball and minimize the risk. But peeling at the back of the line-out, if done properly, and if one has the back of the line-out jumper to guide the ball and someone with a certain amount of mobility to take it on with a bit of pace or power, can open up a lot of options for the threequarters from the resulting loose play. In the Irish team in the last couple of years prior to Lenihan coming into the side, we've had to vary our line-out positions and our line-out jumpers quite a lot and we were more intent on trying to out-think the opposition rather than relying on our natural ability to jump. Consequently, the role of the props wasn't the traditional role in the sense that the props often changed positions. I think the better your jumpers and the more specialized they are, the greater importance one attaches to the role of the props as supporters or as protectors of the jumpers. I think it requires a lot of skill on the part of the outside backs, and particularly now the fly half, to curtail his tendency to try to attack from set positions. He needs the patience to capitalize on the quick ball from loose play with the opposing defence lying flat because this can have its advantages in the sense that with a sidestep one can be away. On the other hand, when the player is

tackling you from 10 yards, one tends to rely on either a change of pace or a swerve.

*Q. What kind of defensive organization is applicable to the Irish game?*

**A.** One would cover all one's priorities in defence, particularly at international level, where you are bringing players together for three or four games a year and where they may not be as coordinated as a club side, and I think players themselves like to cover all eventualities in attack right through from back-row defence, through the defensive screen and mid-field and trying to counteract the opponent's variations.

*Q. Do you work on a number of defensive tactics before a game or are you far more concerned with the business of attacking?*

**A.** This is covered as a matter of form, and one just gets on with one's own business and one's own creative play and attacking options. I don't think that the defensive priorities outweigh the tendency towards maximizing the advantages that might occur to one.

*Q. We hear quite often of players who are very good at going forward and not so good at going back; obviously you go for people who can do both – but would you tend to go for the good defensive player rather than the attacking player, or would you be looking for a balance between your two flankers?*

**A.** You try to get a balance to some extent, but the likes of Tommy David to me were very much attacking players; they were instinctively attacking and aggressive players who were capable of snapping up and supporting attacking moves. I think the best thinkers amongst back-row players tend to foresee the eventualities which can happen in defensive situations and have greater anticipation in defence than the guys who tend to go forward most of the time. But what one does look for in a good back-row player is one who is capable of reading the game as it evolves and consequently of being in attacking positions when required or in a cover defence position.

*Q. Looking now at the practical aspects of running an international team, can you tell me what happens in the week leading up to an international match?*

**A.** We meet on a Thursday at lunchtime and we have a brief meeting setting out details of the weekend – the times of team meetings, asking people to be punctual at various meetings because this can be frustrating to other people, and we suggest the training arrangements which usually incorporate two sessions – one reasonable session on a Thursday afternoon and another very light session on the Friday. We usually have a full team meeting on the Friday evening, after which the coach more or less makes his departure. After that it's very much in the hands of the captain – on the day of the game he has his own meeting, after lunch again, where meetings tend to be more or less sessions reminding players of various signals, of variations, planned moves and so forth and the captain really motivates the team on the day of the game right up to the kick-off.

**Q.** *Can you describe a Thursday training session?*
**A.** One primary objective of the Thursday training is to get the players into the mood of the forthcoming international. One has to use one's judgement as to the requirements of what goes on at a session. One may feel that the players need a fairly stiff session in order to bring them to the realities of the international occasion, or perhaps in midstream in an international series one may have achieved this earlier on, and one may be trying merely to brush up on scrummaging or threequarter play or coordination if some new players have been introduced to the team. But generally speaking the basics are covered in training sessions, and after a warm-up session the threequarters tend to like thirty or forty minutes on their own going through their various plays. The forwards take off for seven, eight or ten scrummages and then tend to concentrate on some line-out play to get their thinking right in this area, particularly the throwing from touch which is now so vital to the success of line-out play; and they tend to come together then in a game of unopposed rugby for twenty to thirty minutes to wind up the proceedings.

**Q.** *What is your role as coach in the dressing room prior to the match?*
**A.** Personally, I vacate the dressing room quite early on the day of the game as I feel I've more or less completed my job, but I do try to be available in case people want last-minute items or whatever.

**Q.** *A hypothetical situation: you've just lost to Wales 27–0. You're on the way to the dressing room – how do you act as the coach?*
**A.** There's not much difficulty in coming to terms when you are beaten 27–0, Carwyn! But when you are beaten by a point in the last minute, it's much more difficult. I think one looks at defeat with a certain amount of self-criticism depending upon the manner in which defeat is inflicted, but I think that overall one has to try to consider it twenty-four or forty-eight hours after the event so that one is not emotionally involved in coming to one's conclusions about the game, because this can be a huge factor. We change our opinions so often in the twenty-four hours after the game, particularly if we see a rerun of events, but there is nothing worse in sport than defeat. It's such a disappointment, and the disappointment of defeat is far greater than the thrill of winning. It is a great help if one knows the sensitivities of the individual players and usually, when you come onto the scene, the grapevine is a great help here – talking to the former coach or perhaps selectors who have been involved in the previous couple of years. But at the end of the day one has to be very careful in case one is influenced by other people's judgement of players which may not coincide with one's own, and I think more people tend to take players and their personalities as they see them; in rugby football (and I don't say this in a patronizing way) most rugby players of international calibre tend to be basically very decent, brave and courageous guys, who are able to take the knocks as well as the bouquets, and there is not usually too much difficulty in coming to terms with personalities.

**Q.** *On the question of discipline, how do you and the selectors react to certain psychopathic tendencies in certain players?*
**A.** I haven't much experience of dealing with players with those tendencies, particularly my own players, but I would think that most selectors in my experience abhor violence on the field for two reasons. One being that it is contrary to the spirit of the game and, the most important one, the injuries that may be inflicted. Secondly, that the player is not able to maintain his control over his own emotions on the field and consequently is not concentrating as he should be on the game in hand.

**Q.** *What kind of attitude should players have towards the referee?*

**A.** Well, I feel like a poacher turned preacher in this one, in so far as I wasn't slow to talk to the referees myself. But, broadly speaking, it is again a lapse of concentration on the player's part. There are frustrations on the field particularly with the tension of the occasions of international matches when so much is at stake. Again, the different interpretations which different referees have on different aspects of the game make it more difficult for players to understand them. But at the end of the day one sees very little questioning of referees.

**Q.** *What would be your priorities, Tom, to make the game a better game?*

**A.** I think you make the game a better game by having more people playing it with greater ability, but the problem in Ireland in a sense is that we don't have too many people playing the game and we have to maximize the resources of those promising people who do play. Indeed, we are currently examining the systems by which we might maximize these limited resources right from school up to the availability for the Irish side.

**Q.** *Do you feel that the future of Irish rugby is probably brighter now than it ever was?*

**A.** It has been bright for a few years now. The Triple Crown probably came at an ideal time to inspire those numerous people who were giving their time to teaching those boys, and I think the combination of the youth rugby and the schools rugby will lead to a much stronger position in Irish rugby in the foreseeable future.

**Q.** *If the International Board were to write to you, Tom, and say: 'We allow you to change one law in order to make it a better game – we'll call it the 'Kiernan Law' – what would it be?*

**A.** I would like to revert back to the tackle law just from the point of view of rugby without going into its dangerous aspects or its medical implications, because I believe that one of the greatest sights in rugby is the continuity of play by players who have the ability in tackle situations to get the ball away. Now that comes to mind because it's the more recent law which has acted to the detriment of the game. Two other areas in which I would like to see greater clarification are (a) the line-out and (b) if possible either a greater interpretation of the laws by the referee or a different attitude of the referee towards the laws. Now I realize that I could be asking for the impossible. I think that refereeing, as much as rugby, is an attitude of mind with the ultimate result of allowing the play to flow. I would imagine that if we could get a change of attitude like we did when the Australian dispensation law and the 10-yard rule were brought into the home countries in the late sixties, it would improve our rugby. It really was a change of attitude by the players that improved the game, not the laws themselves. They were certainly a help, and I would dearly like to see that attitude now coming through the referees.

**Q.** *Could you sum up your feelings about rugby and what makes it enjoyable for you?*

**A.** It's very difficult for me to illustrate what really makes me enjoy rugby because I've been involved in it since I was a child, but I think the unpredictability of it to a great extent and the physical contact which takes place between players of different sizes, speed and strength; and of course the fact that it is an amateur game and the comradeship and friendship one creates during one's career are enough to satisfy me.

# 12 Physical Conditioning for Rugby Football

*Tom Hudson and Bruce Davies*

'Soccer is a contact sport, rugby a collision sport.' These modified words of a very successful American football coach emphasize the need for positive thinking in the game of rugby football.

Collision sports such as rugby football, played with continuity, require the attainment of high levels of physical fitness. Although the game is highly susceptible to manipulation, via the perception and insight of an innovative coach, the prerequisites of a successful team are *aerobic power, anaerobic power* and *muscular power*. In the eighty-minute game these fitness characteristics can be identified simply as the ability to support, to generate speed and acceleration at random intervals and to produce controlled strength and power in order to gain possession at the first, second and concomitant phases.

The ball is in play approximately one third of the game and this play ranges from 100 to 150 activity periods; 56 per cent of these activities last less than 10 seconds, 85 per cent less than 15 seconds, with a very small percentage lasting longer than 30 seconds. There are approximately forty scrums and seventy line-outs per game lasting 5–20 seconds each. The forwards spend a total of 7½ minutes in the scrums and 40–50 per cent of their total game activity is spent in line-outs, scrummaging, rucking and mauling.

A back can expect to handle the ball for no more than a minute and will spend 15 per cent of the game at jogging pace. During the game he will cover approximately 6 kilometres of which 2 kilometres will be sprinting, 2 kilometres jogging and 2 kilometres walking. His heart rate will range between 135–180 beats/minute and his caloric expenditure for the game approximately 1600 Kcalories.

About 85 per cent of recovery intervals during the game last less than 40 seconds. It would seem from the game analysis just described. that a large proportion of the energy used in rugby football must be provided by anaerobic metabolism, and specifically from the energy stored in adenosine triphosphate and phosphocreatine (ATP–PC system). Although the amount of energy available from ATP–PC is extremely limited (0–10 seconds), this system has a large power capacity, i.e. it is capable of supplying a large amount of energy per unit of time. This makes it ideal for maximum power over 0–40 metres. There is a need for at least a minute to partly replenish muscle ATP–PC following an exhaustive exercise. The 40 seconds recovery between activities in rugby will facilitate about 70 per cent repletion of phosphogen stores. Following several short bursts with minimum recovery, glycogen may be called in to supply the energy anaerobically, with a corresponding decrease in power output. Glycogen used in this way (anaerobic) will provide energy for the longer, spectacular runs of 60–70 metres at 70–80 per cent maximum for as long as two minutes, but the critical 'precision acceleration' over 0–20 metres drops away with phosphogen depletion. The jogging support runs at 60–75 per cent maximum are maintained by aerobic breakdown of glycogen and with the correct prematch diet and training can be repeated throughout the match.

Although the game lasts for 80 minutes with substantial aerobic demands, the game analysis emphasizes the need for high-quality anaerobic work during all training sessions.

At any one moment during the game, the players' ability successfully to execute an individual or unit skill depends on their readiness to perform. The player's maximum fitness level and the fatigue accrued throughout the game interact to produce a player's readiness to perform. Maximum readiness to perform would be achieved when the fatigue level is zero and the player has attained his maximum level of fitness. In the training and game situation this condition never occurs, but the coach must strive to maximize the difference between fatigue and peak fitness.

The fatigue level accrued during the game can be influenced by efficient execution of individual and unit skills, a high level of team organization and individual fitness capacity. In order to facilitate a player's maximum readiness to perform before and during the game, a high level of skill and organization must be acquired in conjunction with a high level of general and *specific* fitness.

To obtain fitness objectively, it is essential to monitor the team before and at selected intervals throughout the season. Ideally, the monitoring should be done in a laboratory with scientists experienced in athletic monitoring, but sadly Britain is lacking in the facilities required to do this work. However, several field tests have been developed which are very useful for monitoring key features of the fitness profile. These will be discussed at length later in this chapter.

Players should be encouraged to maintain their aerobic fitness throughout the off season and, if possible, clubs should encourage this with ongoing group running sessions throughout the summer months. Soccer, volleyball and, in particular, basketball are excellent activities to create enthusiasm and good fitness.

In order to maintain winter aerobic power (i.e. cardiovascular endurance) a minimum of two 30–40 minute exercise sessions are required per week. During these sessions the pulse rate should range between 130–180 beats/minute, with an average pulse rate over the complete 30-minute session approximating 150 beats/minute. During soccer or basketball sessions, a low pulse would indicate an 800-metre run at 80 per cent maximum interspersed at selected intervals during the game. When a continuous aerobic programme is maintained throughout the off season, players should arrive in mid-July for pre-season training at 70–80 per cent of their maximal aerobic fitness. This gives the coach two weeks to intensify the training for aerobic fitness and use the month of August to concentrate on quality work (ATP–PC and lactic acid systems), leading towards the more specific training with the ball.

It is during the off season that players should be given individual strength-training programmes. Coaches should be seeking out the weight-training facilities within the vicinity and encouraging players to use these. Two to three 1½ hour sessions per week would be ideal. These sessions should be volume orientated. Players who are able to handle greater loads are usually more able to absorb and transmit energy during the game situation.

A typical strength-endurance weight-training routine would be as follows:

| | Exercise | Repeats | Sets | Load |
|---|---|---|---|---|
| 1. | Leg press | 6–10 | 3 | 80–90% rep-max |
| 2. | Leg extension | 6–10 | 3 | 80–90% rep-max |
| 3. | Bench press | 6–10 | 3 | 80–90% rep-max |
| 4. | Shoulder shrugs | 6–10 | 3 | 80–90% rep-max |
| 5. | Lat. pull-downs | 6–10 | 3 | 80–90% rep-max |
| 6. | Clean and jerk | 6–10 | 3 | 80–90% rep-max |
| 7. | Triceps extension | 6–10 | 3 | 80–90% rep-max |
| 8. | Biceps curl | 6–10 | 3 | 80–90% rep-max |
| 9. | Abdominals | 10–20 | 3 | 60–70% rep-max |
| 10. | Back arches | 10–20 | 3 | 80–90% rep-max |
| 11. | Squat thrusts | 6–10 | 3 | 80–90% rep-max |

The maximum strength in a specific exercise represents the total weight that can be moved through one repetition (REP-MAX).

It is important to teach the correct technique, i.e. correct breathing, smooth continuous movement and no cheating movements. We do not intend to cover the indepth knowledge for effective weight training in this chapter. However, we do recommend some excellent books in our suggested reading (see p. 185)

The coach must encourage the players to strive for maximum work; quantity (training volume) is very important. A player motivated in the weight-training room usually produces on the field. The game is about self-generated power, and a hard weight-training session develops specific strength, tenacity and confidence.

## Pre-season assessment

Laboratory assessment is the most objective and meaningful method of ascertaining the maximum physical capacity of an athlete, but, if this is not available, several field tests have been developed which are useful indicators of physical fitness. These tests should be used at regular intervals throughout the season. A significant decrease in performance in these tests will indicate a decrease in the readiness to perform, and players should be told that this will be a negative consideration at team selection. Too many players are allowed the luxury of slow metamorphosis towards a state of poor match fitness as the season progresses.

### Aerobic power (cardiovascular endurance)
In well-motivated young men this can be estimated quite well with distance run in 12 minutes. 1·5 miles would be the absolute minimum distance expected for an elite player, and the majority of the squad should be running 1·75 miles to greater than 2 miles. What is important is to get a genuine maximum distance, and this distance should be attained or improved at subsequent testing sessions.

### Muscular endurance
This depends partly on the extent of initial glycogen reserves within the active muscle, and the bloodflow through these muscles. When the stores are depleted, the anaerobic work (powerful sprints), so crucial and characteristic to the game, are reduced. In the last quarter of the game, it is probable that blood lactate levels are significantly decreased, indicating an important decrease in muscle glycogen. A useful indicator of tolerance of anaerobic work can be ascertained by comparing a 600-yard 'drop off' time before and after a hard training session. The first run must be a genuine maximum and a high level of motivation is required to ensure this.

### Anaerobic power
This is a key feature in rugby football and should be an essential characteristic in the majority of the players. The time to run 50 yards, with a 15 yard running start, is a good indicator of the immediate energy stores (i.e. ATP–PC) in the muscle. Competitive running in threes ensures maximum performance.

### Muscular endurance in the abdominals
Strong stomach muscles are crucial to the rugby player. Not only do they assist in breathing, but they absorb a lot of energy from tackles. A simple test of abdominal fitness is the maximum bent knee sit-up in 60 seconds. Competition in threes for motivation will facilitate maximum effort.

*Flexibility* is crucial in the prevention of injuries. Two tests that provide a good estimate of flexi-

bility in the hamstrings, hip and lower back are the sit and reach and back arch, or extension.

### Flexibility
### Standards for sit-and-reach flexibility test

| Category | Sit-and-reach |
| --- | --- |
| Excellent | +8 inches or greater |
| Good | +5 to +7 inches |
| Average | Toe line to +4 inches |
| Fair | −2 to −1 inch from toe line |
| Poor | −3 inches or more above toe line |

*These standards were developed by Michael Tichy at Portland State University, Oregon*

Scale attached to square box

+6 +5 +4 +3 +2 +1 0 -1 -2 -3 -4 -5

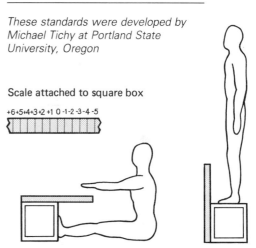

Toe-touch position          Trunk-flexion position

*This instrument to measure flexibility can be constructed with a minimum amount of effort*

## Some suggested stretching exercises

Stretching exercises for rugby football should involve the major muscle groups and joints of the body, including back, neck, achilles tendon, hips, chest, groin, spine, quadriceps, shoulders, arms, abdominals, ankles, knees.

Stretching exercises should be performed smoothly and jerky actions should be avoided. Hold the final stretch position for approximately 30 seconds duration, repeat the exercise five or six times. Stretching should be performed before competition and training (warm up and warm down). There are many stretching exercises that may be used, the following are only suggestions.

## Neck

Neck stretching, rotate the head, first in one direction and then in another. Rotate slowly and repeat several times.

## Ham strings

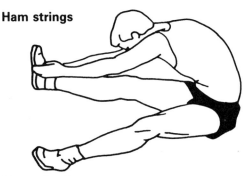

Sit on the floor with legs spread, reach for one foot, hold, and reach for the other and hold. Attempt when you reach to touch and hold the head and chest as closely as possible to the thigh of the leg. You are trying to hold at the foot. Repeat. Continue reaching, first for one foot and then for the other.

## Quadriceps

Lying on your left side, flex the knee of your right leg and catch the ankle with the right hand. Slowly move the hips forward until a good stretch is felt on the thigh. Hold, repeat with your left leg by lying on your right side.

## Groin

Sit on the floor with the soles of the feet touching in front of you. Slowly push down on the knees as far as possible, hold the final stretch position. Try each day to push the knee closer to the floor.

## Spine and waist

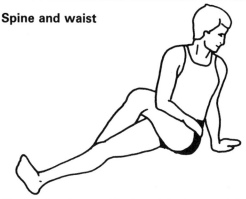

Sit on the floor with the right leg straight and across the left leg, placing the left foot flat on the floor. Using the right hand, reach around the left leg towards your left hip. Put the left arm directly behind you, slowly turn the head. Sit up straight, continue looking over the left shoulder. Hold, then stretch to the side by pressing the right leg over the left.

## Achilles tendon

Stand several feet in front of a wall, the feet several inches apart. Lean forward, place hands outstretched on the wall, keep the feet flat on the floor. Move away gradually from the wall, but keep the feet flat on the floor. The final stretch position should be held. Try each day to increase the distance you move from the wall.

**Back**

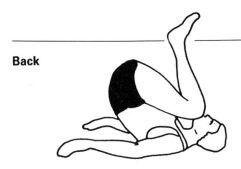

Lying on the back, with the arms extended to the sides, bring the knees as far as possible to the chin. Do not raise the arms off the floor. Hold position, then repeat.

### Percentage body fat

By purchasing a pair of skinfold calipers, fat measurement can be ascertained, to assess the muscle mass and fat mass of the player. This is very helpful when considering the weight of a player. Many coaches are asking players to lose muscle mass. Most backs should be 12–14 per cent fat, with forwards no greater than 20 per cent fat.

The authors have recently designed a rugby circuit, (see pages 186–8) which should give the coach an excellent indication of the player's all-round fitness.

The circuit has been designed to give the coach an immediate indicator of the player's readiness to perform.

At present there is a need to establish norms on British players. This will make the circuit a more meaningful and objective guide. We believe that the circuit has all the prerequisites of rugby fitness and will serve as a good guide to training effectiveness. Individual sections of the circuit can be analysed to examine specific weaknesses or strengths. From our recent work with international and county players, split times of 5 minutes for part one (exercises) and part two (1500-metre run) should be expected for top-level players.

## The one-year training cycle

*Pre-season*: Individual and team conditioning. Game preparation – early matches.
*Mid season*: Readiness to perform.
*Peak season*: Readiness to perform for important matches.
*Active recovery period*: Maintaining physical conditioning throughout active rest from competitive rugby football.

## Pre-season training

### Phase one

Commencing at the beginning of the third week in May.* Two half days per week. One and a half hours' duration each session.

### Phase two

Commencing at the beginning of the third week in June. Four sessions per week. One and a half hours' duration each session.

### Phase three

Commencing at the beginning of the second week in July. One and a half hours' duration each session.

### Phase four

Commencing at the beginning of the fourth week in July. Full training including tactical training.

### Phase five

April to mid-May – active recovery.

## Phase one

### Days one and two

The training session should progress in the following sequence. Ten minutes' flexibility exercises and callisthenics. The session should also involve some game activities such as basketball, soccer, volleyball, handball, slow running with the ball while passing and catching and practising other individual skills.

10 v. 10 rugby practice, 60 minutes' duration.

In addition three 30-minute sessions of weight training should be continued throughout this phase.

## Phase two

### Day one

Repeat day one, phase one, plus 30 minutes' weight training.

### Day two

10 minutes' warm-up, flexibility and callisthenics. 45 minutes' touch rugby, using a quarter of the pitch. 20 minutes' individual skill practice. Weight training, 30 minutes.

*Dates given apply, of course, to the British season and should be adjusted to suit other countries' seasons.

### Day three

Swimming only. *Suggested programme*: Multi-stroke, 200 metres front crawl, 200 metres back-stroke, 50 metres legs only, front crawl, 50 metres legs only, backcrawl. Non-swimmers should repeat day one, but should include circuit training.

### Day four

Fartlek running 45 minutes, while passing and catching the ball. Players should be organized in to groups of eight to ten. Weight training 30 minutes.

## Phase three

### Day one

Warm-up 10 minutes. Flexibility and callisthenics. 45 minutes five-a-side soccer or seven-a-side rugby. Weight training 30 minutes.

### Day two

Fartlek, approximately 9–10 miles. Players in groups of six to ten using ball, passing and catching. 10 × 25 metre running, stride only, concentrating on technique.

### Day three

Weight training, 60 minutes including warm-up of flexibility and callisthenics.

### Day four

Flexibility and callisthenics, 10 minutes. 45 minutes' touch rugby. 30 minutes' individual technique practice, which should include passing, catching, grid practice, individual and unit skills, concentrating on fitness with skill and specificity of training. Group practice split into forwards and backs. Backs should concentrate on goal-line attacks, 40–50 metres out attacking and defensive play. Forwards concentrate on specific scrums, rucks, mauls, line-outs, practice dribbling, rushes, organized opposition where possible.

## Phase four

### Week one, day one

80 minutes' match practice. 30 minutes' interval training, must be specifically related to the game.

### Day two

25 minutes' fartlek running, 5–10 minutes' recovery. Circuit training, 20 minutes, game related. 10 × 100 metre hard runs. 45 seconds' recovery time between each run.

### Day three

Warm-up, flexibility and callisthenics, 10 minutes. 20 minutes' game-related practice i.e., change in direction, sprinting, tackling, scrummaging, passing and catching, kicking, sidestepping, dribbling, etc. 5 minutes' recovery.

Speed training, 6 × 25-metre sprints, 6 × 50-metre sprints, 10 × 200-metre sprints. 3 minutes' recovery between each set. Walk back after each repetition.

### Day four

30 minutes' weight training. 10 minutes' recovery. 60 minutes' match practice. 5 minutes' recovery. 45 minutes' individual skill and technique practice, related to the individual player's position. 20 mintues' unit skills practice.

### Day five

Recreational swimming, golf or tennis.

### Week two, day one

Team discussion, 20 minutes. Conditioned game 10 v. 10, 30 minutes. 40 minutes' individual practice (specificity of training).

### Day two

Speed training, 10 × 50-metre sprints, 10 × 25-metre sprints, 10 × 50-metre sprints, 2 × 100-metre sprints. 3 minutes' recovery between each set. Walk back after each repetition.

### Day three

25 minutes' related skill practice. 40 minutes' match practice using a quarter of the pitch.

### Day four

25 minutes' circuit training or weight training. 100 minutes' full match practice.

### Day five

30 minutes' basketball using rugby ball. Recreational swimming if possible.

### Day six

Conditioned match practice, 90 minutes.

### Week three, day one

Team discussion, 25 minutes' unit skill practice. 25 minutes' individual skills related to areas of position. 30 minutes, all players will practice unit skills. Coaches and players to evaluate and review.

**Day two**
Fartlek running, 30 minutes.

**Day three**
Skill practice, individual and team, related to the game. Whichever form of endurance programme is used during week three of this training phase should be used for the next four to five weeks.

**Day four**
Team discussion, 20 minutes. Weight training, 30 minutes. Match practice, 80 minutes, conditioned game.

**Day five**
10 minutes' warm-up, flexibility and callisthenics. 30 minutes' individual skill practice. 20 minutes' team and unit skills practice.

**Day six**
Match practice.

**Week four, day one**
Team discussion, 30 minutes, and match inquest. 40 minutes' game-related skill practice. 30 minutes' fartlek training followed by 10 × 20-metre sprints. 10 × 15-yard sprints, 10 × 100-yard sprints. 3 minutes' recovery between each set. Walk back after each repetition.

**Day two**
As for day one, excluding team discussion.

**Day three**
Speed training. 6 × 15 metres, 6 × 20 metres, 10 × 50 metres, 2 × 100 metres, 1 × 120 metres. 3–5 minutes' recovery between each set. All splits should be timed and recorded.

## Phase five

Approximately three to four days per week of relaxing activities, such as cycling, swimming, running to maintain aerobic fitness.

## Mid-season programme

**Monday**
Team and individual coaching session. Weight training, 30 minutes.

**Tuesday**
Individual skill practices. Fast interval training, 20 minutes. Circuit training.

**Wednesday**
Team practice and individual coaching.

**Thursday and Friday**
Complete rest.

**Saturday**
Game.

**Sunday**
Weight training, endurance, 30 minutes.

## Peak season programme

**Monday**
Individual coaching and team practice. Speed training.

**Wednesday**
Team practice, 50 minutes. Fast interval training, sprints.

**Sunday**
Weight training, 30 minutes.

Serial testing in a laboratory for lung function, maximum oxygen consumption and body fatness provides excellent information for the coach and, in conjunction with the field tests, gives the necessary feedback required to assess the player's physiological fitness.

The observant coach may from time to time notice that individual players may demonstrate a distinct drop-off in performance, despite intense effort during training. From our experiences, more laboratory tests for blood haematocrit and haemoglobin can sometimes indicate anaemia. Reversal of this problem, with iron supplement, results in an immediate improvement in performance. In many cases players are not providing themselves with adequate nutrition; this can have a considerable negative effect on endurance performance.

# Nutrition

Nutritionists are well aware of the problem of the 'athletic diet'. It is always difficult to assess the effect of a single food component on physical performance because of the interference of such variables as motivation, physical fitness and skill.

It is essential that the food must be chosen in quantities and varieties to provide the nutrients for growth maturation tissue repair and maintenance, and to provide the energy for training and competition.

Daily energy turnover among rugby players varies in range from about 3000 to 4500 calories/day and are obviously dependent on the individual's size and training programme. Although it is unlikely that the rugby player training correctly throughout the season will gain weight, excessive calorie intake above the daily energy expenditure will bring about fat deposition (obesity) with a corresponding decrease in performance. There are no special food sources which supply extra reserves of energy that are not supplied by other foods with the same nutrients. An adequate guide on which the rugby player should base his food selection is the basic food groups: proteins, fats, carbohydrates, vitamins, minerals and water.

When more than 3500 calories/day are consumed the proportion of fat should be raised to approximately 35 per cent of the diet. Generally the protein:fat:carbohydrate ratio should be about 20:20:60, with vitamins, minerals and trace elements given in optimal proportions.

There is obviously controversy surrounding proportions of food classes but generally it would seem that Yakovlov's recommendations are a good guide for rugby players. He suggests that the calorie content of the daily diet should be as follows:

| Total cal/kg/ day | Protein | Fats | Carbohydrates |
| --- | --- | --- | --- |
| 63–7 calories | 2 g/kg | 2 g/kg | 9–16 g/kg |

These figures are expressed as grams per kilogram of body weight so a 70-kg (154-lb) rugby player would have a total daily calorie expenditure of approximately 4550 calories (65 × 70 kg). This would be made up of 140 grams of protein (574 calories) and 140 grams of fat (1302 calories) with the remaining 2674 calories coming from carbo-

hydrates. Of the total carbohydrates, approximately 10 per cent should come from refined sugars, with the remainder made up of starches. Vitamin therapy is once again an area of controversy, many medical doctors in the UK say there is no need for additional vitamins because of the quantities in the normal British diet. We tend to believe that a moderate increase via a multi-vitamin tablet will be of benefit to the active rugby player; this is certainly the opinion of many Eastern Bloc physiologists.

In addition to the obvious need for adequate nutrient intake by the rugby player, the psychological aspects of eating are of equal importance. It is important that meals be palatable and presented at appropriate and suitable times. Some fat in foods makes food more palatable to most persons, so that a decrease in dietary fat can lead to inadequate intake of other nutrients. A total lack of fat would make it very difficult to maintain adequate energy levels because of the large quantities of carbohydrates and proteins that would be required to supply up to 4000+ calories. It has been suggested that athletes have frequent light meals rather than three heavy meals.

In planning your diet for a weekly game it would be wise to consume 60–70 per cent of your total weekly intake as carbohydrates. Be sure to consume plenty of water.

The following diets are modifications of a regular, well-balanced diet, i.e. high calorie, high protein and high carbohydrate. These are guidelines and obviously substitutes can be made to suit economy and convenience.

**High-calorie diet** (approximately 4000 calories)
In a high-calorie diet emphasis is placed on increasing the calories rather than on increasing any particular nutrient. A full meal should be eaten three times a day, with a substantial snack in the afternoon and in the evening. This fifth meal may consist of a sandwich and milk shake or whatever else the person may wish.

This diet is adequate in all nutrients. The following foods should be included in the daily diet (other foods may be eaten as desired).

| | |
| --- | --- |
| beverages | 4 cups milk, 1 large glass fruit juice |
| bread | 6 slices, wholewheat or enriched |
| butter/margarine | 2 lbs or more |

| cereal | 1 large serving, wholewheat or enriched |
|---|---|
| cheese | as desired |
| cream | ½ cup at breakfast |
| desserts | pie, cake, ice cream, or cookies as desired |
| eggs | 1 daily |
| fruit | 1 serving fruit in addition to large glass fruit juice at breakfast |
| meat, fish, or poultry | 2 large servings |
| potato or potato substitutes | 2 servings daily |
| soups | as desired |
| vegetables | at least 3 vegetables (1 raw and 1 green or yellow) |

## Sample menu

*Breakfast*
1 large glass orange juice
3/4 cup oatmeal
1/4 cup light cream
1 soft cooked egg with butter/margarine
3 tsp sugar
2 slices bacon
1 slice toast
1 tsp butter/margarine
1 cup milk
coffee if desired

*Lunch*
3½ oz portion leg of lamb
3/4 cup mashed potatoes
½ cup peas and carrots with butter
pineapple and cream cheese salad
hot roll
1 tsp butter or margarine
lemon meringue pie
1 cup milk

*3 p.m.*
½ cup ice cream
2 sugar cookies
1 glass milk

*Dinner*
1 medium club steak, broiled
large baked potato with butter/margarine
spinach with vinegar
tomato salad with 1 tbs French dressing
1 slice bread

1 tsp butter/margarine
baked apple with cream
1 glass milk

*8 p.m.*
chocolate malted drink

**High-protein diet** (approximately 100 grams)
A high-protein diet is a normal diet with added amounts of meat, milk, eggs, cheese, fish or poultry. Non-fat dry milk may be added to soups or to regular milk, thereby increasing the protein without increasing the fat. This diet is adequate in all nutrients. The daily diet should include the following foods:

| beverages | 3 glasses milk |
|---|---|
| bread, butter or margarine, desserts, and soups | as desired |
| cereals | 1 wholegrain or enriched |
| cheese | may be used freely |
| eggs | 3 eggs (1 or 2 may be used in cooking) |
| fruit | at least 2 servings (1 a citrus fruit or fruit juice) |
| meat, fish or poultry | 2 large servings each day |
| potatoes or potato substitutes | 1 serving daily |
| vegetables | 3 servings (1 raw and 1 green or yellow) |

## Sample menu

*Breakfast*
½ grapefruit
2 eggs
2 slices crisp bacon
toast
butter/margarine
coffee with cream
milk

*Lunch*
4 oz roast beef
mashed potatoes
buttered peas
combination vegetable salad
wholewheat bread
butter/margarine
fruit cup
milk

*Dinner*
beef and vegetable soup
2 lamb chops
buttered asparagus
peach and cottage cheese salad
wholewheat bread
butter/margarine
baked custard
milk

## High-carbohydrate diet

The high-carbohydrate diet should include the following foods in the daily diet:

| | |
|---|---|
| beverages | fruit juice as desired, 1 qt milk |
| bread | 2 slices at each meal |
| butter, cheese and soups | as desired |
| cereals | 1 large serving wholegrain or enriched |
| desserts | cake, cookies, ice cream, sherbet, pastries that are not too rich, and puddings |
| eggs | 1 daily |
| meat, fish, or poultry | 2 servings |
| fruits | 2 servings (1 a citrus fruit or fruit juice) |
| potatoes or potato substitute | 2 servings |
| vegetables | 3 servings (1 raw and 1 green or yellow) |

### Sample menu

*Breakfast*
orange juice
stewed fruit
oatmeal with cream
scrambled eggs
2 slices toast
butter/margarine
jelly
coffee
milk

*Lunch*
fruit juice cocktail
meat cooked in sauce on toast
baked potato with butter/margarine
glazed carrots
apple and celery salad
sherbet
milk

*Dinner*
broiled chicken
candied sweet potatoes
buttered peas
pineapple and banana salad
2 slices wholewheat bread
butter/margarine
caramel cake
milk

During the two games/week, a high carbohydrate diet should be consumed throughout the week with an absolute minimum of exercise between the Wednesday and Saturday games.

## Water

There are occasions when the rugby player's response is an inadequate gauge of water loss and he may become chronically dehydrated. Man's delayed thirst pattern normally causes him to be slow in replacing sweat losses but twenty-four hours is usually adequate for athletes to rehydrate voluntarily. This may not be the case when the rugby player trains twice each day during warm weather; under these circumstances he must force himself to ingest fluid well in excess of thirst. With such efforts it is possible to replace 6–7 lbs sweat loss in four hours. This means that the rugby player can rehydrate adequately even when training twice a day.

## Pre-match diet

Breakfast should be eaten on the day of the match. The problem of providing the rugby player with a nutritionally adequate diet is complicated by the emotional tension that so often accompanies the prematch preparation. Solid prematch meals may be in the process of digestion four hours after consumption because of this stress. Basic considerations for the prematch meal should include:

1. A meal light enough in calories to prevent hunger during the match (900–1000 calories).

2. A minimum of fat, as it slows down emptying time of stomach.

3. Elimination of foods which form gas (this is an individual judgement).

4. A minimum of protein (prematch steak) and bulky foods. Protein is a source of acids which can only be eliminated by urinary excretion.

5. Whatever the meal, it should be consumed 3–4 hours before the match.

6. The meal should consist mainly of carbohydrates. Toast with marmalade or honey would be an ideal choice.

Eating at a training table can be beneficial for a player if meals are professionally planned, nutritious and served in an atmosphere conducive to enjoyment of food.

Recent evidence would suggest that two cups of strong coffee drunk one hour prior to the game mobilizes fats and in doing so prolongs the muscle glycogen store. This would be advantageous to second-half performance.

Avoid large quantities of sugar 60 minutes before the game as this can bring about a drop in blood sugar which would definitely impede performance.

Both quantity and quality of food consumed by the athlete are important and maintenance of good diet should be year round. But a balanced diet cannot compensate for poor skill development or a poor training programme.

## Contra-indications to exercise

As a general principle, players should be feeling well when they train or play. Too many coaches put pressure on players to sweat out colds and flu-like illness. It is quite possible that the heart can be affected during or after a non-specific respiratory infection. It is probable that all viral illness, including the common cold, will respond negatively to exercise.

Following pyrexial (i.e. oral temperature in excess of 37° C) illness, exercise should be forbidden for at least ten days. The coach should give the benefit of the doubt to the player. If a player has a localized nose or throat infection, the coach should demonstrate understanding; a few days' rest will probably save a substantial amount of time in the quest towards optimal readiness to perform.

## Suggested reading

BAWLA, *Know the Game: Weight Lifting*, E. P. Publishing Ltd, Wakefield.

M. Fallon, *Weight Training for Sport and Fitness*, Kaye & Ward, Tadworth.

J. Lear and A. Murray, *Power Training for Sport*, J. Batsford Ltd, London.

A. Murray, *Modern Weight Training*, Kaye & Ward, Tadworth.

George Popplewell, *Modern Weight Lifting and Power Lifting*, Faber & Faber, London.

William J. Stone and William A. Kroll, *Sports Conditioning and Weight Training*, Allyn & Bacon, Boston, Mass.

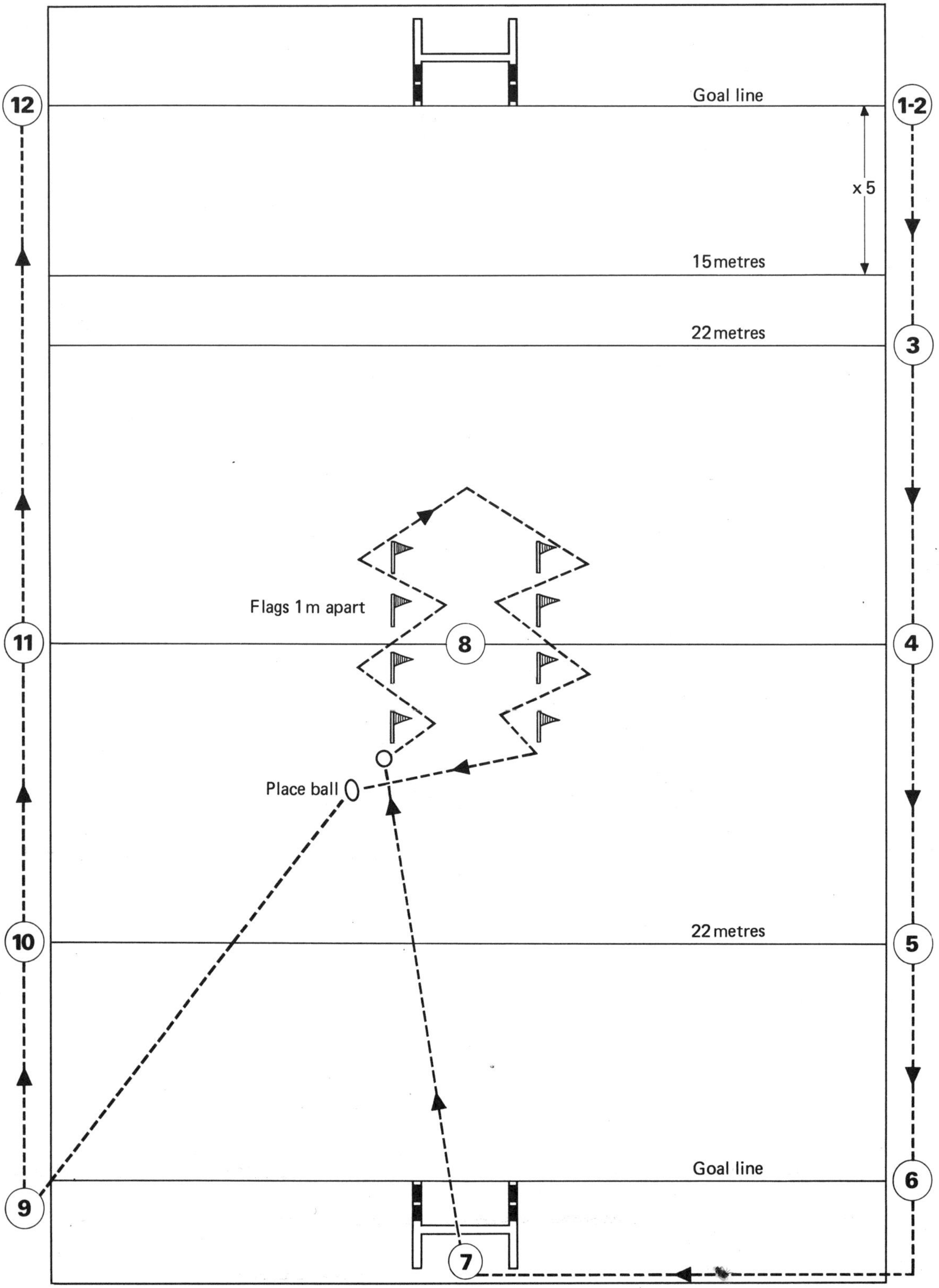

Goal line

1-2

x 5

15 metres

22 metres

3

Flags 1 m apart

8

4

Place ball

22 metres

5

Goal line

6

7

9    10    11    12

# The Davies–Hudson Rugby Readiness Circuit

The circuit is performed against the clock. It is essential that all the exercises are done with the correct technique.

**Station 1** Ten standard press-ups.

**Station 2** Five continuous 15-metre runs are designed to create an oxygen debt which the player must carry through the circuit.

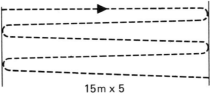

15m x 5

**Station 3** Fifteen sit-ups measuring muscular endurance of the abdominal muscles. These are key muscles for rugby players.

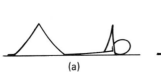
(a)

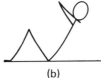
(b)

**Station 4** Fifteen back extensions measuring muscular endurance of lower-back extensors.

(a)                              (b)

**Station 5** Five continuous 6-foot standing broad jumps. Another measure of leg power and anaerobic work.

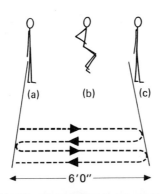

(a)        (b)        (c)

6'0"

**Station 6** The crucifix (× 20). An excellent measure of dynamic hip flexibility.

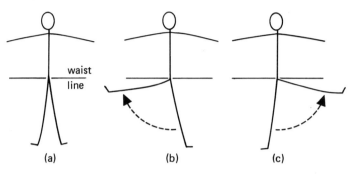

**Station 7** Leg abduction (× 20) and adduction (× 20). A good measure of endurance in leg adductors and abductors.

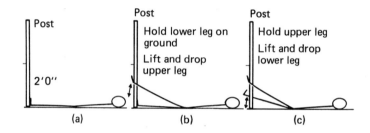

**Station 8** Agility run with the ball. High level of specific speed and power required for a good time.

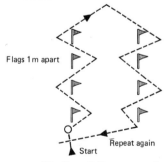

**Station 9** Knees to chest (× 10). Muscular endurance in the lower abdominal muscles which are particularly susceptible to the hard low tackle.

**Station 10** Modified burpee (× 15). A good measure of dynamic extension and flexibility in the back.

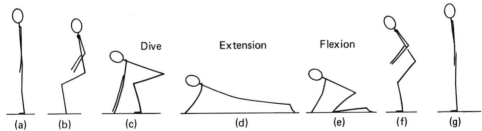

**Station 11** Hip raises with feet over head, through to full flexion (× 10). Good for stretching the muscles of shoulder, back and hips, prior to the endurance run.

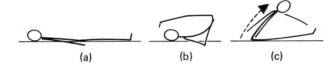

**Station 12** 1500-metre run. Very good indicator of aerobic power.

1500 m run